BEING BRETT

ALSO BY DOUGLAS HOBBIE

Boomfell

The Day

A JOHN MACRAE BOOK

Henry Holt and Company

New York

BEING

BRETT

Chronicle

of a

Daughter's

Death

DOUGLAS HOBBIE

The author wishes to thank Dr. Andrew Leavitt of the University of
California, San Francisco, who, with characteristic thoroughness and
care, proofread this book for technical medical accuracy.

Henry Holt and Company, Inc.
Publishers since 1866
115 West 18th Street
New York, New York 10011

Henry Holt® is a registered trademark of
Henry Holt and Company, Inc.

Library of Congress Cataloging-in-Publication Data
Hobbie, Douglas.
Being Brett: chronicle of a daughter's death/Douglas Hobbie.
p.   cm.
"A John Macrae book."
1. Hobbie, Brett, 1965–1992—Health.   2. Hodgkin's disease—
Patients—United States—Biography.   I. Title.
RC644.H53H63   1996
362.1'9699446'0092—dc20   95-13280
[B]   CIP
ISBN 0-8050-2520-0

Henry Holt books are available for
special promotions and premiums. For details contact:
Director, Special Markets.

First Edition—1996

Lines from "October" are from *New and Selected Poems* by Mary
Oliver © 1992 Mary Oliver, reprinted by permission of Beacon Press,
and lines from "The Summer Day" are from *House of Light* by Mary
Oliver © 1990 Mary Oliver, reprinted by permission of Beacon Press.

Designed by Paula R. Szafranski

Printed in the United States of America
All first editions are printed on acid-free paper.∞

1   3   5   7   9   10   8   6   4   2

For *Holly, Jocelyn, Nathaniel,*
and for
Beth Wilson

In loving memory of
Brett

JANUARY 11, 1965–OCTOBER 14, 1992

CONTENTS

1. Recurrence   *1*

2. Cure   *37*

3. Alone   *68*

4. Distance   *94*

5. Marrow   *117*

6. Pain   *152*

7. Home   *197*

8. Autumn   *237*

9. Snow   *274*

. . . I want to love this world
as though it's the last chance I'm ever going to get
to be alive
and know it.

—Mary Oliver

1

RECURRENCE

My life is supposed to be happening again, he thought, strapped into his seat as the early-morning westbound flight lifted into the air.

They were his older daughter's recent words and they made his heart race. A year and a half before, one year after her graduation from Smith College, Brett had flown to San Francisco, the chosen setting for her next big adventure, the quest for "real" work, financial independence, selfhood—a dazzling young woman, as she appeared to him, hastening to a world of possibilities. Just six months after her arrival on the West Coast and only weeks after she'd finally come into a challenging job on a small out-of-the-mainstream newspaper—"I have homework again," she reported—she discovered a small lump above her collarbone. Actually her girlfriend, Eve, had been the first to notice it. As if a powerful switch had been thrown, her life veered, not out of control, but onto a different, scarier track where events speeded up and everyday existence was perilously heightened.

The perplexing lump was an enlarged lymph node, possibly a symptom of some innocuous virus, she was told, or a relatively nonthreatening thyroiditis or—the ominous word became more frightening the longer they avoided it in their long-distance phone calls—cancer. A lymphoma. Alone in San Francisco with Eve, she went through the initial diagnostic procedures, soon becoming entangled in the frustrating bureaucracy of a large city hospital. The tape recorder purchased for her newspaper job she now brought to her interview with a Dr. Leavitt. The lump was removed under general anesthesia for biopsy. She'd never been under general anesthesia before or experienced surgery of any kind. She'd never spent a day in a hospital. Following the surgery, she called from her apartment, sounding exhausted and distant and remarkably calm. "When I woke up, my doctor was at my bedside. He said he was quite certain it was Hodgkin's and I should know that. He was pretty emphatic about it." The cancer of young adults, someone had called it. Unlike other, more aggressive and stubborn lymphomas, she'd learned, Hodgkin's was curable ninety percent of the time if diagnosed at an early stage, often requiring no more than six weeks of radiation therapy. Instead of feeling only fearful and helpless, she had already begun to be determined. Back in Massachusetts, he promptly contacted experts at the Dana Farber Cancer Institute to develop a plan of action now that this unthinkable turn— unthinkable despite how accustomed one was to tragic misfortune constantly befalling others—was happening to them, to his daughter.

She'd returned to New England for Christmas and to have her illness staged in Boston. CAT scans, a splenectomy, for Hodgkin's can hide in the spleen, the oncologist explained. When it was established that she had Stage II Hodgkin's disease and her sole treatment would be the six weeks of radiation therapy, she decided to return to San Francisco and resume her newly independent life there. In fact, the course of treatment did not go smoothly. This so-called curable disease was far more complicated, plain trickier, than anyone had suggested. Doctors at the Medical Center at the University of California, San Francisco, found Dana Farber's assessment of his daughter's disease inaccurate. Six weeks of treatment became six months, beginning with dreaded chemotherapy and ending with radiation. Brett did what she had to do.

"Today begins with the usual burning gut and bent-overness of morning," she wrote, once the spooky, poisonous chemo had begun.

Scrambled eggs and toast and fifteen pills and a tall glass of something fresh-squeezed to ward off the evil spirits. My body begins to feel like a hive or a fist. . . . Rawness inside my veins. . . . Afternoons are sleepy, incoherent. I walk on the beach with my eyes closed. . . . I wait for hunger and sleep like holidays. This is so hard! . . . I'm trying to keep my head on my shoulders, my hair on my head, my hair on my chinny chin chin. . . . This body isn't helping, but I try to love it, to trust it. Driving me crazy, though—the internal limp . . . always the pain or the absence of pain, while everyone around me goes to work or play or grumbles about the weather. Yesterday I got bundled up and went to watch a soccer game—came home all freckled and bummed out. I couldn't remember the feeling of being able to run, kick a ball, and breathe deep. . . . Leavitt thinks I'm "tough." I joke around with him. I use words like "appreciable" and "morbidity." I've learned some things. I ask him if all oncologists wear pink shirts. He's cute.

Things that help: chocolate frozen yogurt; hot baths and mineral salts; talking to you both on the phone; the idea of flying to Italy as soon as this stuff is over; yes, the Hobbies in Roma in beautiful shoes eating big plates of pasta and looking at big art with big hearts. . . . Oops—my side effects are starting up—pins and needles, dry mouth, dizziness—gotta go. I'm thinking of you all the time. Stay warm. Stay healthy for Christ's sake. All my love.

When she began to lose her hair, she had her head shaved—a hairdresser's fantasy, the hairdresser told her—and found she was quite beautiful bald, her eyes bigger and bluer. A fashion designer in a Cole Valley boutique, mistaking the consequences of chemo for a new hip style, asked her to model his dresses at Nordstrom's. There were emergency hospitalizations, once for a virulent, inexplicable skin eruption and several other times, each more frightening than the last, for variously mysterious fevers. There were numerous invasive proddings and pokings, repeated X-rays and CAT scans, the dark claustrophobia of the MRI, the grueling torment of bone-marrow biopsies, the anxiety of treatment postponed while her white count fluctuated uncooperatively. By June, despite the pain and fear and loss associated with the whole ordeal—her life on hold—she had come through. It was over and done with. The sacrifice of her spleen carried a burden of caution. Her radiologist warned ominously that she could perish of a bacterial infection within forty-eight hours. Any fever above 101 degrees required emergency attention. The chemo and radiation had impaired her heart and scarred her lungs. This formerly strong, athletic young woman was now plagued by a harsh, nagging cough and severe shortness of breath.

When the course of treatment ended, though, and the MRI, among other tests, showed that the cancer was indeed gone, she was ecstatic, that was the word for it, and shouldered her losses without bitterness. On the last page of the journal that had seen her through those months, she wrote *thank you* and *goodbye*.

She spent a restorative month with the whole family and a lineup of friends in New England, where, undeterred by the condition of her lungs, she settled into a self-disciplined routine of long daily walks. By Labor Day, sitting in the sunny garden waiting for the hour of her departure for San Francisco, she was in great form. Stoically, she endured another bone-marrow biopsy at UCSF and submitted to the precautionary procedure of a bone-marrow harvest. Healthy bone marrow, one and a half quarts of it, was extracted from her backside and preserved, frozen, against a possible recurrence of the disease. While her doctors told her there was an eighty percent chance that she was completely cured—George Canellos of Dana Farber, with whom he'd kept in touch throughout Brett's treatment, therefore considered

the procedure eighty percent unnecessary and didn't recommend it—
they insisted it was smart to have healthy marrow in the bank. For
Brett it marked the end of the whole process, the final detail, a last
cause for celebration. "Back to the intrigue, moral complexities, black
humor, irony, grainy realism . . . of urban adulthood," she wrote them.
She was especially excited about the spacious apartment she'd located,
"clean and sunny enough to be happily empty for a while . . . until
we're raking in the dough."

In October she flew to Santa Fe, where she hooked up with a new
roommate, Beth Wilson, who had driven from the East Coast. They
had connected that summer through a mutual friend, Edgar McIntosh,
who was also moving to San Francisco after the new year. In Santa Fe
their friendship quickly flowered into a relationship, something they
both must have been anticipating for a while. Their ensuing trip was
a lovers' whirlwind tour of the West, which his daughter saw as a
transitional adventure, her passage to a fresh start on the Coast. "Sun-
burned, agnostic, earthquake-proof, with a chipmunk on my knee, and
evolution all around," she wrote from Bryce Canyon. "I'm one big iron
pill in denim, thank you. Feeling very sunkissed and hearty. . . . Love
and blisses, tall in the saddle, Brett." Earthquake-proof: the Great
Quake of '89 had struck San Francisco on October 17; they'd missed
it. One big iron pill: the marrow harvest had left her anemic.

In mid-November, a month after the bone-marrow harvest and less
than five months since the conclusion of her treatment for Hodgkin's,
she began to experience the same symptoms that had come down on
her almost exactly one year before. Fevers, night sweats, tightness in
her chest. It terrified him to imagine her fear on awakening at night,
soaking wet, alone with what the eerie and unmistakably familiar sen-
sations might mean. "Don't worry, kids," she told her parents long-
distance. Only the week before she'd had her monthly checkup and
everything seemed fine. She didn't believe the disease could recur so

soon after being done with it. It had to be pneumonitis again, which she'd had before as a result of radiation therapy. The next time she called she said, "I'm not panicking, but there's something in the X-ray."

Now, en route to her adopted city, enclosed in the muffled reverberation of flight, how vividly he remembered her call the following afternoon. It was still morning in San Francisco. Both he and his wife, Holly, were on the phone. Brett had just spoken with Andrew Leavitt, her doctor at UCSF.

"I have Hodgkin's," she stated flatly. She began to cry. "I can't face this again. I can't take it. I don't want it."

She'd been so sure that she'd done all she could and that the awful year was over. She had a new girlfriend and the new apartment, which they'd been painting and fixing up for weeks. Beth had made her a desk that looked like she was about to embark on some serious work. She'd been getting her résumé together. "I don't want to be the sick person," she said, "I don't want to be the one who needs help and support." She had always played the opposite role among her friends. "Now I'm always going to hate this time of year." Fall, the best-loved time of year, the season of beginnings. Her emotion was raw. "At last I've got this wonderful apartment," she cried, *"to be sick in.* I can't take the chemo, my veins can't take it. Symbolically, it scares me—all the repercussions of it. . . . I don't want to make Beth and Edgar go through this." She had persuaded them to take up with her on the West Coast, she'd found the apartment. She didn't want these new people in her life to see her unwell. "I'm beginning to feel like a sick person. I know I'm healthy mentally, but I'm not a normal person with this." She felt herself becoming jealous of her friends just because they were normal and healthy. "My life is supposed to be happening again."

Carefully turned from the person beside him, a young woman he had yet to look at directly, he inwardly shuddered at his daughter's pain. He had never heard her cry as she cried then, not even as a small child. Throughout all the frustration and anxiety of the preceding year she had never wept as she did during that phone call. At one point she was sobbing so uncontrollably she wanted to get off the line.

"No, stay here," he said. "Stay and talk." He wanted to rescue her from this anguish, but the words he attempted to pile against it—words of reassurance and understanding and encouragement—felt hollow, useless.

Pulling herself together, she asked them, "My having cancer doesn't put too much stress on your relationship, does it?"

They talked, the three of them, until it seemed she had regained her composure, the rawness abated.

"Are you going on with your plans for Thanksgiving?" Holly asked. Brett was expecting twenty people to attend a traditional feast in the new apartment.

"Yes!" Her voice bristled with defiance.

"What are you going to do this afternoon?" he asked, anxious that she would be alone with her impossible knowledge.

"I'm going to squirt Visine into my eyes and go out on the street and look at people."

He and Holly had wanted to fly out immediately, the very day their daughter had delivered her disastrous news. But Brett wanted to carry on with the Thanksgiving she'd planned with her friends. One of them would fly out for a weekend right after the holiday, they decided.

The plane began its descent, shredding clouds, and the unfamiliar landscape below gradually emerged. *Now I'm always going to hate this time of year.* No you aren't, he'd insisted to her. In six months it will be over, really over, and you'll have your whole life ahead of you. How were any of them going to get through what lay ahead, especially Brett? During those confusing first months of treatment and afterward, he'd grieved the loss of her spleen, the brutal assault of chemo and radiation on her splendid body, her young life thrown offtrack by illness just as she was coming into her own. He'd grieved her loss of innocence, the loneliness of her suffering, the unfairness of the whole ordeal. But the tears he'd cried recently sprang from an intimation of loss too profound to contemplate at all. "We're disappointed," one of her doctors had said concerning the recurrence, "but we think you have a good chance." That shocked and angered him. Chance of what? Brett's ultimate survival had never been in question, no matter what she might have to endure.

That day of rage and tears when she'd first learned she had Hodgkin's again, she said as their conversation came to an end, "I'm never going to be sick when I'm old. I'm doing it all now."

In blue jeans, with short, dark hair, Beth was waiting at the arrival gate as he got off the plane. As if to skirt his disappointment—he'd been anticipating the sight of his daughter's face—he approached her too impetuously, maybe, for someone who had only laid eyes on her twice before, and she seemed shy of his he-man embrace. He was grateful to this young woman for the impossible part she seemed willing to undertake. Within weeks of their Santa Fe rendezvous, surely with no idea of what she was in for, Beth found herself entering the frightening world of serious illness. I want to be there for her, she'd told him over the phone. They'd been together all of a month, and yet their relationship had already been subjected to extreme emotions and events, the sort of intensity that tore people apart if it didn't forge enduring bonds. Beth had comforted his daughter through the initial shock of the recurrence. They'd thrown their first big Thanksgiving dinner together despite their sudden unhappiness. She had bravely accompanied Brett to the exacting grind of yet another bone-marrow biopsy—evidently Andrew Leavitt was getting better at that; the first time, the table shook as he put his weight behind the instrument, the thickness of a pencil, trying to penetrate the bone in her backside— and earlier in the week, on Tuesday, she was there for Brett's first chemo infusion and its grisly aftermath. That, it seemed to him, would have been plenty to discourage most people, especially young people intent on their pleasure and entitled to be free, hopefully for decades, from the daily miseries of arduous illness. Yet here she was greeting this stranger, Brett's anxious and overeager father, with a smile.

"How is she?" he asked.

"She wanted to be here to meet you but just couldn't make it." The intense nausea following the infusion on Tuesday—vomiting every ten minutes as if she'd suffered food poisoning—had let up by the following morning, but Brett was still exhausted and feverish two days later, and this morning, stomach cramps had immobilized her. "But she's pretty amazing," Beth said. While Leavitt was extracting marrow from her bones, she was asking him how his Thanksgiving had been.

Driving to the city, Beth talked about how much she liked San Francisco so far, job prospects, their apartment—as if everything in her life here were going according to plan.

Their apartment on Central Avenue, a steep block above Haight Street and just below Buena Vista Park, was in a newly painted three-story Victorian building with typically elaborate moldings and handsome pillars. At a glance this was a welcome improvement on his daughter's previous address. The apartment was on the first floor, a wide flight of steps above the street. He took a breath to calm himself.

She was still in pajamas this sunny blue day when she opened the door to greet him—the Black Watch plaid pajamas he'd been given one year, he realized, but had passed on to her. His last sight of his daughter had been at the airport only three months earlier. Striding down the wide carpeted concourse to board her flight to another start in California, she had turned to wave confidently. "I feel I can do any-thing now," she'd told him one afternoon that summer. She would need every ounce of that self-assurance in the months ahead.

"Hi," she smiled.

After the past two weeks, it was a relief finally to put his arms around her.

The new place was fairly spacious and light-filled, with tall ceilings, two fireplaces, unusually fancy oak floors, and a glassed-in back porch.

"Don't you love it, Dad?"

They drove through Golden Gate Park, lushly tropical to him—sequoia, eucalyptus, palm trees, fern, and rhododendron. When they reached the beach they decided to get out of the car.

"I love to come here." She hadn't been outdoors since her chemotherapy infusion on Tuesday.

The previous Easter the whole family, the five of them, had come to this beach. Dressed in gold blousy pants and a colorful antique kimono and beautifully bald, Brett looked then like a member of some Eastern religious sect. Her treatment was under way at that point, following considerable debate, but she'd been an indefatigable host. There was a wonderful photograph of her standing on the beach with her arms outstretched in an expansive, even triumphant, gesture: hallelujah. They'd taken many pictures to commemorate that day. Everyone looked well, everyone was smiling—an optimistic and youthful family striving on under temporarily troubled circumstances. Now that batch of snapshots captured an innocence that he'd never suspected at the time.

She took his arm as they walked down the wide beach, the wind in their faces. She moved slowly, slightly stooped—the chemo hunch, one of her friends called it—her black tam tugged down on her head. Surfers wearing black wetsuits, both men and women, bobbed on the water like seals, waiting for a wave. Kites high above the beach wagged in the air as if impatient to sail free. A tireless dog acrobatically fielded a tossed Frisbee. His daughter walked as if walking hurt. You had to go along, shooting the breeze, as though you weren't dismayed and crushed by the people here, the sky, the ocean, everything. He hated seeing her this way. Typically, she would have run directly to the water, splashing up to her knees in the cold surf.

She wanted to hear about her younger sister and brother.

Jocelyn was in Florence for her junior year of college, studying art. As they continued along the beach, he summarized what he knew about her life abroad so far—her ancient apartment, the unbelievably good food, trips to Rome and Venice, a man she'd met in the program, also an American, and fallen in love with—as in a fairy tale, it must have seemed to Brett.

"That little artist," she smiled. She hadn't said how she felt about her sister being out of the country while she undertook another hellish course of cancer treatment. She'd never suggest that Jocelyn return to the States.

In September, Nathaniel, the youngest, instead of starting college like most of his friends, had sailed out of Newport on a tall ship.

"The Salty Dog," she said.

They discussed additional measures that might help her through the next six months. Megavitamins, acupuncture, support groups. She had already begun to pursue those possibilities. The fear was that her body wouldn't be able to withstand the normally prescribed six cycles of chemotherapy. Judging from her response to her initial treatment, her doctors didn't believe her white count would bear up. They intended to take the therapy as far as possible, but one specialist had told her to prepare herself for a bone-marrow transplant, which sounded nightmarish.

"Three times," and she laughed to tell it, "he's told me I could die in a transplant." No, such last-ditch options weren't something she had to think about now.

Several surfers began frantically paddling as a wall of water arose behind them. Two of them caught the wave. A young woman, powerful-looking in her black wetsuit, took it the farthest.

When they returned to Central Avenue, she sat on the steps waiting for Beth to unlock the door, pale, her breathing stressed. Their brief stroll down the beach had seemed leisurely and relaxed. In fact she had extended herself, inspired by his presence, eager to seem okay, and the modest outing had tired her.

It was easier, he realized—easier for him—to be with her in this trouble than to be apart from her. Separation made him prey to impossible imaginings, anxiety, and guilt. But to find her so altered, all her youthful fire subdued, following one blast of the fucking chemo. The first time around the doctors had decided a combination of four chemicals, collectively called MOPP, was the appropriate regimen for Brett's case. The first of these, mechlorethamine, was a derivative of the agents they'd used to make mustard gas in World War I. This time they were hoping another recipe, ABVD, would be kinder to her body as well as to her white count. The evidence following the first infusion wasn't encouraging.

"Damn it," she said, exasperated by her fatigue.

But an hour later, showered and changed for the evening, she appeared transformed, her complexion rosy, lips brightened with color. They found a festive restaurant in North Beach—nouvelle California Italian, Brett called it. She devoured an appetizer, salad, her whole hunk of swordfish—"It's so good to see you eat," Beth said—and they began to have fun, talking about the trip out west, Eastern Europe unraveling, Bush's language, lesbianism, the San Francisco art scene, new love. Before returning to the apartment they spent an hour browsing in a bookstore. He bought her a new volume of poetry by Sharon Olds, which she especially wanted, and an anthology of spiritual writings, a handsomely packaged book entitled *The Enlightened Heart*. By ten, the three of them were ready to turn in. They had avoided Hodgkin's disease for this evening out, and the evening was better for it.

Alone in his daughter's room—Brett would sleep in Beth's bedroom while he was there—he was moved to observe the life she had begun to put together here. She'd painted the room a warm off-white. There was a beveled mirror over the ornate Victorian mantel. In addition to the desk, Beth had made a bookcase and a night table, all painted white. Brett's aquamarine comforter contributed to the feeling of being near the ocean. Her grandmother's hooked rugs provided textured color on the inlaid oak floors. Jocelyn was present in a large self-portrait in oils, which the painter disclaimed at this point in her artistic development but which was a vivid and enjoyable likeness nonetheless. Everything here was orderly and cared for. She had arranged special stones, sand dollars, and shells, mementos of her travels and times of her life, on top of the bookcase and the mantelpiece, like sacred objects. They *were* sacred, he supposed. Her collection of poetry books represented an authentic passion. There were numerous cards and photographs and manila envelopes containing letters and important papers. There was a shelf of her journals in various sizes and shapes. Her violin, on the bottom shelf of the bookcase, was another crucial element of her inner life. She had hoped this year to get involved with a chamber group, something. There was a soccer ball in the corner on the floor. Long braids flying, he thought. He wanted her to play the violin again, if only for herself; he wanted her to play soccer again, a Sunday afternoon in the park, three or four to a side, just to open the lungs and stir the blood. Healthy blood.

The cowboy hat from Santa Fe—how happy she appeared in photographs from that trip a month ago!—hung on the wall, and a used, broken-in pair of cowboy boots from the same journey stood by the fireplace looking like old friends. It was an aesthete's spare, ascetic room, which conveyed what was important to her. She wasn't motivated by material things. The room represented her idea of home, everything she needed to make her life here. On her desk, along with books, photographs, various papers, there was a folder of information from UCSF pertaining to her course of treatment.

Now I have this wonderful apartment . . . to be sick in.

. . .

The previous December, almost a year earlier, he'd gone into her bedroom in Conway her first night back home in Massachusetts after her brief venture on the West Coast. The evening felt incomplete to him, her loneliness unacknowledged in the cheerful banter of everyone's being together again. She was lying on her back with her eyes open. They embraced, and tears momentarily surfaced as he pressed his face against her shoulder.

"It's going to be all right," she said. Spontaneously, she moved her hand to the back of his head, pushing her fingers through his hair, comforting him, the father, who had come into her room to offer comfort. The intimate, unexpected gesture startled him, and rather than shield her from his fear, he wanted to confide it.

"It's so scary," he said. "It hurts, it really hurts."

A moment later, as he straightened up to leave the room, she said, "Thanks for coming in." As he pulled her bedroom door shut behind him, she added, "It's good to be home."

It's going to be all right. That was the assurance they'd received from the medical establishment from the beginning. "I have every reason to believe that she'll be cured," Andrew Leavitt had boldly told them during a minor setback that first year of treatment. Leavitt's wife, a psychiatrist, had had Hodgkin's disease many years before, a fact that contributed to their confidence in the man's determined outlook. He believed his daughter would come through, unquestionably, but the additional cumulative costs frightened him, her immediate suffering as well as the long-term repercussions.

Why Brett had gotten Hodgkin's disease was a question he'd given up—but why had the disease so suddenly recurred? What had been overlooked or misjudged? What could have been done to make a difference? He'd been over these issues repeatedly, and now, wishing to sleep, he found himself futilely going over them again.

In Canada Hodgkin's patients automatically received six months of chemotherapy as the sole treatment, which avoided the whole splenectomy issue. The Canadian approach had something to do with the costs and contingencies of socialized medicine but was also posited on the supposition that diagnostic surgery to examine the lymph nodes and the spleen might fail to uncover microscopic disease. Doctors in the United States, however, sought to avoid chemotherapy because of the greater severity and duration of treatment, as well as possible side effects such as sterility and, years later, secondary tumors, namely leukemia. Empirically, the surgeon at Dana Farber had informed them, the chance of missing disease was very low, and Brett's preliminary scans had indicated that the risk of the operation was worth taking.

The surgeon had also assured Brett that her disease could not be progressing as rapidly as she, who was sensitive to her body, believed it was. The cancer had taken years to develop, he explained—this wasn't an emergency; a few weeks made no difference. Nor had George Canellos been concerned about the short term when they'd contacted him before the holiday. Subsequent X-rays and CAT scans showed that Brett had been right. The oncological surgeon was wrong. In particular, the tumor in her chest, which they'd known about from the outset, had enlarged in a startlingly short time. If it continued to grow, radiation would soon be ruled out because of the risk to her heart and lungs. Suddenly it seemed to have been a mistake not to have acted as promptly as possible—before Christmas rather than after. In the end, additional scans persuaded the doctors that the laparotomy, involving a splenectomy, was still appropriate. The date of the operation was moved up.

As it turned out, no disease was discovered below the diaphragm. Brett recuperated from the surgery rapidly. Soon she was on her way back to San Francisco to begin radiation. Within two months this would all be over—that was the thing to bear in mind. The transition from Dana Farber to Moffitt Hospital at UCSF couldn't have gone more smoothly.

Doctors at Moffitt, however, continued to be concerned about the growth in her chest. They decided to put her through an MRI, which provided a more precise image of the heart. That procedure detected a "layer" of cancerous cells too near her heart to risk radiation therapy. She would need chemotherapy after all. That had been shattering, the first major blow since she'd been diagnosed.

Of course, the disease in her chest had been *the* question at Dana Farber. Why hadn't they employed magnetic resonance imaging there? Canellos explained that they didn't use that technology for such cases in Massachusetts, not yet anyway.

"So if Brett had remained at Dana Farber for radiation therapy, the undetected and untreated cancer would have recurred?"

"It's conceivable," Canellos suggested, "that the scatter or broadcast of radiation would have gotten those cells without damaging the heart."

"That sounds awfully arbitrary."

"Unfortunately, for patients with tumors in the center of the chest, like Brett's, there's a thirty percent chance of recurrence in any case."

This was the first anyone had mentioned such a statistic to either of them. "Is that due to the very predicament we're talking about—the radiation inevitably fails to address those cells too close to the heart?"

Canellos said, "That isn't clear."

"Maybe it's worth taking the chance on radiation now and sparing Brett the chemo. That was the whole point of the laparotomy, wasn't it?"

"When the data is staring you in the face," he said, "you can't ignore it." As for Brett's laparotomy, that hadn't been in vain. The knowledge gained would be crucial to designing the most appropriate treatment. "You don't need the spleen," Canellos told him. "That's over." It was possible she would require only minimal chemo, along with radiation. "It would be worse," he said, "to have the disease recur following radiation, forcing her to go through the maximum chemo treatment then."

"The bottom line in all this is that she'll be cured, one way or the other." His bold assertion pleaded for confirmation.

"It's not a hundred percent," Canellos replied, "as I told you."

Dana Farber was universally recognized as one of the premier cancer treatment centers. In his daughter's case they had missed what UCSF had discovered, and they would have treated her unsuccessfully. They might have gotten lucky, Canellos had suggested. How much was luck and nothing but luck? What had they overlooked in San Francisco, for all their high-tech apparatus, because they didn't know how to look?

He'd called Sloan-Kettering in New York and managed to speak to a woman who specialized in Hodgkin's disease. Sloan-Kettering didn't use MRI in such cases either. As the doctor got the drift of his phone call—Had Dana Farber culpably omitted necessary procedures?—her tone became impatient. Look on the bright side, she advised. It was fortunate they'd seen the cancer in California. His daughter's prognosis was very good. As for the most suitable chemo regimen, George Canellos was the man to consult. He knew more about MOPP and ABVD than anyone in the field.

Francine Halberg, Brett's radiation oncologist at UCSF, had said that there they would have reduced the tumor in her chest with radiation immediately, before the surgery, just to be sure they had it under control. There was no way of knowing whether that would have happened or not. It seemed the radiation oncologist wouldn't have been called in until the staging had been done. Would they have taken an MRI prior to the splenectomy to establish the need for preliminary radiation? And if they had, would they have found the cancer to be too near the heart at that time? The truth was, they began to see, this so-called curable disease was far more complicated than they'd imagined or anyone had yet made them realize.

And it was lucky, wasn't it, that she had returned to San Francisco after all. At least, that's what he'd attempted to argue long-distance to somehow alleviate his daughter's anguish over the whole mess. Far from being comforted, she may have felt more alone with the ominous new verdict. All her luck! She was lucky it was Hodgkin's, she'd been told, instead of some worse lymphoma, lucky she'd discovered it at an early stage, lucky to have received the best available care at Dana Farber, and then she was lucky to be at UCSF where they could reevaluate all her previous luck. Andrew Leavitt had called him at that time, when they were developing a plan of treatment, and insisted that between Dana Farber, UCSF, and Stanford, with whom they frequently communicated, his daughter's case was getting the best possible attention. That thought was no longer as reassuring as it had been.

Following two cycles of MOPP, two months, an MRI scan showed the disease had been substantially reduced, and the consensus was—people at Moffitt had conferred with Stanford at something called a Tumor Board—that the risks of further chemo outweighed the benefits. They were convinced radiation was the best choice to complete the therapy. "I feel like I've won an Oscar," he remembered Brett saying. But radiation, once it began, turned out to be more problematic than they'd foreseen. Treatment had to be postponed when Brett's white count was down. In the first month, out of a possible twenty-seven treatments, she had received only fifteen. Francine Halberg spoke of her as an atypical case, a person with very sensitive bone marrow.

But then her white count did stabilize, she received the balance of radiation therapy on schedule, visualizing like mad, she said, and praying to a Chinese goddess. And then it was over. He had called George Canellos for the last time, he believed, and summarized the successful outcome. At UCSF they believed she stood an eighty percent chance of being completely cured. Those were good odds.

"We're assuming it's over," he said.

"You can't assume that," Canellos replied in the firm, rather dignified manner he'd cultivated over the years for just such sensitive discussions. He added, "A cure is a function of time."

And now ... the disease was present again in less than five months, not years, and his daughter was facing the maximum chemotherapy on top of what she'd already been subjected to. If she'd done the six cycles in the first place and been spared the splenectomy, spared radiation, everything might be different. It might really be over. There had been no way to make that call at the time.

Change one detail, and everything might be otherwise—or nothing might be otherwise. Questions oppressed him, and yet he was unable to see how they could have proceeded, detail for detail, differently. Throughout the past year he and his daughter had been as determined, vigilant, and questioning as possible, it seemed to him. He also believed that in Boston and then in San Francisco her doctors had done—they continued to do—all they could for her. In many respects, the sad truth was, they didn't know what they were doing.

They'd insisted on the bone-marrow harvest because they'd feared recurrence. Did that imply that something might have been, should have been, done differently? What did the doctors know or suspect now concerning his daughter's illness that they weren't revealing?

Leavitt had recently told him that the prognosis was less positive with patients who recurred so suddenly.

But it was not as though Brett's disease had recurred after maximum treatment or had turned up in a new site. The disease had arisen in exactly the same place in her chest. Wasn't it plausible that her recurrence represented cancer cells that survived the initial treatment? Two cycles of chemotherapy hadn't been enough, apparently, and the cells near the heart hadn't been subject to radiation. "Six cycles of chemotherapy will be a different story." Surely such considerations improved his daughter's prognosis.

Leavitt stuck to the available research. "There are more plausible hypotheses than data to support them," he said. In his view Brett had received appropriate and thorough treatment for her illness. There was a fifty percent chance of recurrence for Hodgkin's patients, he said now, presumably including all cases of the disease, and for those cancers that did recur, there was a fifty percent chance of cure. In essence you could say that Brett had a fifty-fifty chance. The fortunate thing was that Hodgkin's, unlike most other cancers, was subject to secondary treatment.

But what did the numbers mean to the flesh-and-blood sufferer? Brett had started out with a ninety percent chance, and following her treatment they decided it was eighty percent. The truth was that whatever happened to each and every individual patient happened one hundred percent, and that was all that mattered. His own explanation for the recurrence made the renewed onset of disease seem less terrifying, less out of control; maximum chemotherapy was bound to be conclusive. There was no other way to think about it.

And for all the frustration and pain, for all his skepticism concerning his daughter's *luck*, there had been luck of a kind. Brett's health insurance under their family plan had ended, predictably, the moment she graduated from college, and in that interval between school and *real work*, before she could secure health-care benefits or afford private insurance, unimaginable illness had struck, leaving her, financially, in no-man's-land. Fortunately, they'd been able to cover her personal living expenses, and they were prepared to do so as long as necessary, but the state of California had covered the extravagant medical costs so far, and it seemed that coverage would continue. Otherwise they would be wiped out.

He awoke with a start, and it was long seconds before he realized he was in his daughter's apartment in San Francisco. Light from the street insinuated itself through the closed blinds, casting narrow horizontal shadows across the room. He was discouraged to find it was only midnight. A sadness came down on him as his eyes adjusted to the partial dark and he observed her new room again. He imagined her awakening in this room only weeks before and finding herself drenched with perspiration, so soaking wet she had to get up and change her clothes: her terror, her already rapid pulse racing faster.

One memory suited the imminent season: a girl with long strawberry-blond hair in a white dress intensely playing the Corelli "Christmas Concerto" to a hushed crowd while he held his breath. Randomly, he saw her racing around the corner of their former house in denim overalls, ten years old, trying out new sneakers, and grinning with her original smile, as yet unaltered by braces . . . or painstakingly selecting stones and shells on a bright beach, wearing shorts and a T-shirt—in Maine, Massachusetts, the Caribbean. A tall, thin girl with braids, her face flushed pink, nimbly dancing a soccer ball down the green—that was another image—or seated at the kitchen table, frowning over outspread homework. Most of life became school. For a couple of years he frequently took her to grade school on the crossbar of his ten-speed bike, still a kid himself in those days. Then, for a time, he drove her to school every morning, along with her sister and brother as they came of age, because they attended school in a neighboring town where the public education seemed better. Mainly, he loved those twenty minutes in the car each morning discussing everything that mattered—friends and teachers, a project, politics, problems, the meanings of words, looks, feelings.

He recalled the sound of her coming down the long, narrow hall, home from school, to enter his study again and again, bringing him all her exciting news of the world. More than his other two children, his oldest daughter wanted to tell him about her day and she was eager to hear his responses. At the end of the day she would be sitting up in her bed, furiously writing in her journal, getting her most important thoughts on paper. He saw her waving from the gracious porch of a dormitory . . . waving from the parade of classmates, laughing in her black, tasseled mortarboard . . . waving from the concourse of the airline terminal.

He opened his eyes to stop the slide show of arbitrary, out-of-focus images. She might take issue with such a selectively sanguine view of her growing up, yet it was those pictures, rather than less happy ones, that came to mind as he lay awake in her room. Perhaps because she was now so far from being that child, the kid in braids, a student of the violin and literature, his sidekick.

In the next room she began to cough, the harsh cough she'd been left with since radiation. He listened to her walk down the hallway to the bathroom and feared she was going to be sick after the large meal he'd urged her to finish in the restaurant. That didn't happen. Her cough was like a wound that wouldn't heal.

The traffic from Haight Street was a constant background noise. You adapted to that, but he couldn't block out the voices that repeatedly intruded—laughter, a shout, a gang of contending male voices at one point that sounded on the verge of violence. If, intermittently, he dozed, he woke up almost immediately to new disturbances, people drunk, complaining, angry.

He quietly made his way down the hall. The window in the bathroom opened onto a quadrangle. Somewhere above or below him a woman was in the heedless, unmistakable throes of an enviable orgasm. Normal life, he thought. His absence of desire reflected how removed he felt from it.

I'm not a normal person with this. All her intelligence and strength and ambition and love of life—all she had achieved so far—going into this impossible labor. The stakes had never been greater, and yet it felt like you were working for nothing—no awards, no promotion, nothing to show. Thankless drudgery that went on behind the scenes of ordinary endeavor, squandering precious resources. When he was her age, twenty-four, he'd been in graduate school, the anxious father of a child aged three. The thought of serious illness had never crossed his mind. Cancer was as remote as old age or sudden death.

At seven o'clock he showered, then let himself out into the street, which was quiet now, forsaken by the host of phantoms that had disrupted his fitful night's sleep. He turned up Cole, the route his daughter walked to the UCSF complex, which stood at the top of Parnassus, overlooking the park and the bay with its famous bridge. The proximity of the hospital, as well as of the park and the ocean, spoke in favor of her living here. He stopped at an already busy, almost festive café, people meeting for coffee on Saturday morning. He had nothing in common with them. He didn't need to climb Parnassus to the medical center in an effort to identify with his daughter's familiar routine. He returned along Frederick to Buena Vista Park, a quiet neighborhood of attractive homes one block above Brett's address. Such a mild, sunny morning in December felt like a deception.

With confident panache, Beth steered them through the steep streets of the town in her small blue car. Damage from the earthquake to some of the Marina District's pastel stucco homes didn't look like the end of the world. They were lucky to find a parking place in North Beach. Brett led them down Grant through the swarming exotica of Chinatown. Ginseng, ivory, dangling chickens, junk. They entered a brick building through an open side door. A man shrunken with age was furiously whipping up food in a tiny kitchen. A narrow, twisting staircase led to the cramped restaurant, a handful of tables, on the second floor. The Hou Temple, the oldest Chinese temple in the city, was on the third floor, with a balcony that looked out onto the thronged street. The dim red room was pungent with incense. Prayer signs hung from the ceiling like banners. There were many small altars, laden with offerings of oranges and tea, and numerous candles. Brett knelt at one of the enclosures while he browsed like a casual visitor to a bizarre museum. The world of the temple was too remote to move him. When had she discovered this place? What did it give her?

They bought several cartons of Chinese food and walked to Washington Square, the small park there, to eat it. Wasted-looking men slept on the grass or sat huddled over paper bags. A person maybe thirty, aged by neglect, approached their bench and asked for change.

They gave him their carton of Chinese noodles and a plastic fork. He hungrily ate with his fingers.

Beth went off to run an errand, and they were alone in the car for a moment. Brett leaned forward from the backseat. "I've been having these dreams lately," she said. "Sometimes nightmares. My fevers seem to bring them on."

"Dreams or nightmares?" he asked.

"In one dream I entered a large room, a gathering of some kind. Everyone was there, our family, friends, everyone, and everyone was clearly older. The Littles' sons were there, for example. You know?" The youngest son of that family had been Jocelyn's boyfriend in high school. "I came into the room and tried to participate. I was there, but no one paid any attention to me, no one acknowledged me." Quietly she added, "I was a ghost."

He didn't want to appear alarmed, to credit dreams with significance; a cool attitude toward these unwanted visitations might diminish their power to frighten her. "That must be inevitable," he said, "the subconscious working overtime." Bad dreams were normal.

"It was so strange," she told him. "Everybody was there, and they couldn't see me."

She decided to try to nap before they went out to dinner. He walked down to Haight Street, as teeming late Saturday afternoon as Chinatown had been at midday. Die-hard hippies. Bands of lingering kids. The street was a refuge for the derelict and adrift, the mentally ill and mortally ill, drunks, addicts, the lost, wretched, who huddled in sociable groups or sprawled on the sidewalk under sheets of cardboard, out cold. Street musicians played up a storm that was lost in the general din. Plenty of leather, chains, torn denim, rings on ears, noses, fingers, numerous rings, bracelets, beads, the nostalgic—to him—scent of marijuana. Mainstream types were clearly in the majority—for all the visible remnants of the old days, the street was essentially a shopping district—but the upper Haight was still a show, exhilarating to someone as unaccustomed as he was to crowds of any kind. More than anything else, he noticed the young women, inventively togged up, with wild hair and vivid, bee-stung lips, exuberantly pawing through racks of goods, laughing, excited, or presenting made-up faces ridiculously bored, but mostly just being themselves, young, out on the street. The sight of them made him wince.

Beth came toward him as he let himself into the apartment. "Would you go and see Brett? She wants to see you."

She lay on her back on the bed in Beth's darkened room. Left to herself here she had tumbled into a bad moment. He sat on the edge of the bed and embraced her.

"I was lying here thinking about Maine this summer," she said. "About how wonderful it was, lying on the rocks in the sun, and the boys climbing the cliffs." She had gone to Maine with him and Holly to revisit the landscape of many summers. They'd hiked the perimeter of Monhegan and the cliffs of Acadia. At the Otter Cliffs they'd sunned themselves while lithe teenage boys ascended vertical rock faces, dipping their fingers into leather bags of chalk. The surf spray showered them at Scootic Point as it had on excursions there for almost a decade of summers, and at Grindstone Neck in Winter Harbor they collected beautiful smooth stones for mementos and gifts and built cairns on prominent rock formations to celebrate their visit. "I believed I was better."

"I know."

"It was over, and now this. Why?" That was a cry of emotion, not a question. "Cancer, Dad."

"It's not fair. It hurts. You were always healthy and strong," he said. "You will be again."

She touched his chest. "I feel very close to you, you know," she said, "but I feel so alone with this. It's so lonely."

The only way he could think to comfort her was to commiserate. She was right, it *was* lonely.

25

She remembered going in for an infusion last year. Doctors came into the clinic and told the woman next to her that the only possibility left was a transplant, and the woman broke down. Brett felt sad for her, but she also felt, That's not me. I'm better off than she is. "And now it *is* me," she said. "I've had these setbacks from the beginning—these *atypical* setbacks."

"There is no typical experience of cancer. The doctors have their idea of what's typical, their ideal sequence of events, but there's no such thing. Everyone suffers their own setbacks and disappointments." And the bone-marrow transplant wasn't inevitable. They had to wait and see. Right now they were planning to get through the chemo.

"It can't get any worse, Dad."

"I know." He gently rubbed her shoulder, momentarily avoiding her eyes. At a loss, he said, "People suffer." Did she need to be reminded that people suffered? "People have suffered so much in every conceivable way." He didn't need to enumerate plagues, wars, death camps, the daily horror of starvation and violence overwhelming humans moment by moment. "We've been fortunate. For years, you know, your whole life. Now this is our burden, except it's happening to you. And no one can do it for you." That hadn't come out right, not what he meant somehow.

"It's hard to believe in what I believed before—visualization, all that. My body, my self. The doctors. I trusted them."

He nodded.

"I feel out of control. I feel like I'm losing control of my life. I don't know what I should be doing or if I'm doing the right things."

He decided to respond at the most literal level. "No, you are in control," he told her. "Undergoing the treatment is taking control. You're doing everything you should be doing right now. The right thing is to trust Leavitt and go with his view. He's your doctor."

They had not seriously considered alternatives to mainstream Western medicine, mainly because it was the conventional allopathic approach that promised a cure for Hodgkin's. Other therapies, whether experimental or traditional, didn't. With the recurrence, the proven treatment seemed even more imperative. And now, more than ever, time was of the essence. She was in no position to set off on some wild-goose chase while her disease progressed.

"They have the drugs that will destroy the disease," he said. "The issue is that you must endure it."

"Everyone talks about how brave I am. I don't want to be brave, I can't be brave all the time."

This talk had begun, he realized, with mention of her frightening dreams earlier that day. She didn't want to perform bravely all week-end in the interest of a congenial visit. She wanted him to know what she was going through; she needed him to grasp her pain.

She took his hand and twisted the silver band on his middle finger. "I wanted children, you know. I always thought someday I'd have children."

Infertility had been a major concern during her first treatment when chemotherapy became inevitable, and that concern had influenced the decision to stop after two cycles. With the recurrence the whole immense question, Brett's possible children, was simply dropped. The stakes had changed.

She frowned, thinking, then met his eyes again. "I don't want my life to be divided between before cancer and after cancer. Do you know what I mean by that?"

Again, he felt an urgency to respond, to rescue her from her own discerning insights, and he felt pressured, inadequate. "There's no be-fore and after. It's all one." The year before she'd made him a card with a Neruda poem inside. "I always gained something from making myself better / . . . to search once more for the light that sings / inside of me, the unwavering light." Somehow all this was going to contribute positively to her life, he'd told her, as in the Neruda poem. Below the poem she wrote, "Everything you have done for me . . . I will be there for you." Now he said to her, "You're going to get better, you're going to be well. Words are cheap, I know, but . . . This will be over, and you'll go on. No before and after. All one life."

Several times, with a certain deliberateness, she said, "I love you, Dad." Those words were like a gift in a box—something she wanted him to have, he felt, in case she didn't get better. She'd been crying at first and he had struggled not to cry, holding her, her moist, heated face near his. They gradually came out of that, the heaviness, the oppressiveness lifted.

"These moments recur," she said, emphasizing the new word that had entered their vocabulary. "At first I was crying all the time, then you begin to adapt. Now I go along just fine, and suddenly it strikes me down again."

Moments later, on her way to the shower, she gave him a wonderful smile. "I'm all right," she said. "I have to do that, I have to get it out. Afterwards I feel so much better." And ten minutes after that she emerged from her room looking absolutely beautiful, he thought, in a white silk blouse, her short red hair still damp, her complexion glowing.

They spent part of the next morning reading in the Sunday *Times* about momentous, almost unimaginable events, Eastern Europe unraveling now that the Berlin Wall, the month before, had collapsed, as if the whole damn world was about to be set free. Brett couldn't get as excited about such global upheavals as he was. It was another gloriously blue, sunny day. She longed for clouds, she said, and rain. Back in Massachusetts, when he called home, it was zero.

Eve Arbogast met them for brunch. She and Brett had met during their sophomore year at Smith, when a house near campus had burned down in the middle of the night. In the midst of that beauty and danger, Brett reached out and took the hand of the girl standing beside her. Sometime afterward she marched into her parents' living room, decked out to go dancing that night, and announced to them, I'm in love with Eve. In vivid contrast to Brett's red-blond fairness, Eve had black hair and dark eyes. They went through school together, lived in Ireland for some months, traveled through Europe, and when it was time to get serious about living somewhere, they came to San Francisco together. That first year on the West Coast, while his daughter struggled with the advent of illness, the relationship suffered a crisis, Brett became involved with someone else, and by the time that infatuation had run its course, there was no going back to first love, the original flame, although they remained important friends.

"You look great," he told Eve. The picture of ripe youth. Thick, tangled hair, shapely, unshaved legs, a thoroughly wholehearted, almost goofy smile.

Walking down Haight Street in a tweed jacket between these two young women, he felt like an outsider being given safe escort in a strange land.

She was teaching English as a second language to adults.

"All the men are in love with her," Brett said. "Señorita Eve."

They spent the afternoon in the park again, a vast playground on Sundays, when cars were barred from the wide, smooth blacktop and the place streamed with all manner of runners and joggers and walkers, people on skateboards, bikes, rollerskates. He fell back a step for just a moment and observed his daughter in the midst of all this normal exuberance: her careful, tentative posture as she walked, the pallor of her skin outdoors as the day wore on, her constrained smile. Christ! he thought, stricken for her.

For an hour they sat on a grassy bank and watched rollerskaters dance to rhythm and blues, rock and roll. A beautiful black woman dressed in slick black pants and a leotard top was a show. Gradually, a man insinuated himself into the sphere of the woman's scene, she adapted to his moves, and what ensued was something like mating, their insistent corresponding rhythms playing off one another, all nuance—subtle, cadenced, mesmerizing—each attuned gesture emphatic. When the music stopped, the woman threw her head back, her arms dropped limp at her sides, and she broke up, laughing, slapping the man's hand a slow whack.

"They're so great," Brett said.

On the way back she went up to Eve's apartment on Page Street to use the bathroom while he and Eve waited outside.

"I'm glad you came," she said. "Brett is a lot more relaxed with you here. It's obvious."

"It's impossible," he said. "We want to be here, of course, but how can we? We'll all be here for a week at Christmas, then we'll just have to play it by ear." If Brett's situation changed again—if the dreaded transplant became the only option—they'd do what they needed to do. "How are you managing?" he asked.

"At first I was in a state of shock. Now I'm scared. Last year it was Hodgkin's disease," she said. "Now it's cancer."

"I think we're all feeling that."

"I'm going to begin attending a support group for the families and loved ones of cancer patients. I hope that helps."

"Thanks for sticking by her," he said. "I know how much you mean to her."

They watched Brett descend the stairs of Eve's building and come toward them, not her former self. Eve gave each of them strong hugs. She hurriedly crossed the street and climbed the stairs without looking back. Following the pleasant afternoon, the abrupt sadness of their parting stung him.

"She's been a loyal friend," he said as they continued back to Central Avenue.

But the relationship was more complicated for Brett. "Eve's wonderful," she said. "She was fine this afternoon, but she can be difficult and emotional. She's still hurt, and that's not what I need now."

That night she made the salad while Beth, dancing in the kitchen, prepared pasta. A Bonnie Raitt tape was playing: love, just in the nick of time. They ate on the glass-enclosed porch by candlelight, off a black-and-white tablecloth. Later, she wanted him to view San Francisco at night, another of her discoveries, so they drove to Twin Peaks and got out and stood there looking at the glittering city below them without saying anything. On the way back they picked up a video, some psychological thriller; he never learned the title. The two girlfriends cuddled up on the couch together. Thank goodness for Beth, he thought. She caressed the back of his daughter's dense, coppery-red hair. It had grown in darker and coarser following the first bout of chemotherapy months before. She'd hardly gotten it back when she was about to lose it again. Beth had never known Brett with her wonderful pre-chemo hair. In some ways she'd never quite grasp that "original" person, would she? It occurred to him that these two young women wouldn't have entered into a relationship if the cancer had been known. *I believed I was better.* Their window of opportunity, their chance for love, had been narrow; they'd just squeezed through.

"I think you're awfully lucky you ran into Beth," he told her.

Brett touched her girlfriend's face affectionately. "Isn't she a sweetie?"

Beth said, "I'm the one that feels lucky."

His last night's sleep was as fitful as the preceding two had been, haunted by the images he'd acquired from being with her. He got up at five. He showered and dressed, putting on a tie this morning. He sat at his daughter's desk and inscribed the book he'd bought her the night in North Beach, thanking her for this weekend in her house. He looked around the room again carefully, committing its contents to memory. He closed his eyes, wishing her well here. Within half an hour, he heard the girls—he was still capable of thinking of them that way, he was afraid—getting up, shuffling back and forth to the bathroom, then Brett getting ready.

"Are you all set? We should be going."

"Now or never," she said.

Beth was on her way back to bed as they left. It was still dark, and they drove the brief route she typically walked—up Waller, left onto Cole, then right onto Parnassus. Moffit-Long Hospital was at the crest of the hill, directly across the street from the clinic. The place was familiar to her, and she didn't seem anxious as they entered. He was less calm. His only experience of hospitals was as a visitor, never as a patient. To him they seemed forbidding institutions where unfortunate people mysteriously languished in dehumanizing isolation, confined to cells, until they were released. Despite the semblance of order and efficiency, there was, in the odors and polished corridors and the very look of people, an air of anxiety and imminent disarray.

In her individual curtained cubicle, his daughter stripped and donned a white-and-blue hospital tunic and got into the narrow hospital bed. He drew a white cotton blanket over her, but she was still cold; she was usually cold in these buildings. He grabbed two more blankets from a supply cart in the hall and tucked them firmly around her.

The enormity of her experience came down on him again. Monday morning. Instead of starting a new workweek, she had to check into the damn hospital. This was her work. Illness.

"Are you nervous?"

She smiled. "No."

"I am." The general anesthesia spooked him.

She had been similarly calm at Dana Farber one year earlier, when she faced the splenectomy. That exploratory operation had seemed the worst of her trials then.

Today's procedure, insertion of a subcutaneous port, was minor, but it was yet another invasive assault to be passively endured. Another scar. That was the least of it, of course: scar tissue. The catheter would be inserted into a vein in her chest. The only thing visible would be a quarter-size disc just beneath the skin, the port through which she'd receive her subsequent chemotherapy infusions, thereby sparing the already diminished veins in her arms. Her composure implied that she had already dealt with what he was feeling now, she was prepared for this next detail. She wanted to get it done.

"I like Beth a lot," he told her.

"She's smart, and she makes me laugh, which is a switch. We have fun together. It's good."

A tallish blond nurse in her thirties arrived with a blue notebook the thickness of the Manhattan phone directory: his daughter's UCSF medical record. The nurse braceleted the patient, then took her vital signs. Brett's pulse was ninety-two.

"Do you feel tense now?" he asked.

"No, I'm relaxed actually."

When the nurse left, he cursorily flipped through the medical record. Countless impersonal notations chronicled her soul-wrenching struggle, reducing it to a series of clinical problems. Toward the end of the book he stumbled on the result of the recent test that had been done to evaluate the condition of her heart.

"What's it say?" she asked.

"Small normal ventricles."

"Small?"

Francine Halberg had also noted that there might be evidence of an obstruction, but that was very uncertain. "Very" underlined. He didn't mention that to her.

"Your heart is fine," he said.

"It better be."

At age twenty-three his wife had also been calm, uncomplaining, brave as she lay in the hospital and endured a twelve-hour labor, giving birth to their first child. The Boston Lying-in Hospital. Eight pounds, ten ounces. Red hair. Love at first sight. January 11, 1965.

Was that where the root of his daughter's illness lay, in the innocent lovemaking of two kids almost twenty-five years earlier, their genetic matchup planting the seed of an impossibly misguided cell? How did you begin to think about that?

He checked his watch. They'd guessed that there'd be just enough time for him to take her to the hospital before heading out to the airport to catch his plane. He was cutting it close. "I can't stay." His flight was at seven-thirty.

"You better get going. I'm fine. They'll be taking me in a minute anyway."

"Call tonight, okay, and let us know how it went."

"Okay."

"The apartment is terrific. I think you're doing wonderfully. It was a good weekend. I'm glad I came."

"Me too."

"In a couple of weeks we'll all be back. That's going to be fun." The whole family, except Jocelyn, would return for the Christmas holiday.

"Beth and I will look for a tree. They must have them around here."

He parted the drawn curtain, glancing back for just a second—she raised her hand good-bye, smiling—and left. That was the hardest moment of his visit, more difficult than their talk Saturday afternoon in Beth's room. He hated leaving her lying in the cubicle of the pre-op room, waiting, thinking about everything, seeing the many aspects of her situation—the pain, the uncertainty, the impossible irony— too clearly.

Lurching through the corridors, hastening from the hospital, he avoided making eye contact with anyone, like a wounded man ashamed of his injuries.

His flight from San Francisco felt like escape, reprehensible. Once he was above the clouds the sense of separation disturbed him. Looking out at the billowing oceanic whiteness, he imagined her succumbing to the anesthesia—going under—too distracted by the operating-room ambience to be particularly anxious. Yes, he'd told her, it's lonely, that's the truth. Undergoing surgery, the implantation of a device intended to facilitate chemotherapy.

I don't want my life to be divided between before and after cancer.
That's not going to happen.

He opened the book he'd packed for this journey, a novelistic medi-
tation by Thomas Bernhard, a brilliant, endearing misanthrope, but
he found the prose too dense and relentless in his present mood. The
epigraph was from Kierkegaard: "The punishment matches the guilt:
to be deprived of all appetite for life, to be brought to the highest degree of weariness of life." Despair.

From the inside breast pocket of his jacket he took the envelope
containing three photographs that his daughter had given him. He
had asked her for them. Color snapshots of her in her Central Avenue
kitchen, busily working over the stove. She was dressed up in a dark-
green jumper and an earthy-colored sweater, lovely with her red hair,
and over her clothing she wore a vivid blue-and-white-striped bib
apron. Surprised, smiling, he recognized the pendant around her neck,
a piece of picture jasper that looked like a miniature Western landscape, a canyon under a vast sky, set in silver. He'd given that to Holly
years ago. It had become one of his wife's favorite pieces of jewelry,
and she was upset to realize, after considerable searching, that she'd
evidently lost it somehow. Perhaps the clasp had broken. Here it was!
The devil. The pendant epitomized their relationship: what's mine is
yours. Brett was smiling in each of the pictures, not for the camera but
authentically, happy. She looked rosy, gorgeous really. Her old self, for
all intents and purposes. The pictures had been taken at her big
Thanksgiving feast one week after Andrew Leavitt had told her she
had Hodgkin's again.

She had been anticipating the Christmas holiday in Massachusetts
as a celebratory occasion, in marked contrast to the year before. That
wasn't going to happen. So you let it go, you began figuring out the
next thing. He counted the months. She could be done with her therapy by May. In the context of the rest of her life, that wasn't the end
of the world: six months. They would have to accept whatever costs,
whatever permanent damage, attended her getting through them. All

right, they could do that. They would accept anything. He wanted her to have her life, that's all.

I don't want my life, he thought, to be divided between before and after cancer. Please, he muttered to the limitless nothingness beyond the oval plastic window.

By the time he changed planes in Pittsburgh, she was in recovery, he figured. She might even be ready to leave the hospital, provided the morning had gone smoothly.

He had placed the photographs in the book. He opened it to look at them again. To be brought to the highest degree of weariness of life . . . She glowed in these pictures, bravely forging ahead with her holiday plans. Thanksgiving. To be deprived of all appetite for life . . . In one snapshot she was grinning from ear to ear as she shoved a tablespoonful of something creamy directly at the camera, hamming it up.

She was going to be all right. It was right there in those pictures.

It was dark by the time the plane began its descent over New England. His wife would be waiting at the airport, eager for a full report of his visit. She would be happy for the photographs, for the little surprise they contained—the lost pendant found—and she would be happy, he supposed, for the way he seemed tonight, this unexpected optimism he'd brought back with him. Only three days before, as he'd left for San Francisco, he was like a man in despair.

2

CURE

Two infusions of chemotherapy, composed of adriamycin, bleomycin, vinblastine, and DITC, ideally administered twice a month, fifteen days apart, represented one cycle of treatment. All he knew about these chemicals was their names and certain effects of their toxicity. Six cycles, ideally carried out in six months, was the prescribed maximum treatment for Hodgkin's disease. Empirically, that regimen promised the best hope for a cure within limits that a normal patient could be expected to endure. Every two weeks, ideally, his daughter could count on being vilely ill for eight hours or so, followed by gradual recuperation. The impact of the therapy was cumulative, physically and psychologically, each month worse than the last. In addition to weight loss, hair loss, general debilitation, and fatigue, there was bound to be long-term damage to the heart and lungs. Infertility was a major concern. There was possibly a ten percent risk that the chemotherapy would cause leukemia within twenty years. His daughter would be forty-five in twenty years. And there were bound to be adverse and startling complications no one could anticipate. On the other hand, as far as they—or anyone they'd consulted—knew, there was no plausible alternative. If the disease were not eradicated, the patient would perish. Six cycles of chemotherapy had proven successful in cases of Hodgkin's significantly more advanced than his daughter's disease. Her cancer had not invaded organs such as the lungs, for example, or, worse, the bone marrow, and it was still confined to the lymphatic system above the diaphragm. Following the shock of recurrence, they were entitled to be hopeful.

Brett's white count plummeted after the very first infusion. If 5,000 was a number that stood for the normal sum of mature white cells and 3,000 was the minimum necessary to allow the next infusion to proceed, her count was 1,600. The doctors, hoping she would handle ABVD better than MOPP, hadn't expected such a dramatically negative impact after the first treatment. The harvest of her marrow in October had been a prescient move, after all; the bone-marrow transplant now seemed inevitable. The prognosis for that radical and experimental alternative was substantially improved, presumably, if the disease was already in retreat, so they intended to coax Brett through the first two cycles of chemo anyway. The grisly details she'd learned concerning the bone-marrow transplant—patients quarantined in sealed hospital rooms for months, profoundly ill, unable to eat or even drink for weeks—were too frightening to think about. A nuclear bomb set off inside you was how one nurse at the clinic crudely and inconsiderately described it. That wasn't happening yet, he insisted, despite his daughter's disappointing white count. Wait and see.

"Are you discouraged?" he asked Leavitt long-distance.

"I don't get discouraged. My job is to encourage people." But the man sounded disconsolate.

The following week her second infusion was postponed, but her white count began to recover. And they decided next time to substitute Oncovin, which she'd managed pretty well the year before, for vinblastine, which was brutal to white cells. On balance, that day in the clinic, a Tuesday, had been a pretty good one. She and Beth were having friends for dinner.

The phone went off at seven-thirty Wednesday morning. Four-thirty on the West Coast, he calculated automatically.

"We've just returned from the emergency room." Her voice was shaky. The night before she'd experienced severe chest pain, radiating to her shoulder and neck. "A dagger in the chest, Dad." Strangulation of the heart, pressure, breathlessness. When they established that she wasn't having a heart attack, they sent her home with Demerol. Another bizarre setback. Just then Beth was with her; she was still badly frightened.

Her heart? he thought. Her heart?

"Call us when you know something." He was afraid for her, and useless.

"I will."

By the end of the day, the people at Moffitt decided she'd suffered an attack of pericarditis, an inflammation of the sac enclosing the heart, possibly provoked by the cancer growing or shrinking. The symptoms were often indistinguishable from a heart attack. When he checked in the next night, she sounded fully recovered, the anti-inflammatory was working; she and Beth had been out looking at Victorian houses all bedazzled for the holiday. Her relief reflected how terrified she'd been by the inexplicable hand that had reached into her chest and squeezed and wouldn't let go. Anything could happen. Without warning.

When they arrived in San Francisco for the Christmas holiday, they were amazed at how well she seemed only two days after her second infusion. Bald again, she looked beautiful, physically strong and energetic. They tramped through the park, hiked the cliffs along the bay, and, another day, the Marin headlands—writing JOCELYN, enclosed in a giant heart, in the sand on Brett's favorite beach. Brett in blue jeans, black shoes, black beret, oversized gray-brown jacket. Christmas morning they drove to Muir Woods and climbed the steep trails there, heads bent back, celestial shafts of light, no less, piercing the ancient stand of awesome redwoods, until Holly, not Brett, became short of breath and they had to turn back.

Their daughter seemed to have achieved a new confidence, some inner peace. She was excavating the resources necessary to see her through whatever the coming months demanded. Nathaniel began to adore her this trip, it seemed, seeking out, for the first time, what she saw in the thin volumes of poetry that lined her bookshelves.

She was feeling great when she called home a week after their return to Massachusetts. She and Leavitt had looked at her most recent X-ray together. Following only one cycle of chemotherapy, the discernible disease in her chest—the size of a thumb, she said, on one side of her windpipe and smaller on the other—had been reduced by half, an excellent response. And her white count had held its own, so she was scheduled for another infusion the following day. The best possible news.

"Dad, do you realize?" she said, hooting two long sweet notes of celebration. For this day, the specter of the transplant backed off.

On her twenty-fifth birthday, she and Beth went off for an outing—dinner and romance in a B and B somewhere—and she continued to sound on top of things. A few days later she completed the second cycle, weathering the hours of intense illness—continuous convulsive vomiting, sore throat, sore ribs, headache, gut pain—with stoic resolve. When he next talked with Leavitt long-distance, the doctor was clearly pleased with how she was doing. Her sed rate, one blood measurement of inflammation, had returned almost to normal. Yes, possibly the transplant could be avoided after all. Ten days later, when Brett's white count wasn't adequate to begin the third cycle, no one panicked.

At the end of January she called to tell them that she'd left a front window unlocked and someone had entered the apartment in broad daylight and made off with a new CD player. Definitely a drag, but no big deal. She called again the next morning. What she hadn't realized at first: the thief had also taken her violin.

"My violin, Dad." A piece of her, of the resonant halcyon past, one of the few unsevered ties to her youth. "I feel invaded."

Despite his alarm, he didn't want to fuel her emotion in this. "Don't read too much into it. It's a personal blow, I know—your violin—and hitting you when you're down, but it's not a symbolic event, Brett, it's more like a lousy accident. In terms of what you're going through, it's really not that important, is it? I feel much worse about the loss of your spleen."

"I'll probably never play the violin again."

"Of course you will. Wednesday nights with some chamber group for recreation. When you get involved with music again, you'll get another violin, that's all there is to it."

But when he hung up he wanted a gun, he wanted a thief, he wanted revenge. All he could do was march down the long drive, his exasperated breath visibly expelled in the frigid air.

As far as he knew, Brett let the incident go.

At the beginning of the third cycle of chemotherapy she learned that Leavitt had succeeded on her behalf in securing GCSF, granulo-cyte colony-stimulating factor, which promoted the growth of infec-tion-fighting white cells. She would receive as much GCSF as she required, and—I'm making medical history, folks—the carefully monitored results would become a study bearing her initials. Brett would give herself an injection once a day, seven days a week, typically in the abdomen. One week later, she was elated. For the first time since treatment began, her white count was normal.

D ay by day, however, week after week, the mental and physical costs accrued. One Thursday she reported that, owing to her compromised immune system, she'd developed shingles, a painful virus rooted in the nerve endings, and she was feeling low. When he called on Saturday to see if there had been any improvement, it was clear that he'd under-estimated this latest affliction. She was in constant pain, unable to sleep. And shingles, in this case extending from her shoulder up her neck to the back of her head, was also messy, ugly, and would probably leave scars. AIDS patients often received morphine to cope with the discomfort. The psychological damage, it seemed to him, was the worst of it. Having struggled on so gamely through the past three months, upbeat and undaunted, she was brought down by this new twist. The other day, she said, Beth had gone to pieces, crying hard about everything for the first time. The way this fucking business wouldn't let up.

"I suggested she call you. She has no one to talk to."

"Of course." He was quite sure Beth wouldn't call him.

"I feel alone," she said bluntly, as if getting the truth on the table. "Brett, I know . . ."

"I can't believe it's happening, Dad. I talk about it intelligently all the time, I know the lingo, but I really can't believe it. Cancer," she said, pronouncing the word as though what it denoted was unthinkable. "I'm not depressed, but I'm so sad. What I feel most is a sense of loss. That invincibility of youth, you know, the happiness of being young. I see all these young people going about their lives without ever thinking about being sick, and I feel jealous. I'm running a fever, which makes everything worse. I just got a letter from Jocelyn Emerson. She's been admitted to grad school. I was in the same place, at the same point, as my friends, and now I'm not."

His attempt to respond—"You're young," he began, "you have it all ahead of you"—didn't penetrate her grief.

"Dad, cancer . . . If it came back again . . . I try to be positive, but I can't help these thoughts . . . If it came back again, I don't think I could go through this any longer. I don't think I could do it."

"You won't have to go through it again. You've been doing well, Brett. You might have been in the transplant by now."

Her stomach was black and blue from sticking a syringe into it every morning. "I go to the hospital all the time and see people in various stages . . . People die. I try to remain positive, but the whole thing . . . I'm just sad, I feel lonely. It's like . . . a loss of innocence, I suppose. I didn't want to know all this—at twenty-five. I didn't want to know this pain and fear, my vulnerability."

Unable to summon words, yet compelled to answer, he spoke of the universality of suffering, random, meaningless, relentless suffering—death and destruction occurring to people of all ages all over the world constantly. Desperate platitudes.

"Suddenly when this ends I'm supposed to get back into my life and be normal again." She'd been reading her notebook and had discovered a premonition of the recurrence in its pages. "I think about my life—I just get out of college and . . . get cancer."

"There isn't any good time to get it."

"I don't want to depress you," she said. "I'm not telling you this because I feel an obligation to tell you. But because I want you to know. I mean, I don't want to be separated from you and Mom in that way—because you don't know what's happening."

"I want to know," he said. "Of course I want to know everything. So does your mother."

"I have to talk about it. It's important to me." The pain and confinement of shingles had triggered her immediate sorrow, she knew, but it was always there at some level.

"The shingles will pass. You're halfway through."

"I know. Halfway. I don't see how I can take another six infusions. I hate it so much."

They talked for an hour and a half. By the time they hung up he believed she was a little better than she had been at first. He didn't know. There was so much you didn't know, couldn't know.

Whom could she share her unwanted knowledge with? The women in a support group she'd attended at Stanford seemed preoccupied with matters she couldn't relate to—appearances—and she hadn't gone back. She attended another group, women in their forties with breast cancer, two of whom were terminal patients. Brett felt helpful in their company, able to articulate thoughts and emotions on behalf of everyone present. She felt especially close to one member of the group, who called her once to wish her luck before an infusion. The woman was facing the end of her life and toiling with the question of additional chemotherapy. Not to do it was a guilt trip. "She didn't care about baldness the first time," Brett said, "when she believed she'd get better, but she doesn't want to die bald." Brett found being with these older women too overwhelming. She didn't want to identify—she couldn't identify, she said—with the terminally ill. She met another woman, only three years older than she was, who had also been diagnosed with Hodgkin's six months after her arrival in San Francisco. She'd undergone six weeks of radiation therapy, which had proved successful so far. For all the circumstances they uncannily shared, this woman chose to distance herself from Brett's more troublesome story.

At the beginning of April, just when some encouragement had become imperative, she called with ecstatic news. After four cycles of chemotherapy, the MRI revealed no disease.

"I feel cancer-free!" She hooted a whoop of joy. Her doctors were now confident that the transplant wouldn't be necessary. The four final infusions were crucial, of course, but at last the end seemed in sight.

When lung complications briefly postponed treatment, she was unable to return to the East Coast for the Easter holiday as planned. She received an infusion on Good Friday. This time she threw up twice while the drugs were being injected. That happened again two weeks later—the end of the fifth cycle. And blood clots developed in the subcutaneous port, requiring repeated stabs with something the size of a knitting needle. Uncontrollably, her weight was going down. And the impact of the chemo had jacked her resting pulse up to 112. "I can't take any more of this," she said, "but I have to."

And yet in the Easter snapshots Brett sent them, taken less than forty-eight hours after chemotherapy, she and Beth and Edgar, all dressed up for the occasion, appeared happy as they strolled in the park and gallivanted on the bright beach and posed at their dining table before their Easter spread. In one picture Brett stood alone in a flower garden, wearing a long lemony-green skirt and a white blouse. Large, round pinkish earrings dangled beneath her perfectly bald head. She was wearing bright lipstick and smiling broadly as she waved toward the camera. The shoulder-high, open-palmed wave that appeared in so many pictures of her. She looked thinner than he had imagined, almost spindly, otherworldly somehow, and heartbreakingly innocent, for all her loss of innocence. On the back of the picture she'd written "Egomaniac."

The familiar walk to the clinic for her chemotherapy—Waller to Cole, then the steep, laborious climb up Parnassus—had become a dreaded gauntlet of nauseating associations. Smells along the way, especially the sweet scent of flowering privet, reviled her. Now when she received the infusion she could taste the awful chemicals, she was so steeped in them. He and Holly and Jocelyn, who had recently returned from Italy, each on a different phone in the house, cheered her on to the first infusion of the sixth cycle.

It was May. Another spring.

That night, after they'd gone to bed, Brett called, sounding beat up. "I wanted to hear your voices," she said. In the past they'd always spoken to her before and after her treatment but not while she was in the throes of sickness. She wanted them to glimpse, to hear, what it was like for her. To each of her parents, taking the phone in turn, she asked, "Do you love me?"

The next day she sounded like a different person. Laughing, she described the little old woman, at least eighty, getting an infusion in the bed beside her. Loudly, angrily, she accosted every doctor and nurse who entered the room with the same demand: "I want to know where the hell all this cancer is coming from." Brett loved her.

"This is really almost over," he said.

Leavitt told her she'd have to stay in San Francisco for a year to monitor her condition. That was all right with her. "I really haven't experienced San Francisco yet," she said. "I think I'll check it out."

"Daily life as a normal citizen, isn't that going to be something else?"

"I guess."

The day of her last infusion everyone at the clinic congratulated her, she related. At six o'clock the following morning she made phone calls to her grandparents and to friends across the country, delivering her message: It's over. She'd been up all night.

He stepped outside, a spring morning in Conway, that new lovely green, tulips, narcissus, viburnum in sunstruck bloom.

"It's over," he said to Holly. "She did it."

She didn't turn to him.

"Holly?"

She raised her clenched fists to her temples, her face was tortured. "I'm going crazy," she cried. "I am." Desperation in her voice.

"What is it?"

"I'm terrified that it's not over." Her arms were trembling. "I can't help it."

He embraced her. Such fears were inevitable, but having them didn't mean they'd turn out to be true. As he'd argued so often—to her, their daughter, himself—there was every reason to be hopeful, to believe that six cycles of chemotherapy administered on schedule would be conclusive. "After only four cycles there was no evidence of disease, was there? She's going to be all right now."

Since Brett's recurrence, Holly had been plagued by scary, inexplicable symptoms—sudden bouts of nauseating dizziness, seizures of vertigo that had caused her to collapse without warning and left her temporarily unable to function. This had happened once in San Francisco when she'd gone there alone, once as she stood in the kitchen after a meal, and again at a friend's memorial service. The following day she would feel weak, unfocused, hung over. These events had seemed so uncontrollable and so uncharacteristic—she was physically tough, sturdy, and levelheaded—that they assumed there had to be a physical cause. A thorough workup in February suggested stress was the only explanation. Professionally, as an illustrator and designer with a promotional schedule, she'd been working hard to meet the demands of an important recent contract, but that was not the heart of it. Although she'd seen a therapist briefly, what she was suffering as a mother seemed to be unapproachable through therapy or other ordinary means of so-called stress management.

"Brett is happy today," he said. "We've got to be as brave and determined as she is."

She didn't want these feelings, she said, these oppressive premonitions. Her crisis in Muir Woods during their Christmas holiday with Brett was something she'd kept to herself until they'd returned to Massachusetts. On that occasion she and Brett had gone on ahead, ascending a steep grade through towering redwoods, the morning illuminated by dramatic shafts of fanned light pouring down through the dark trees. As Holly watched her daughter calmly precede her, the back of her bald head beneath her exotically ornamental beaded cap vulnerable-seeming, she was seized with the notion, a deafening sensation, that she and Brett were in heaven, alone together, climbing a hill. Her heart was pounding, she couldn't get her breath, she had to get out of there. It still disturbed her, powerfully, to recall the incident.

"It's over," he urged, "we have to believe it's over."

"I want to. Don't you think I want to?"

She told him, "I couldn't live without Brett."

Black tam, denim jacket, green pants. In contrast to the last time they'd seen her, she looked thin, even frail, as she deplaned in Hartford. Hurt by these months of chemo. She was smiling.

"I'm so excited I'm shaking," she said, as the whole family, except Nathaniel, embraced her. Her brother had recently left for summer work in Wyoming.

Brett's incessant cough, a dry, hoarse bark originating in her chest, was disturbing. The doctors had told her it would be a year before she felt right. But now she would steadily recuperate; that was the infinitely more desirable work ahead.

The first night Holly and Jocelyn slept with her in Joce's double bed. Good for them, he thought. The next night the four of them drove to a restaurant in Vermont to celebrate Holly and his wedding anniversary. Every head in that staid establishment, the Newfane Inn, turned as Brett walked to their table—skinny, bald, in a bright-colored ankle-length skirt, the member of a weird tribe or cultish religious sect. Brett's appetite steadily improved as she gained confidence in her stomach's ability to handle all kinds of food. Each day, without fail, she took herself off for a good walk. One day she and Beth, who had come east separately, went off to a wedding dolled up in floral dresses and straw hats.

As Brett was getting to the end of her chemotherapy, he'd been approaching the end of a novel, working seven days a week as he closed in. Since spring he'd introduced a thread that hadn't been in the original weave of the book, a bisexual character named April whose life was given new direction following her mother's breast cancer. Everything pertaining to the new pages was grounded in his daughter's experience. She was both the girl and the girl's mother. In a sense, he was the girl and the girl's mother. He wanted the pages to convey his daughter's wit, her passion, and to evoke something of the life she shared with her friends. That he felt permitted to write these pages, which ended so positively concerning the cancer, was a measure of his belief, his certainty, that his daughter was okay, the Hodgkin's was indeed behind her. She read the April sections of his manuscript one afternoon, then climbed the plank stairs to his summer workroom in the small barn, and, frowning thoughtfully, pronounced them the best part of his book.

The last day of this brief visit she took a five-mile walk with her mother. In only two weeks, it seemed to him, the cough was less harsh, her bearing sturdier, her stride more energetic, and her complexion, more freckled than ever because of the chemo, fresher. Coming east, she'd checked her blue backpack for the flight and let her father carry it to the car. Now, when he dropped her at the airport, she shouldered the pack as she walked toward the departure gate.

On July 2 she had the portocath removed, the last detail—"Now it feels really over," she told them, happy, really happy—and on Independence Day she and friends had a picnic on her favorite beach across the bay. Bonfire! Shooting stars! Hurrahs!

Now let her be well, he pleaded in bed at night, awake with fears too ingrained over the past two years to be suddenly assuaged.

Toward the end of July Brett returned to Massachusetts for a month, skinny, coughing, but still toting her own gear and doing well. Her face had acquired a temporary fuzziness, possibly from weight loss, as occurred with people afflicted by anorexia. The close-cropped hair on her head, as it grew back, had lost something of its vibrancy and color. "My beige hair," she called it. They assumed that was also temporary. Their place in Conway, isolated on its hill, surrounded by woods and pastures, with woodland trails, shaded dirt roads, streams, was a retreat compared to city life, a good setting to begin the long journey back to normality. From his workroom he watched her go down the private road each day, wearing a wide-brimmed straw hat, one of his long-sleeved shirts, and baggy pants, for her arduous five-mile hike. One day he jogged past her as she marched along a dirt road canopied by old maples, hickory, oak. A wave. When he returned to where he'd left the car, there was a bouquet of red clover and Queen Anne's lace on the front seat.

She cooked regularly—various pastas, Indian dishes, concoctions from whatever the garden provided. When the zucchini began its prolific season, she made loaves of bread and sent them off to Beth and Eve in San Francisco.

She visited the Cape with a friend for a long weekend: the healing ocean.

For a spell in August, as the air grew oppressively humid, her breathing became that much more labored, the stress visible in her pallor. That didn't prevent her from being the comic relief at a family get-together in Connecticut, borrowing her cousin's guitar to give them all a couple of songs on her uncle's deck. "How many out there tonight are from Connecticut?" she asked, her fist a mike. "This one is going out to the fans in Connecticut." That got a rise out of her grandfather, who was even more distressed by the heavy air. Emphysema. With keen empathy now, Brett told them, "You have no idea what it's like." Her identification with his father in this vital concern— breath!—was horrible to him.

"Our beautiful daughter," Holly said, "when I think of what she was like . . ." They were reluctant to speak about the dramatic physical costs of the last two years, as though such superficial observations, in the context of what she'd been through, were beneath them.

"It was a matter of life or death," he said. "Time will heal."

That didn't diminish the wave of sadness that could unpredictably crash over them like grief. Each day they watched her go down the road, doggedly self-disciplined, as though she had a mission: find the missing person and bring her back.

She drove to Bennington, Vermont, with a friend, Richard Shaw, to hear Mary Oliver read from her work. Richard described Brett's excitement—she grabbed his hand and squeezed—as Mary Oliver read her poem "The Summer Day," which described walking through fields, in part, and ended with questions:

> *Tell me, what else should I have done?*
> *Doesn't everything die at last, and too soon?*
> *Tell me, what is it you plan to do*
> *with your one wild and precious life?*

Toward the end of her month in Conway, he asked her, "Do you worry about recurrence?" They were in a crowded club in Northampton, The Iron Horse, where they'd come to hear Shawn Colvin, a new singer-songwriter Brett liked. He knew the answer, but he hadn't put the question to her in so many words. He didn't know how constant or tolerable the strain was.

"I've had my moments of crisis. You deal with it somehow. I'm dreading the MRI in September." She and Beth were traveling to British Columbia and Seattle for a holiday, a pre-MRI spree.

She gestured across the room of crowded tables. "The teacher I had for that course on cancer is sitting over there. Remember?"

The course, which she'd taken as a college junior, was called The Biology of Cancer, and it had made Albey Reiner, the lecturer, something of a local guru on the subjects of illness, healing, dying. Brett had been impressed by the testimony of guest speakers who had waged, or who were continuing to wage, remarkable battles against disease. He remembered her stories of mysterious remissions and miraculous cures.

Albey Reiner and his female companion looked subdued, like foreign travelers unacquainted with the local customs here.

"He's a great guy," she said.

"Do you want to speak to him?"

"No." It had been a large lecture; he wouldn't know her.

"You could be one of his guest speakers now."

She nodded, not smiling.

Two years before, a November night, he had unearthed one of her texts from that course, *The Misguided Cell,* desperate for any insight into Hodgkin's disease. What moved him most was his daughter's marginalia, her underlinings, her typically responsible studiousness, though she never could have dreamed this would have any real bearing on her life.

. . .

The hike into Garnet Canyon was a relief after the valley. Beyond a field of massive white boulders, they had a good view of their objective, Middle Teton, with its vertical black dike. There had been intermittent showers most of the way up, but by late afternoon, as they reached the Meadows, above the tree line, the day had cleared. They'd climbed most of the way in silence, beneath the weight of their backpacks, acknowledging the lakes below, a pair of deer, the changing, increasingly spectacular vista with few words. In the Meadows there was a lively stream and wildflowers he couldn't identify. Nathaniel immediately unpacked the tent and began setting their site, the sheltered area beneath a hanging rock, to rights. He'd been trekking into the Tetons all summer; he was the guide. Although two million visitors came through this park each year, the valley crawling with RVs, there was no one else here in the canyon at just over nine thousand feet. They ate sardines and cooked noodles for supper. Nathaniel was master of his small stove. By dusk four other campers had arrived. When the wind dropped the evening became tranquil. A waterfall ran down a canyon wall to the west. The constant babble of the stream near them was pleasant company. The mountain towered straight up behind them. They sat and watched the light change on the walls of the canyon—rose-red, pink, orange—and grow radiant over the distant valley, a vast blue-green lake of light. He felt they'd entered the landscape of a Rexroth poem and was sorry he didn't have some lines by heart.

His daughter had introduced him to Rexroth. The Christmas she was first diagnosed with Hodgkin's disease, she'd given him a copy of the collected shorter poems. "Believe in Orion, believe in the night, the moon, the crowded earth, . . ." she had written as an inscription. They were words from a Christmas poem Rexroth had composed for his young daughter. Brett added, "Everything is possible."

He hadn't slept his first two nights in Wyoming, and even now, following a day on an uphill trail, while his son was sound asleep, he remained awake in the small domed tent, rehearsing major themes of his life. In the end he managed maybe two or three fitful hours. Taking a piss in the wee hours, he was amazed by the inky sky of stars. Believe, Brett, you've got to. . . .

It was sunny but cold in the morning. They set off by eight, Nathaniel leading the way along a steep route up the southerly approach. He marched across the scree powerfully—at nineteen, twice as fit as his father for this adventure. Getting to the saddle at 11,500 feet was arduous but not unmanageable. It was clear, though, as they traversed a narrow ice field that a slip of the foot would tumble you straight down. Unlike his father, whose only experience of mountains was the friendly hill-like Monadnocks in New England, Nathaniel had done four peaks already this summer, including Grand, but he'd been blown off Middle by an intense thunderstorm just short of the top, and so wanted to return for another try. From the rock field, the couloir they intended to follow looked too steep to climb without support, but once they entered it, the way became visible. It grew cold and windy; they pulled on windbreakers and wool hats. Eventually the ascent became fairly vertical and it was necessary to use their hands to climb. As they approached the summit, the old man—he was forty-six—had to stop every so many steps, short of breath, to collect himself for the next short haul. Christ!

"I know," his son called down to him, shouting in the wind, "I couldn't breathe very well in the beginning either." Now this mountain was a piece of cake.

He rested his weight against rock, holding on, his lungs unexpectedly shallow. My father, he thought, my daughter. *You have no idea what it's like.* Glancing below, he wondered how he was going to get down. His shortness of breath and the cold wind, which blunted his senses, heightened his anxiety. At one steep reach, requiring a full stretch, his legs became a little wobbly and he clung there for a minute, not sure he could handle the move.

"Come on," his son called, "don't crap out on me now." The boy was taking pictures.

And after I snapped that shot of him, he imagined his son telling family and friends sometime after the tragic mishap, he fell.

There was clear ice in places and at another tricky spot, when he reached to pull himself onto a boulder, the large rock moved. He might have pulled it back on his chest. Loose rocks were a major danger. One boy Nathaniel had climbed with earlier in the summer and never again—the kid had no antennae, he explained—had carelessly kicked a boulder back on him. Nathaniel managed to deflect it with his shoulder, sustaining a good bump. The rock could have sent him flying.

Middle Teton rose to a sharp, prominent peak just big enough for one person to sit on, which made getting there particularly satisfying. The final pull to the top was a rush. Nathaniel mounted the summit, swinging his leg over, like getting into the saddle. There was a circular brass marker embedded in the rock between his legs. Grand stood tall directly to the north. Typically, the ascent of Grand was a guided climb along a technical route; Nathaniel and two friends had free-climbed, without protection, attacking the summit along a narrow snow-covered shelf that led to a perfectly vertical hundred-foot chimney three feet square. The oldest of them, a twenty-eight-year-old recovering from a divorce, lost his handhold going up the chimney and almost fell, catching himself with his back against the rock, so shaken he didn't reveal the close call to his buddies for two days. Almost every year experienced climbers, as well as adventuresome novices, died on the Tetons. Nathaniel had reported his exploits over the phone, but only now, squatting at the summit of Middle, did his father appreciate the danger. He remembered a haunting story that appeared in *The New Yorker* about four students climbing Moran years before. Both girls on the outing, students from Brown, had lost hold with their ice axes on a snowfield, one after the other, and fallen. One girl was killed, and the other critically injured. The parents who had lost their daughter—how did they go on living? he'd thought at the time. Nathaniel claimed he'd felt confident on the mountains most of the time. The truth was, disaster could have easily befallen their amateur expedition at any moment.

After a few minutes in humbling wind, they wanted to start down. As it turned out, the descent wasn't difficult, just long and hard on the knees and feet. They encountered two experienced mountaineers on their way up, climbing with poles, who greeted them breezily, as though strolling on a beach. Just where the climb grew steep they passed another couple, who had also been in the Meadows the night before. The woman was huddled out of the wind, not sure she wanted to go for the top.

"You can do it," he told her. "Believe me, you can do it."

Back in the rented platform tent in Colter Bay that night, he became feverish and had to get out of his sleeping bag when he started sweating. What's this about? He was wasted from the outing, his feet blistered and his toenails blackened from the descent, and yet sleep wouldn't come. The serenity of Garnet Canyon the night before was an unreachable memory. He'd begun to loathe the sight of people on vacation here, the tidy, cheerful, middle-aged middle class on holiday who came to Jackson Hole to shop, for whom the mountains were as remote as the moon. And then he loathed himself for entertaining such thoughts, for failing to sleep, for lying there feverish. You needed sleep to carry on with what had to be done. His son was out like a light.

This body . . . I try to love it, to trust it, his daughter had written. This self, she might have said. There were layers of sadness, he saw, that she couldn't talk about. *Cancer, Dad!* The struggle to love the cast-out, ailing self.

They hiked through Cascade Canyon, through wildflowers in a half-dozen colors, to Lake Solitude. Moose grazed in the river, marmots darted among rocks. He asked a woman on horseback, in a single-file party of six, where she was headed. I don't know, she said, as though the question hadn't yet occurred to her. Hostage. The hike through Cascade offered majestic views of the Tetons—Owen, Middle, Grand. Again they were the only campers in the area for the night.

From their site Nathaniel pointed out the route he'd taken to the summit of Grand. This clear view of the chimney—a just discernible vertical mark on the mighty, distant peak—and the thought of his son invisibly struggling up through that shaft, relying on only his body, frightened him now more than ever. Climbing Buck Mountain early in the season, Nathaniel and his companion got caught in cold rain and lost their way, finally bushwhacking for hours until they hit a trail, almost midnight before they returned. At one point the other boy stretched out on the ground and refused to go any farther. Nathaniel knew they were at risk for hypothermia and forced him to keep moving. The next time out, the storm struck on Middle, petrifying them by its ferocity, the unreal crashes of lightning forcing them to race to lower ground when they had a chance. Then there was the incident of the rock striking him from above and, finally, the clear danger on Grand. Four opportunities for catastrophe. Take care of yourself, he'd told Nathaniel over the phone, don't take foolish chances. He'd had no idea. The kid had been risking his life.

He no more knew what his son had been confronting on the Teton range in Wyoming than he knew what his older daughter had been contending with, the real terror in her heart and mind, three thousand miles away in San Francisco. For all his diligence and earnestness to be there for her, he couldn't know. All evening, as the Tetons glowed rose-pink in the waning light, then dark, he kept looking to the vertical line that rose from the thin white shelf to the summit. His son set up the tent, hoisted the food bag into a tree, got the stove going for water and canned stew, then sat back on his haunches looking down the canyon, holding a steel mug of herbal tea.

"Not bad out here, huh, Dad."

His flesh and blood: separate, unknown.

. . .

In September Brett began to experience severe lower-back pain that seemed to occur only at night. She attributed it to a muscular or nerve-related injury from hiking, moderately, on Mount Rainier just about the time he was in the Tetons. The pain became so severe one night that she ended up in the emergency room, where they failed to establish the cause. A subsequent CAT scan was normal. The following week she had the MRI. He went through the day thinking of her in that black tube again. With what had been going on all month it wasn't possible to think of the test as merely routine. Finally she called with the results: the MRI was fine. The three of them cheered their happiness.

"Now you can resume your life."

"It's about time."

In mid-October she and Beth went to Yosemite for a weekend. The following Tuesday when she called, there were tears in her voice. She'd been to the clinic because of chest pain. Leavitt heard a "rub," and her sed rate was elevated. If he had to give a diagnosis without further tests, he told her, he'd say the cancer had recurred.

Everything had been fine at Yosemite, she explained, until Sunday night, when pain similar to the pericarditis she'd had last winter suddenly seized her.

"Where's Beth?" he asked.

"She's here with me."

"Only three weeks ago the MRI was clear. Could something have developed in three weeks?" he asked. "You've been through six cycles, Brett, the maximum."

The last time, Leavitt had reminded her, there'd only been a week between a negative and then a positive X-ray. Evidently, the disease could become discernible that quickly.

"Now everything has changed. I can't go through it again. I'm afraid of the pain."

"Maybe Leavitt is mistaken. You never had pain associated with the disease. The sed rate is irrelevant. And there are no fevers."

She didn't think her circumspect doctor would make such a disturbing statement if he wasn't very concerned. "I became emotional in his office. He put his arm around me and said, We've been through a lot, we'll get through this."

"You will."

"I need you out here," she told them, and they assured her that they would be there.

"I was convinced it was over," he said.

"I've been getting better all along. I wanted to jog, my lungs felt so good. I did jog a little one day. I was beginning to think about what I was going to do now—that's what I was starting to worry about." She'd been revising her résumé: the most tactful way to account for her past two years of unemployment. "I feel like I'm losing ground," she said. "With each step I get set back. I don't think I can believe in the process anymore. I believed in the six cycles. I endured that, and now . . . How can I believe in the transplant?"

There had been doctors who argued the transplant was necessary even after six cycles, he reminded her. She could do it if she had to— just the way she'd done everything else. "But listen," he said, "we don't know yet. We have to wait and see."

It was a wrenching phone call. At one point Brett said to her mother, "Don't blame yourself."

"I won't." As if it was a mother's burden, Holly had days when she did blame herself.

"I have to get something to eat," Brett announced suddenly. "I've been completely out of it all day. I can't get a handle on it this time, I don't know how to think about it."

Each of them said, "I love you." He imagined that phrase weaving a web of sound across the nation as it pulsed through electronic lines of communication, uttered by countless loved ones, a promise, a plea, a prayer—a helpless keening.

He and Holly turned to each other. Everything that had seemed possible now seemed impossible. This insidious malignancy had begun to seem evil, that was the only word for it, a black fate. It was wearing her down, destroying her—my daughter! he thought—and it was destroying them. He didn't know where to go with the feelings squeezing his chest, pressing on his throat. He walked outside into the fall night, the sky above their domed hill dazzling. *Believe in Orion . . .*

He didn't believe anything anymore, that was the feeling. As his vision passed over their place here, the home they'd made for themselves and their children, and now struggled to hold onto, he thought, Why do we live?

The next morning the ordinary beauty of the fall day was grotesque.

She called soon after nine that evening. She was scheduled for an MRI tomorrow at ten. Leavitt had been businesslike; they didn't really talk.

"How are you?" he asked.

"I'm good. This morning Eve came over. She cried. Then we took a walk and ended up having fun, laughing. I went to S.J., my therapist, this afternoon. She's great. I'm sad about what you're going through, she told me, but I don't scare easy. Really, I'm feeling okay." She paused before she said, "The cancer is not me." She intended to take each day as it came. Tonight she and Beth were going out to dinner.

The following day, a Thursday, he and Holly moped, wounded, trying to work, waiting to hear from Brett or Leavitt. They didn't hear. It would take a day to get the MRI results.

Friday was another long stint of apprehension. A storm had struck the night before, taking down a sixty-foot pine at the edge of the top field, and the dangerous wind continued throughout the daylight hours. Every time the phone rang, his arms and shoulders jumped as though wired. Brett reached them late in the afternoon, and he could hear her overwhelming news in her greeting. The MRI revealed no disease, period. According to Halberg, radiation could cause an episode of pericarditis a year and a half later. Leavitt had overreacted. He'd been thinking out loud when he examined her, he explained apologetically; he'd let his patient in on his worst fears, and that was a mistake. He was awfully glad to be in the wrong now. Brett forgave him.

"I don't have cancer," she shouted, her happiness now as wild as her despair had been two days earlier. "I'm free."

As if fate were real, though, November lived up to its dark place in Brett's mind. She detected a swollen lymph node in her neck, her cough seemed more severe, but mostly she just felt exhausted all the time. Stress, she thought, could account for part of her fatigue. She was simply spooked this time of year, and Leavitt wasn't particularly encouraging. He viewed her situation as uncertain and ordered additional X-rays.

"I'm worn out from walking this tightrope. I want it to end."

"Get past Thanksgiving, come home for Christmas, and the new year will begin to look like something you can believe in."

Please let this happen, he pleaded. Enough.

The following week was more disturbing. She had fevers. The scar tissue on her lungs made X-rays ambiguous. A neurologist established that the ongoing pain in her hip wasn't a nerve problem. Leavitt said, "We're in the dark. We don't know what's going on." The doctor talked about restaging her.

"Look, the fever and sed rate could reflect something that has nothing to do with cancer." Like a zealous grunt digging into the front lines, he maintained his position. "Leavitt's job is to be vigilant—there's no room for error—but his uncertainty is only that," he implored his daughter, attempting to conceal his own dread.

"I take my temperature and note my condition each morning. Writing it down seems to take care of it for the day, so I can get on to other things."

Following five days of impossible waiting, she called on a Tuesday right after she spoke with Leavitt. The X-ray was fine, the sed rate was going down. "I'm okay," she said.

The plunging twists and turns of this roller coaster never seemed repetitious or predictable. Only brutal and exhausting. Their relief after each scare was like a dagger at the throat withdrawn; their happiness at such times was real.

"Next week is Thanksgiving," he said, "and you don't have Hodgkin's."

"Do you realize?" She was having a dozen people for the occasion. Feasting, dancing.

One night she announced an upcoming interview for a job as director of communications at the San Francisco Art Institute. A long shot, to be sure. Her excitement was a measure of her remove from the ordinary workaday world. She'd done well, she reported later—*I did jog a little*—and felt proud of herself for taking the leap: a formal discussion of her past and future with someone who wasn't a doctor.

The very next morning, a Sunday, she awoke to discover that her neck was swollen. That night she had friends over to trim a tree and drink mulled wine. An ultrasound and blood work on Monday indicated that the nodes in her neck were normal. Another reprieve, was the feeling. The burden lifted, life could go on. How many more reprieves could there be? She had her ticket to fly home; she'd had it for months.

Thursday she went in for a scheduled MRI as part of her monthly checkup. Following the ultrasound and the blood work, and the repeated false alarms, no one was worried about this one. When he answered the phone Friday morning Brett said, "It's not over yet, Dad."

She reported the facts without emotion. There was significant water around the pericardium, which Leavitt had to assume was disease, a growth inflaming the heart sac, causing it to "weep." Puzzlingly, the lymph nodes appeared normal, apart from a slight swelling in the armpit that seemed to have migrated from her neck. It was incumbent on the doctors to search for the disease and establish just where it was. Another CAT scan below the diaphragm. If necessary, they'd remove the node in her armpit and drain fluid from her chest for biopsy.

"So it looks like I won't be coming home for Christmas, after all. Beth said she'd stay here with me."

"You sound pretty calm."

"I cried last night," she said flatly.

"It might not be Hodgkin's at all," he said doggedly. "Don't give up hope, will you?"

He and Holly clung to each other in the kitchen, disbelieving. This wouldn't stop. How could their daughter endure more?

When they heard from her next she was calling from the cardiac ward of Long Hospital. An echocardiogram had shown that the fluid buildup was quite dangerous—her condition required careful monitoring—but they wanted to hold off draining it until they could examine the fluid for Hodgkin's. They now believed the swelling in her neck was related to the fluid in the pericardial space. The cardiology people had been great. One doctor, a flamboyant, chin-up woman in her fifties, brought her a red rose from her garden. Andy Leavitt had turned up for every procedure, ubiquitous, concerned.

"They described me to the heart specialists as a smart, eloquent patient. How about it, Dad?" She sounded relaxed. "I'm the only young person on a floor of ancient men," she said, "fighting for their lives."

On Monday, Brett had a catheter inserted into her chest and a quart of thick yellowish fluid drained from it. That night she was too uncomfortable to get excited about unknowns. They wouldn't have test results for a few days, but they thought the chance of discovering cancer was fifty-fifty. As always Beth was with her.

He made arrangements to fly to San Francisco.

On Thursday, December 20, Brett called at about five in the afternoon. "The fluid was benign," she declared. "I'm coming home tomorrow with Beth." She would have to return for an echocardiogram the day after Christmas, but everyone seemed pretty confident that it was safe for her to be away for five days. She wasn't worried. She could endure anything as long as it wasn't cancer. "So we should arrive in Hartford at about five-thirty," she said. "Can you wait?"

The cheerful surface of the eagerly awaited holiday was genuine but fragile. Their third day back, Brett and Beth went to Edgar's for brunch, a reunion of old friends. Brett returned at noon, carrying the Sunday *Times* into the kitchen. She looked unexpectedly well, he thought, wonderful, considering.... Her hair, as never before, was dense and curly, a dark coppery red, the color his hair had been ten years ago.

"How was everybody?" he asked. "Fun?"

"Actually, it became a little depressing for me." Her face began to lose its composure.

"What is it?"

"Everyone was my age ... my peers, even people I went to high school with ... they were all full of energy, talking about what they've been doing and their plans for the future." Tears.

"I know," he said.

"And I had nothing to say."

He put his arms around her.

"I didn't want to be the black cloud talking about my illness, nothing but my damn illness."

Only days before, she'd been in the hospital waiting for the results of her pericardiocentesis, waiting to know whether her life was going forward or not. Ultimate concerns didn't make for lively chat among the hale and hearty.

"Then we all went for a walk and I couldn't keep up with them. My lungs. I had to stop, so naturally everyone returned to the house with me. I hate being the person who can't keep up. People try to be considerate and thoughtful, but no one can really understand. Naturally, everyone is absorbed with their own lives."

Holly and Jocelyn had come into the room. She'd been so strong, they said, they were so proud of the way she'd come through the past two years. As if avowals of love could smother this sorrow.

She and Jocelyn embraced. "I want to be in touch with you more," Brett said. Then she asked, "Do you love me?" Not to elicit from her sister an everyday sentiment, he realized. For Brett the audacious question had become vital, an affirmation of self.

Later she told them, as she'd explained to him before, that she needed to break down every so often, she needed the release, she needed them to know the truth.

She'd begun to discover another way to share her truth. On Christmas Eve, taking everyone completely by surprise, she unveiled for them the body of artwork, perhaps twenty pieces, that she'd accumulated only since September. The pieces were small, largely black-and-white, and while they were done with charcoal and oil pastels, they had the density and contrast and depth of woodblocks or etchings. The work seemed to have arrived as a fully formed vision. Where did this come from? he thought. Yet he knew.

Brett had never considered art a serious possibility, in contrast to Jocelyn, who was clearly destined to become an artist of one kind or another since she was a small child. Writing had always been Brett's creative domain. Now, for the first time, she found herself unable to convey her feelings adequately in words, she explained. There was her journal, but that was private and spontaneous. Words now seemed elusive, stubborn, and they echoed too much the words of others. She needed a new mode to get at what, despite its seeming universality, she experienced as unutterably personal, and unique. Making the drawings was a release, absorbingly physical in a way that writing had never been, the actual process, rubbing on paper, an act of exploration and discovery. The resulting work was original, mysterious, coherent, and gratifyingly tangible; its power persuaded the viewer that it came from an authentic and authoritative source.

And I had nothing to say.

The moment his father arrived Christmas Day, he sat in the ladderback chair just inside the kitchen door, breathless, his enormous hands on his knees, his shoulders hunched. In addition to advanced emphysema, his father had been ill with what his doctor called a hot spot, a vulnerable site in the lung where inflammation had established itself. His father had been hospitalized twice in recent months, but a few days' hospitalization to get an infection under control didn't seem unusual or unexpected. One day his mother reported finding her husband in a depressed state. "What's wrong?" she asked. "I just feel so forlorn," he said. Coming from him, that precise word was an alarm. *Forlorn!* He couldn't breathe. He would be awakened at night, frightened by his inability to take a breath. The night they'd finally called the ambulance, his breathlessness had prevented him from eating. "My breathing," he complained. "My breathing." His mother had lived with her husband's ill health for so long her patience was exhausted. She blamed him for his state as much as she sympathized with him, misreading his physical crisis as anxiety. "What we have here is a case of nerves," she said. "Your mother says I'm ruining her life," he told his son, "ruining everything. But . . . I . . . can't . . . help . . . it," he pleaded, enunciating each word as though speaking to someone who barely understood English. "I'm *sick*."

At that point his father's pulmonary physician, Golden, recommended a specialist in Providence but didn't consider the patient's condition that grave. The lungs were supplying enough oxygen to the body, he said. When he and Holly visited his parents on the Cape in early December, his father seemed relatively better. So at Christmas they were shocked to find the man's condition had deteriorated so radically within only a few weeks. The trip to Providence hadn't worked any wonders. He shouldn't have attempted the Christmas trip at all, except they had missed the family Thanksgiving, these aging parents, and they seemed to view that omission as a crisis worse than illness. His father, the cause of it all, was bound and determined to make the next holiday.

The man could hardly cross the room, his cough was impossible, his cheeks almost bluish. They had never seen him so wiped out. Ordinarily gregarious, he had little to say to anyone, even his eldest granddaughter, who had been as bound and determined to get here as he was. Following the meal of the day, he fell asleep sitting up in the library, which was unusual for him.

He urged his mother to become aggressive about his father's condition. Consult someone at Lahey or Massachusetts General. Something had to be done.

When his father hung his head over his bowl of cereal in the morning, she impatiently asked, "Are you all right?"

He blew up. "She's going to drive me crazy."

He had to sit by the door to collect himself before struggling to his car.

"You're a positive person," her grandmother told Brett, as they were saying good-bye. "That's the way you have to be. And here's a negative person," she said, indicating her husband.

He clasped his head. Negative! He couldn't breathe! As if, indeed, he had been driven mad, he insisted on getting behind the wheel of the car for the four-hour trip to the Cape.

There had been many turning points, yet Brett's return home for the holiday, after all, after the long season of relentless ups and downs, felt like a crucial break. All right, he thought, enough, the scares are over. And she seemed to concur for the most part, despite her frustration at Edgar's brunch. En route to the airport, they talked about *her* plans and *her* future. She was considering everything from advertising to an internship as a therapist and was holding graduate school—journalism at Berkeley was a thought—in reserve. The next day, her echocardiogram indicated no new accumulation of fluid, and her doctors believed the whole worrisome incident could have been a singular event without further complications. As they spoke, Brett was at her desk, drawing. She sounded good, which to him was a gift, like the sun making an unexpected appearance at the end of a rainy day.

3

ALONE

That evening, his mother called to say they'd taken his father to the hospital in an ambulance. She had never seen him so bad. He complained of angina. That subsided. Then he thought he was going to faint. He looked dreadful. "He was going without his glasses—that's how bad he was. He's blind without them, he'd never leave the house without his glasses. I could follow them in the car, but I don't want to go driving down there at night. Can you understand that?"

"Let me call the hospital," he said. "I'll call you right back."

The specialist who had been summoned to the emergency room came to the phone. The man's lungs were so bad, the doctor explained, that he'd been unable to hear any alarming change when he'd examined him earlier that afternoon. At present he was seriously ill, but stable. If his condition was to worsen overnight it would be due not to his lungs but to his heart. The doctor thought it was pointless for the patient's wife to come to the hospital just then. "She should stay home and get some rest."

He conveyed that to his mother. It also seemed pointless for him to drive out there that night, not to arrive until two in the morning.

"I've been taking down the Christmas tree," she said. "I'm too agitated to do nothing. I've never seen him as bad as he was tonight."

Clearly his distress was far more physical than mental, wasn't it? he asked her. "Maybe he's been more stoic than you gave him credit for."

"You never know what's going on with your father," she said. "I've never known what that man was thinking. He never reveals himself." She added, "I don't know what to do. I couldn't live with him the way he is now, but I could never put him in a nursing home either." After years of the antagonistic stress of chronic illness, these recent months of repeated flights to the hospital—with her husband becoming increasingly incapacitated, disgruntled, and difficult, while less able to maintain the compensating social routines of dining out, bridge, various excursions—had taxed her patience and compassion to the limit. This night's even more terrifying emergency rescue seemed a culmination. Startlingly she said, "God's will be done."

His mother called at eight the next morning, having just spoken to his father's primary physician, Dr. Golden. "He's a hundred percent better," she told him, as exasperated, he thought, as she was reassured. That was all she knew. He spoke with her again in the afternoon, when she returned from the hospital. She couldn't believe how much better he looked compared to the night before. "I wasn't there for ten minutes when he said, If you'd go home I could get some sleep. Isn't he something?"

But Sunday she said, "I've really never seen him so sick. The nurse said he'll be a long time getting over this. You know, he's never been the same since he retired. Everyone used to love him. He's just not the same person. Now he says, Nobody cares about me." There were tears in her voice as she said that. "The other day I said to him, Your trouble is, you don't like yourself, and he said, You're right. There's nothing on his arms, he's so thin. Of course he's alert to everything around him. He knows everything going on in that intensive care unit."

Of course you didn't *like* yourself lying in the hospital unable to breathe, snatched from the mainstream, a sick person. Illness was hateful. That's your trouble, all right.

Cancer, Dad.

. . .

On New Year's Eve, he and Holly drove to the Cape, arriving at the hospital late in the afternoon. They were in the intensive care unit little more than an hour when his father said, "Why don't you get back to the house." It was more important to him, his son thought, that his wife have their company tonight.

The next day as the three of them entered the private room to which he'd been moved, his father greeted them with rage, without lifting his head from the pillows.

"I've been calling you all morning," he shouted at his wife.

"What's wrong?"

He'd had a terrible few hours, *sick as a dog*. He'd been calling the house since eleven, and there was no answer.

His fury was directed at his wife, his full lips trembling as he bitterly vented anger that had been building all morning. In his extremity, he'd been deserted. Why wasn't he consoled now that she was there at last? His son urged him to calm down, his anger only put greater pressure on his galloping heart.

"Try to reach Golden," his father asked him, "will you?"

Outside the room he spoke to his father's blond, middle-aged nurse, Maureen. "There's a lot of fear involved in this disease," she said. Her father had died of emphysema, and she knew what she was talking about. "Eventually he was unable to eat—because you need breath to eat. When he died he weighed sixty-eight pounds. It's horrible," she said, "worse than lung cancer, which goes quicker."

Her grim prognosis suggested how long-term his father's suffering might be. Nausea had discouraged his appetite, but otherwise he was a long way from not eating, a long way from sixty-eight pounds. Spare him such agony, he thought.

"Your nurse is certain everything possible is being done," he said, back in the room. "Golden is aware of what's going on."

He wasn't satisfied. "You people have it all figured out."

"Are you feeling better now?" his wife asked him. "You're more relaxed now, aren't you? Half your trouble is in your head, do you know that? I think you have a terrible case of nerves . . ."

Every word she uttered was like a slap, a blow that he couldn't deflect. It was obvious that she was saying exactly the wrong things.

"All you want to know is, am I feeling better. If I take a pill you want me better in five minutes. There are a million things in between," he told her. "A million things."

His father had told them he didn't want to be alone, he just wanted someone there. Now within an hour of their arrival his wife said, "We're going to go now, okay?"

He looked around the room, baffled.

"We aren't going, Dad. We just got here."

"You go, Rose," he told his wife. "Go home!"

"Aren't you feeling better? We're going to go now."

Was his mother in such a state herself that she hardly knew what she was saying? Or did she actually want out of there, fed up, embarrassed by his initial attack?

"Your father's terrified," Holly whispered. "Hold his hand. Don't be like him."

It was true, in his solitary anguish the man was flailing, craving to be touched. His mother left the room on the pretense of an errand and he and Holly, on either side of the bed, each took one of his large, pale hands. His father returned the pressure and began to relax, to be comforted. He felt humbled by Holly's decency.

"I'm sorry you had to see this," his father told her.

"I understand. Don't be sorry."

That morning, frightening waves of nausea had engulfed him, that was why he'd panicked.

Eventually, as the day grew dark, he seemed fairly composed. By the time they felt they could go home for dinner, he was resting as comfortably as possible.

"I couldn't bear to have him home the way he is," his mother repeated, "but I can't think of anything happening." Then her impatience flared. "You saw for yourself, he's so angry and resentful. I know he hates my nagging . . . but he's made me nag him." Her themes were familiar. "It can be very lonely living with your father," she said. "He's nothing like the man he once was. He's missed a lot of love," she declared, "love we could have shared." Then she cried, "I feel so sorry for him." And she felt guilty about the way she'd treated him these past few weeks. "I didn't know he was so sick," she pleaded. But her most frequent refrain throughout the evening was one of dismay. "I can't believe this is happening. I say these terrible things about him but I can't believe he won't be home. I don't know what I'd do with myself alone here."

Surely she foresaw the difference between being lonely with him and being lonely without him. A few weeks before, the last time he and Holly had been here, his parents had celebrated their fiftieth wedding anniversary. She'd shown him the Christmas card her husband had given her this year. The unrecognizable unsteadiness of the handwriting, the thin, wavering line that formed each word, was what struck him first. But the sentence his father had written, a single line in the blank card, astounded him: "Without you there would be no one."

His father called soon after breakfast. He wanted his wife and son at the hospital right away, he was in a bad way.

"Don't say anything, Mother," he urged as they drove to Hyannis. "Just be there, that's all he wants. Don't upset him."

Yet inexplicably, weirdly, within minutes of entering the hospital room, she said to her husband, "How long do you want us to stay?"

"Go!" he said. "Go!"

"Open your eyes. Are you sleeping?"

"Go!"

Like the morning before, he was overcome by nausea, his breath cut off in his throat, it felt like. He'd been on oxygen all along.

Now a nurse attached a rebreather mask over his nose and mouth to maximize its absorption. Almost immediately he breathed more easily. When it was time to be taken downstairs for an X-ray, he struggled, a tall, hulking man, onto the gurney. He returned from the procedure completely exhausted. Getting back into bed was a difficult chore. Glancing at his wife, he said, "This isn't your bag, is it, Rose?"

"We're going to leave soon. We've been here all morning."

Recklessly, he squandered what little strength remained to fuel his indignation. "You go, Rose. Douglas will stay."

"Open your eyes. Why do you have your eyes closed?"

He ripped the mask from his face. "Will you stop talking!"

"Mother, why don't you and Holly get some lunch?"

He sat by the bed and took his father's hand, watching him gulp shallow breaths in the transparent green mask.

"Why don't you call the doctor," his father said, and it was an intense struggle to speak in that plastic mask, the words emerging haltingly. "I can't believe there's nothing they can do for me."

He called Golden's office—his father had the number by the phone—described his father's state, and told the secretary to tell the doctor that he could be reached at the hospital.

"I think they're doing all they can, Dad. Golden's hoping to get the pneumonia under control. That's the main thing."

If only he could get back to the way he'd been around Halloween, his father proposed, he was *perfect* then. But this . . . "It's too bad they don't have a cot so you could stay the night," he said. "The night gets very long." Hastily he confided, "I thought I was going to die. Twice."

"When?" he asked, taking his hand again.

"The past two mornings." The overwhelming nausea, he explained, the sensation was like dying.

Intermittently, he was racked by a horrendous fit of coughing, once choking up a golfball-sized glob of blood. Without comment he showed his son the soiled tissue before he dropped it in the wastebasket. Concrete evidence. His lungs were being shredded by in-flammation.

"I have confidence in you," he blurted then, grimacing in the mask to form the words, drowning. "I really do."

"Don't talk, Dad. Breathe in the oxygen."

"If this doesn't come out just right," his father went on with urgency, "it won't be your fault."

"It's not anyone's fault. Life's fault," he said. But he knew his father was thinking of his own father, who had gone into a nursing home toward the end of his life and never forgiven his son for it—so the son, who now found himself in that same frightening and impossible place, believed. The man wished to release his own son from the guilt he had suffered.

"I know you never thought I cared about you," he said, harshly thrusting the words through the plastic, like a man trying to make himself heard behind glass, "but I did. In my own way. People don't think I care about them, but I do. I'm just the way I am."

"I know you always cared about me, Dad. I know that." It was true.

Their talk was cut short when the women returned. In the next fifteen minutes, quite suddenly, as though an oppressive weight had been withdrawn, the patient became far more relaxed. He sat up in the bed, discarded the oxygen mask, and consumed the entire hospital lunch of macaroni and cheese.

Thinking his father might want to pick up where they'd left off earlier, he returned to the hospital alone that night, but the man appeared confident now, almost himself, and they didn't talk about anything. They sat and watched David Frost unctuously interview George Bush about the Persian Gulf crisis. Absurdly, war seemed imminent.

"Never happen," his father declared. Having survived the day, he was almost mellow and graciously deigned to address the young nurse as "my dear." That's fine, my dear. Thank you, my dear. Which was almost funny; this "my dear" routine wasn't him. At nine o'clock his father said, "You better be going now."

Back at the house, when he described his father's equanimity, his mother became hopeful. "I have the feeling tonight he's going to pull out of it."

Evidently Golden made his hospital rounds at six in the morning, then called spouses or appropriate relatives to provide brief updates before beginning his office hours. At six-thirty he'd overheard his mother anxiously respond, "Yes, yes, I see, yes, thank you." She had difficulty posing her questions to doctors in the first place, but Golden made her feel hurried, hardly entitled to speak, and she was too groggy and nonplussed, even alarmed by the phone going off at that hour of the morning, to hold a conversation in any case.

Their third morning at his parents' he took the call rather than his mother. He wanted a clearer picture of exactly what was happening to his father.

"He's sick," the doctor said impatiently, petulantly. "His heart is terrible and his lungs are terrible."

He repressed his annoyance. What was the prognosis?

"He could deteriorate rapidly," Golden said, "or he could go on, chronically ill, for weeks, months, even years."

Months? Years? The doctor refused to be more precise or informative. In answer to his next question, yes, the pneumonia was responding somewhat to the medication. With undisguised rudeness, abruptly ending the conversation, Golden said, "All right?"

"Did he say months?" his mother asked in disbelief. "Years? Oh, my God."

When they reached the hospital this morning, his father was suffering much as before. He was not so good, he said.

"Will you open your eyes, and close that mouth."

"Go home, Rose. You have to talk, you can't be quiet."

Open *your* eyes, he wanted to tell his mother. But that was the point, he realized. She couldn't watch this. "How did it go last night, Dad?"

"The nights are long."

By early afternoon his mother was insisting, "You two better go now. You have a long ride home. You'd better be on your way."

He knew perfectly well that his father wanted him to stay, yet the man's wretched condition did seem less precarious than before. Furthermore, replacements were on the way—his sister Janice was driving up from Connecticut the next day. In any case, he could be back out here at a moment's notice if necessary.

The pattern of morning illness, nauseating episodes of breathlessness, followed by some relief in the afternoon, continued. Each evening he checked in with his mother. "A psychiatrist visited your father today," she reported, "and told him that emphysema could kill him."

"What did Dad have to say about that?"

"He said he never wants to see him again."

"Perfect."

"He lies there with his eyes closed. Do you want me to hold your hand? I asked him. No. Do you want me to rub your back? No. Do you want to say anything to me? No. Do you want me to say anything to you? No. What do you do with a man like that? He's so angry toward me. I don't want him to come home, not the way he is, but I can't imagine him not coming home. Do you understand what I'm saying?"

He understood.

Without you there would be no one.

The next morning, when he called him at the hospital, his father was unable to speak on the phone, breathing was so difficult. A little later his mother called back, and she was briefly tearful. "Your father's not doing too well, he wants you to come out."

"When?"

"Now."

By the time he reached the hospital, the acute episode of breathlessness had abated, but his father seemed to have entered a new phase of his ordeal—more exhausted and subdued, less agitated and ornery. He didn't want to talk, he wasn't interested in television, he hadn't eaten all day. The nurse thought he had reached "the end of the line." Evidently his infection, coming on top of full-blown emphysema, was somewhat rare.

"I thought I was going to die," he told his son again. "Yesterday morning and this morning. I can't get my *breath*." He coughed up blood repeatedly, a moist, guttural cough.

"Dad, would you like to see Mary and Henry?" he asked at one point. Mary was his father's only sibling and Henry, her husband, was his father's lifelong friend.

"Sure, I'd like to see them," he said, "but not until I'm out of the hospital."

It was the same reply he had made to friends who wished to visit him. At the moment, to be sure, his condition had cast him out of bounds for mere well-wishers.

By ten that night he seemed more comfortable than he'd been all day. "Now we just need to get the breathing under control." Later he said, "You better get back to be with your mother. I'm sure she's eager to see you."

When his father was on the edge of sleep, he left.

He listened to his mother as she moved about her kitchen at 4:00 A.M. What he heard were the sounds of her impending loneliness in this house.

He took Golden's predictable call at six-thirty. His father was *better* today, the doctor reported. "If you had the pneumonia," he said, "you'd be ready to leave the hospital by now."

"How long can he go on like this? He's been having a terrible time."

"Barring a heart incident, or more of those acute spells, the condition is long term." Golden wanted to get the patient up and out. Medicare wouldn't pay for hospitalization indefinitely, he warned. His father might need to go to a convalescent home to rehabilitate. Part of his problem was that he hadn't moved for eleven days.

His father had been unable to even walk across a room for eleven days. Yesterday his nurse considered him a man in the end stage of his illness. Yet Golden was "optimistic."

His mother said, "Oh God, I don't want to see him home like this."

"I don't think he's going anywhere, Mother." Golden's assessment was based on the X-ray they'd taken yesterday, not reality.

At nine, when he reached the hospital, his father was relatively calm, but within the hour another arduous suffocating crisis began to set in. Very suddenly his chest began to throb rapidly, his breathing grew increasingly shallow, and his son watched the anxiety come over his somber features.

"This is when you need family," the man said, already gasping. He became agitated as his physical stress mounted. He turned onto his side, his knees drawn up, one hand grasping his bald head. Maybe morphine would help. He hadn't had an injection since yesterday.

But Golden had discontinued the morphine. "It could depress the respiratory system," the nurse said.

"Call Golden's office and request it."

She returned in a few moments. "He said no."

His father's distress was now extreme. He struggled for air like a fish out of water, while ravaged coughing racked his body. "What I need you won't give me," he said, pausing between the words.

"Golden has never seen him like this," he told the nurse. "He's never been here for this. Tell him the family insists that he be given morphine. There's something to be gained and nothing to be lost."

Eventually, the doctor conceded a half milligram every two hours.

Blood came now, tissue after tissue of it, with each tearing cough. His father's open mouth was soon like a wound, black with congealing blood—caked on his tongue, his teeth, and his full lips. To anyone looking into the room, he imagined, to a stranger, his father had become a ghastly sight.

The man took off his glasses and handed them to him, then wanted them back again. On and off with the glasses repeatedly. "Glasses," he said, a moment after removing them, like a surgeon asking for a scalpel.

"What do you want your glasses for?"

"I want to see!"

Startlingly, struggling intensely, his father said, "I've got to get up," reaching for his son's arm.

He needed to sit up, he meant. He swung his legs over the side of the bed and leaned over the service table on his elbows, his naked head bowed. He was perspiring. Moments later he laid back in the bed, only to rouse himself, hauling himself up onto the table again. It was as though you could see the wave come down on him, an unbearable crashing weight, forcing him to move—quickly! now!—to sit up. He was like a drowning man fighting for the surface again and again. With both hands his son removed the eyeglasses, put them on again. He handed his father tissues, then discarded them. He raised his father to a sitting position, hunched over the narrow white table, and placed a bathrobe over the man's smooth shoulders, exposed in the hospital johnny. A moment later he lifted his father's thin legs back into the bed. It occurred to him that he and his father had never worked together on anything the way they were working together now.

"This is a hard day, Dad," he said. He wanted his father to know he realized how hard. "A long, hard day." The morning was almost gone.

The man nodded.

Whereas he'd been able to talk at first, it had now become impossible for him to utter a word. He gestured to have the eyeglasses on or off. When the guttural coughing came, he took the tissue automatically handed to him. The whole time his son held his father's hand, as though greeting him with a handshake—that large, familiar grip—and his father tugged when he wished to be raised to a sitting position, the bathrobe draped over his hunched back as though he were a prize-fighter.

He's better today, Golden had said. At six-thirty that morning, the doctor had had his father headed for a convalescent home. Anxiety, panic, was a big part of his problem, Golden had encouraged the man's wife to believe. And the fact that he hadn't moved for eleven days, that was another part of his father's problem, the doctor explained. The fool. His father was fighting for his life.

Believing the end was near, the head nurse had called his mother to tell her to come to the hospital. An appointment with a therapist had prevented her from being there sooner. When she entered the room, she burst into tears at the frightening sight of her husband. "I'm here," she told him, drawing a chair to the side of the bed.

He shrugged his shoulders as if to say, All right, you're here.

"I can't believe this is happening. I don't want to be here when he dies. I don't want to see that."

"Ssh," he whispered, "he can hear you." His father appeared almost comatose, but suddenly he would have to get up, he would need a tissue, he'd want his glasses, a sip of water.

"I didn't know he was so sick. Maybe I pushed him too hard. What will I do without him?" she wept. She had taken his right hand in both of hers. After a moment, watching him gasp for breath, she pressed her forehead to the back of it and cried, "I love you. I love you."

"Ah, bullshit," her husband managed to utter, which was funny, really—not a scornful rebuff but the unexpected emergence of his gruffly good-natured self.

The struggle continued relentlessly all afternoon. It was as though he'd been running up a mountain all day—his pulse was 140—and it didn't seem he could go on much longer. Now, lying there spent, his wife and his son on either side of him, he roused himself to sit up less frequently. The incessant coughing and blood spitting ceased, as if he no longer had the strength for it. By three o'clock, when another nurse came on duty, he lay like a man who'd had the fight pounded out of him. The new nurse promptly decided to clean up her patient. Earlier his father had seemed too agitated to withstand such fussing.

He seemed to be dozing—his arms twitching constantly, like the legs of a dreaming animal—when he suddenly told them, "Go to bed. You're crowding me." A little later he took the oxygen tube out of his nose and pushed it behind his head. "I've had it," he said.

"Have you had it?" This siege had been going on for over eight hours.

He nodded. "I've had it."

His son gently inserted the cannula back into his nostrils.

Unaccountably, over the next few hours he began to rally, to spontaneously come around. He was clearly exhausted, but the horrible breathlessness had passed, and when Janice and her husband arrived from Connecticut at nine, he sat up and engaged his new guests in conversation. Janice, who'd been told to come quickly, he was certainly dying, was baffled to find him pleasantly inquiring about her children.

There was a recurrent phrase in his chart for each day he'd been in the hospital, including today: *Alert. Oriented.* "What's that mean?" his son asked.

"I'm not nuts," the father said.

His will was stubborn. He'd survived another day.

The phone alarmed the household before seven the next morning.

"Oh no," he heard his mother say, and he imagined death had come to his father in the night, after all. A moment later, replacing the receiver, she turned to him. "Golden says he's *better* this morning," she said. "And he told me Medicare won't continue to pay for hospitalization much longer." That especially upset her. Her husband was in no condition to come home—was he?—and yet she couldn't bear to put him in a convalescent home.

That morning his father passed an anxious hour, but by noon, while he was profoundly fatigued, unable to get out of bed, his arms and legs more wasted than ever, his breathing was less fitful, and he appeared to be resting as comfortably as possible. He had only a vague recollection of the day before.

That afternoon Holly called the hospital room from Conway.

"Brett's had a setback," she said. He felt his body constrict. Their daughter's apartment had been broken into again, one year after the first incident. The thieves had cleaned out whatever they could get their hands on—another CD player, a leather bag Jocelyn had brought from Italy, jewelry—but the greatest blow . . . they'd taken the black leather portfolio that held all Brett's artwork. "She's devastated," his wife said. Their daughter had run into the street screaming; she'd smashed a chair in the house.

He hurried to a public phone and called San Francisco. There were no words of consolation. Maybe she could attempt to re-create the most important pieces, he suggested feebly.

"The work was a mirror of my journey through illness," she said. "It was so valuable to me. I couldn't repeat the excitement of discovering each piece for the first time."

What had become of the irreplaceable work was hard to contemplate. The thieves would have cashed in the portfolio for a few bucks. They would have thrown the contents away.

He considered later how it must have seemed to his father. While he lay there desperately ill, his son seemed almost more alarmed about the loss of drawings three thousand miles away.

He and his sister left the Cape toward the end of the day, prepared to return if there was any change. Incredibly, the patient's condition seemed slightly improved for the moment.

Brett called that evening, following another echocardiogram earlier in the day. There was no discernible buildup of fluid. And no evidence of disease. "Leavitt doesn't want to see me for a month." She sounded all right, as if so many blows had made her that much more resilient.

. . .

"For years I've hated what's become of him," his mother said when she too called that night. "Once he was the best dancer. I loved to get back to dance with him after attempting to dance with these shorter men. I feel guilty that I've treated him harshly, I didn't know he was so sick. Today I said to him, I love you. He had all he could do to answer, I love you too. He was so sad. What's the matter? I asked. I don't know, he said. I think he wants to spare me by not talking about his fears or the past. Have you had it? I asked. I've had it, he said. But I don't think he was talking about dying. He always said that: I've had it."

The next day she reported, "Last night I was heartbroken about him. I went in today eager to see him, and he was a little better, but he gives me nothing. He lies there with his eyes closed. I don't understand that. If you're going to come home, I told him, you better practice keeping your eyes open. You better stay home tomorrow, he said. Why does he have his eyes closed? He's turning himself into a nursing-home patient. Of course, he knows all about Kuwait. What I want you to understand, Douglas, is that I go down there to be good and he gives me nothing. He's always been the same way. I'm exhausted too. This is my life too." She couldn't stay away from the hospital for a day, though. "I'm scared—scared he'll die, and scared he'll live."

But the following day, a Thursday, "Your father was excellent today. He can't walk, he needs oxygen, but he was eating and generally much better. The nurses can't believe that he pulled through. Today he told me, I miss you after you leave." Now it seemed likely that he'd be home soon.

For the next two days, his father seemed to be holding his own. When he called the hospital Sunday, however, they had an awkward monosyllabic question-and-answer period, which ended when his father impatiently said, "Everything's fine," and hung up the phone. His mother explained that he'd had an accident the night before. He'd taken a laxative and lost control of his bowels before he could do anything about it. "He was mortified. When I walked into the room today, he said, Last night was the worst night of my life. Then he said to me, I hate myself. He's so depressed. Golden, he says, treats us like a couple of old fools."

Together his parents met with a psychologist. His father only grew infuriated with her, his mother reported. "Will you stop interfering, he shouted at me. It isn't fair of you to come down here and upset me. I'm trying to help, Douglas. When the psychologist asked him what he did for a living, he said, I managed a plant. I could manage four or five hundred men, but I can't handle *her*." She paused. "But then to-night he called me, and he was wonderful, he was like his old self. He said he's been doing a lot of praying."

When he phoned his father later, the nurse was about to take him for a walk, he said. He was expecting the psychologist again tomorrow. "We're working on why I'm reluctant to go home. When she gives me some answers, I'll let you know." Thinking to bring his father news of the larger world, he mentioned the impending Persian Gulf war. His father said, "Don't worry about that."

He called back his mother to reassure her that her husband was sounding more positive tonight. "You know, we really love each other," she said, "we really care about each other."

But on Thursday, a moment into their talk, his father told him, "I have to go."

"Where are you going, Dad?"

"To bed," and he hung up the phone.

"You hate me, don't you? he asked me today," his mother said. "I told him I was sorry about what he'd become in the last fifteen years. He doesn't want to come home tomorrow, but he is coming home, on oxygen. He'll have fifty feet of tubing connected to his nose. I'm just grasping how our life is ending. I'm not ready for this." She was crying. "He's a hard man to care for. He makes it difficult. When I suggested he watch television to get his mind off himself, he said, There's noth-ing on but war."

That indifference reflected a profound loss: it was no longer his world.

He heard from his mother again the next night. His father was home. The oxygen tanks made an impossible humming sound. He was unable to eat his supper, he took an interest in nothing. He'd been sitting in his chair, but of course he couldn't get out of it. Finally, they'd struggled to move him into the bedroom. He sat on the edge of the bed and put his head in his hands and became tearful. "What's the matter? I asked him. I don't know, he said. I asked him if he'd like some tea and toast. Right now he's sleeping. Most of your problem is fear, I told him. He said, I know it."

On Saturday, he and Holly returned to Brewster. His father was sitting in the den in pajamas and bathrobe, thin, pale, tethered to the plastic tubing, which snaked through the house to the bedroom, where the oxygen machine hummed in one corner. His feet and ankles were visibly swollen. They shook hands. Before dinner, his father said he'd have a martini. The drink sat untouched on the table near him, like a talisman. The events in the Persian Gulf, the first made-for-TV war, held no fascination for him. He had no appetite for food either.

"Don't you think you should go to bed now?"

"Pretty soon, Rose," his father said. "I don't want to go into that room. I feel too isolated and alone there."

Hoping to point their time together in a helpful direction, he said, "Do you think you're going to pull out of this, Dad?"

"Don't start talking like that," his father said.

Half-carrying him, the man's large, lanky frame powerless, a dead weight, he helped his father into the bedroom. The effort of leaving one room for the next, fifteen shuffling steps, left him completely spent, and he had to wait until he had the breathing "smoothed out" again. The oxygen rig in the corner, its fretful hum, had the presence of an unwanted observer.

"I'm glad you're here," his father said. "I wish you lived closer."

"I can get here at a moment's notice, Dad—any time. I'm not that far away."

His father sat on the edge of the bed for ten minutes before he was ready to lie down on his side.

"This has been some struggle, Dad. It's been hard, hasn't it?"

"My whole life has been hard."

When he asked him what he meant, his father said, "How would you have liked to lose your hair at seventeen?" This subject, his father's hairlessness, had never been broached between them. He'd locked himself in his room for a year, he said, with a radio. His parents made "very light" of it.

"Did you know what caused it?"

"Nerves probably. It had been building up for years—trouble with my parents."

This was a story he knew something about. His grandfather, who had done well even during the Depression, had been a hard drinker. He'd been involved with another woman, the story went, and his son, around thirteen at the time, had been caught between his parents, trying to serve both of them.

"Did it always hurt?" Their father's complete baldness had never meant much, certainly nothing troublesome, to him or his sisters. To them, the man couldn't have been otherwise.

His father said, "It still hurts."

He'd entered the same manufacturing industry—brass and eventually aluminum—in which his father had achieved prominence. That place, he said now, was his cover, his control, a place to go.

"What did the baldness mean to the rest of your life? How did it affect you?"

Without hesitation he said, "I would have been a better person."

It was a wild remark, coming from this modest, decent man. "You mean it made you an angry person?"

"Yes. I was angry at life. I would have been a kinder person, a better person."

"To who?" His father was kind, he believed, tolerant, generous. "Everyone."

Given the host of annihilating infirmities people were heir to, given the countless forms and colors of human suffering, he was intrigued and perplexed to hear his father attribute so much to the event of permanent hair loss in his youth. It was what had made him the way he was. Not the fact of baldness, surely, so much as what lay behind it. How did the man think of his own granddaughter's ordeal? Fifty years later, here was a young woman who had worn her temporary baldness with aplomb. Yet who was to say? Fifty years later, everything was different. His father's affliction had involved punishing shame and humiliation that he, the son, only glimpsed. Who was to say what wounds mattered most?

"Why haven't you ever talked to me about this? You know, in the last thirty years."

His father said, as though it should have been obvious, "I didn't want to involve you."

They were together for a while longer in silence. "Do you think you'll sleep now?"

"Yes."

All night he listened to his father's restlessness and to his mother's repeatedly, tirelessly, it would seem, running back and forth to the bedroom to check on him. All night he listened to the hum of the oxygen, which churned like an indefatigable engine propelling this dwelling through a sea in turmoil.

The next morning his father asked him, "Don't you have a corner in the barn for me?" Then he whispered, "Don't go home tonight. We can watch *Lonesome Dove*." A TV miniseries based on one of his father's favorite novels.

"I'll be out again soon. Next weekend at the latest." He helped his father move from the den—that word disturbed him—to the bedroom, where the taller man clung to the dresser to get his breath, then on to the bathroom. When his father was done there, they made the laborious journey back. This trip to the toilet took almost an hour.

Later, as he and Holly were leaving, his father shouted his name with startling urgency, and he returned to the room where the immobilized patient sat in his chair in his bathrobe, the pale green oxygen tube descending from his nose. There was a bulletin coming up concerning Scud missiles, his father informed him, hoping to detain him a little longer. A thirty-second news spot. Then, with odd formality, he said, "Sorry to interrupt your leaving."

"I'll call later today. We'll be back soon."

At the front door his mother broke down in tears.

"I hate this," she said. "The oxygen equipment, and your father in his condition, and the house in chaos. I hate all this, and I'm not handling it well."

"Yes, you are. You're doing fine. It's an impossible situation."

"No, I'm not." She hadn't slept since he'd gotten home. This was wearing her out.

That evening she called to say the day had passed calmly. His father had told her a sad story about one Christmas when he was a boy. She'd have to tell him about it sometime. Just then he was sleeping in his chair. "He said Golden told him he'd soon be able to go out to dinner again, and he's looking forward to that. It's sad," she said, "he doesn't know what's happening."

When they talked the next day, Monday, she had already called the doctor and demanded, "Tell me the truth." Her husband couldn't eat, he couldn't move, he was nauseated, his feet swollen. Golden became indignant. He'd always told her the truth; her husband was getting better. "Today he didn't want me to leave him," his mother went on. But she had to keep her appointment with the therapist. "I told her about everything, my marriage, my children, my sister. She wrote it all down."

Tuesday evening, his mother reported that his father had spent the day in bed until his home-care person arrived. "Now he's sitting in his chair. He hasn't eaten all day. I'm more exhausted than ever." She wished her son a happy birthday. He was forty-seven.

At eleven that night Janice called to say that Dad had passed out when Mother took him into the bedroom, slipping from the bed onto the floor. The rescue squad had taken him to the emergency room. "Mother didn't want to disturb you again on your birthday."

When he called the hospital, they were just beginning to evaluate him. Obstinately, he dialed his mother's number.

"He was edgy tonight," she said. "He wanted the TV off, then on. He ate a bit of Jell-O. Do you want to go to bed now? Not yet, not yet. You can help me now, he said a little later. I turned to do something, once I got him to the bed, and the next thing I knew he was on the floor. I thought he'd died."

She called at seven-thirty the next morning. "Your father's going to be home within the hour!" She was exasperated. "Another trip to the emergency room. I'm just strung out. He's got me up to a million. Golden called and told me he isn't helping himself get better. I'll call later. I've got to go and cool down before he gets here."

As though to give him and possibly herself a break, his mother didn't call again that afternoon or evening. It was the first day since Christmas that she hadn't called him. The phone went off by his bed at two-thirty in the morning.

"He's gone," she said, sobbing. His nurse and the social worker had been there in the afternoon. He'd eaten very little all day. She'd helped him into the bedroom—*that room,* he thought—at about eleven. "He said, Talk to me. And I said, It's too late to talk. I haven't been good to him," she said. "We misjudged him. I can't believe it, I just can't believe it. He's lying here. There's Rita now." Just then his mother's friend and neighbor was letting herself into the house.

His sister was already there, several hours later, when he reached the Cape. He wanted to hear the story of the past day.

His father had returned from the hospital and was "set down" in the living room. He had on pajama bottoms, his bathrobe clutched at his throat. He was unable to walk, so she got him onto a chair on a small rug in the hallway and moved him to the other end of the house like a chest of drawers. She changed his pajamas; that exhausted him even more.

"I feel so bad about what's happening to you, I said to him. I feel so bad about this. He said, Me, too."

The nurse's aide arrived at midday to bathe him, which tired him further. He still hadn't eaten, although he'd tried a nutritional drink. "He sat in his chair with his eyes closed and his mouth open; that always drove me crazy." The closed eyes, she ventured, was an attempt to block out the whole thing happening. By the end of the day he looked worse than ever. Yet twice he carefully sorted out his numerous pills with shaking hands, reading the label on each bottle, and he took them on schedule. She asked what he wanted for supper and he told her, "Two hot dogs and a beer." He attempted to eat some toast. She made herself something to eat, and the evening passed without much between them, he sitting in his chair, and she answering his needs as best she could. Eventually she got him to the bed, that long journey again. As he clung to her, he said, "You're better at this than Douglas."

"He said to me," and his mother broke down again at the kitchen table, "Rose, you're my only hope. Just like that: Rose, you're my only hope."

Seated on the edge of the bed, unable to breathe, he told her he was going to faint again. She said, "No, you're not. Just relax, take your time, you're not going to faint." He kept her running back and forth from the other room several times for one thing or another. At nine-thirty he asked her to get his pills for him, telling her which ones he needed, but he didn't take them then because it wasn't time yet to take them.

"He asked me to lie down at his back," she said. He was lying on his side with his back to the center of the bed. "And I did for a minute. But I couldn't sleep with him the way he was." She had been sleeping on the couch in the den.

At some point he said, "Do you want to talk?" or "Let's talk" or "Talk to me." And she said, "It's too late to talk" or "It's a little too late to talk."

Then he wanted the remote control for the TV in the bedroom. He wanted to listen to one of his favorite shows. "Despite everything, he knew that show was on at ten o'clock Wednesday night. I said, Why don't you sit up and watch it, and he said, No, he just wanted to listen to it. He always used to fall asleep listening to Johnny Carson."

When she went to the bathroom to wash up at eleven, she was sure he was asleep, she was sure she saw him breathing, because she'd looked for that. "I fell fast asleep on the couch, and woke up at around two with a start. My first thought was, Why hasn't he called me? Why haven't I heard him?" She found him as she'd last observed him, lying on his right side with his hand under his head, the thumb jammed against his cheek, as he always slept. His eyes were closed, his mouth open. She believed he died in his sleep.

H e was haunted by the last hours of his father's life. *Do you want to talk?* Had he ever asked her such a question before, come to think of it? *Will you lie down at my back?* At last it was the television—a companion of many years—the meaningless voices of some canned drama, that would have to be his comfort. At the very end he'd been aware enough—*Alert. Oriented.*—to tune in to his anticipated show. She last saw him breathing at eleven. So they didn't know whether he had died on Wednesday, the twenty-third of January, or Thursday.

Why hadn't his mother called him that day? He'd wanted, he'd been determined, to be with his father when he died.

"We didn't know how bad he was," his mother lamented. She'd been anxious that he'd end up in a nursing home, after all, when she was no longer able to handle his needs. "I just can't believe this has happened. I wasn't as good as I might have been. It was a case of crying wolf," she explained. He'd been so stressed-out and so ill for so long that she mistook his final struggle for more of the same—it would go on and on. She was convinced, furthermore, that her husband had also been taken unawares. He'd fastidiously taken his pills on that last day, he'd spoken about getting back to bridge, dining out. And Golden had only contributed to the confusion. The optimist.

But wasn't it obvious that his father knew he was dying? *Two hot dogs and a beer.* He didn't know when he'd die or just how. They were all in the same position—knowing yet not knowing. That last day, though, his father surely knew, and then the moment of absolute certainty arrived. He was haunted by that moment, his father in that moment, the man's consciousness in that moment. *Alert. Oriented.* Alone. They had failed, they had all failed. Yet, and this was no excuse, he wasn't sure it could have been otherwise. Had his father been protecting them from his death, from facing his death, or himself? They'd gone along with the pretense.

They decided that it was merciful that his death had come sooner rather than later. Another day or week or month of life would have meant another day or week or month of suffering. And he had been in his own home, after all, not some institution. That didn't diminish the sense of failure. Two months later he experienced a remarkably literal dream in which his father sat in the corner of a couch—it seemed to be the camelback couch in the living room in Conway. He approached him gradually, almost cautiously, until he was seated next to him. He put his arm around him and felt the tall man curl up against him like a child. They were both crying. This should have happened while his father was alive.

Like so much else in his life, the man had died keeping it to himself. *I didn't want to involve you.*

His father often enjoyed driving to the ocean with him and then waiting in the car while he went off for an invigorating walk down the wide, splendid beach. On a mild day, while he was still up to it, his father would go as far as the bench at the end of the boardwalk and wait there. This day, as he returned from his walk toward dusk—he'd wept the whole way down the beach, but now, on his way back, his tears had stopped—he knew the car awaiting him in the parking lot would be empty. He knew—of course!—and yet, when he came down the boardwalk to the asphalt and looked to his car, he caught his breath, stunned to see that his father wasn't there in the passenger seat in his distinctive, ever-present hat, smiling to welcome his son back.

How was it today? he'd ask cheerfully, content to have waited here for most of an hour.

Oh, it's gorgeous, just beautiful. Then, because he knew his father wanted to commiserate, he'd add, It's pretty damn windy, though, pretty cold.

You bet your life it is.

4

DISTANCE

Brett's checkup in February would have been a high—no evidence of disease—except for the inexplicable pain in her hip and back, which had persisted since September. There were appointments with a neurologist, an orthopedist, the pain clinic; they did a sonogram of her abdomen. Discomfort in her chest prompted another echocardiogram. Every time he and his daughter spoke long-distance, at least weekly, she was contending with something, scheduled for yet another appointment, another examination, trapped in the morass of hectic medical procedures.

In March Brett met her mother in Florida to visit Holly's parents for a week; then they flew back to Massachusetts together. She intended to remain through Easter, two weeks away. She looked very well, her hair now wildly curly, a vibrant red. Her running commentary on retirement communities, Florida, airports, and humans of all kinds had kept her mother in stitches all week. The unyielding back pain didn't prevent her from taking a vigorous afternoon hike with her parents and the dog, Ben, through woods and pastures. The next morning, though, Brett announced that she'd made a mistake. Having already been away from San Francisco for more than a week, she didn't want to remain in Conway until Easter, especially while she was continuing to experience these damned aches and pains. She and her mother went to a film that night, and when they returned Brett went directly to her room, disturbed, Holly explained, by the movie's visceral portrayal of a character's death from a sudden feverish illness, a sequence that had taken them completely by surprise. Stay here, the young man's wife had keened as she watched her husband's life being gradually and ineluctably extinguished. Don't die, you can't die, stay here.

In the morning he came upon his daughter in the kitchen arranging a flight to San Francisco for that afternoon. She'd passed a bad night, with pain and numbness in her hip and legs.

"You've only been here two days," he said. "Why are you so eager to get back?"

That was putting his foot in his mouth. Surely his disappointed silence the day before, when she told them that the long holiday she'd planned was a mistake, had annoyed her. Now she blew up at him.

"I don't need this. How can you accuse me of using pain as an excuse to leave? You don't know what this is like. You don't understand what I've been through, lying in that black tube month after month, sick for over two years." Shouting. "I don't need to listen to that." She was holding several black sticks of charcoal in her fist. She flung them clattering to the floor.

He followed her to her bedroom. "That's unfair to me," he said. "I was upset that you wanted to leave and I said so."

"I can't help your problems."

She was wounded, and so was he. His spontaneous regret was acute. He paced the house, trying to get a handle on what was going on here, bewildered by her anger, and finally returned to her room. She was busily packing her belongings. He embraced her.

"I'm sorry," she said.

"My problems?" His biggest problem was the state of her health, for God's sake. "I want to spend time with you, that's all. I'm feeling that more than ever since my father died. I didn't spend enough time with him. I was hurt that you'd decided to leave." Recently he'd written an angry letter to Golden, but he knew that what most troubled him about his father's death had nothing to do with Golden.

He and Brett sat at the kitchen table and had tea together. She needed to get to the bottom of these mysterious pains, she had to resolve the pericarditis issue again—that was why she was eager to return to San Francisco. He understood. They parted lovingly, but her mother drove Brett to the airport.

When she called several days later, her voice was hesitant, uncertain. Her chest felt more constricted, the weird pain in her back and legs was still present, but, most worrisome, for the past two nights she'd been running fevers of over a hundred degrees, fevers that occurred only at night. The next day she would slug it out at the hospital again—more tests—and on Good Friday she'd make the hike up Parnassus to submit to another CAT scan: the hospital garb, the wait, the intravenous needle, the cold sterility of the radiology department, the numbing hum of technology, the glare of fluorescent lights, the pathetic, disassociated aggregation of sick people, the boredom of nurses and technicians, the loss of self as you obediently went through the paces as a good patient, the precious day gone, leaving a wake of frustration, waste, anxiety.

She called to say Happy Easter. She and Beth had been to a brunch where they held twin infants, one for each of them, for an hour. The following Wednesday, Leavitt told her that the CAT scan had discovered four slightly enlarged nodes below the diaphragm. They didn't know what to make of them. Typically, a biopsy would probably have been appropriate, but the nodes were hard to reach, and the doctors didn't believe the situation warranted surgery. An aspirate would be inconclusive. They had decided to wait and take another look in a month. In the meantime, they weren't inclined to see a relation between her pain and the enlarged lymph nodes.

"It can't be Hodgkin's," he told her. Weeks before, they'd thought they'd seen an enlarged node near her pancreas, for example, but no such image had turned up again. Wasn't it unlikely that the disease would appear in such an unexpected place, below the diaphragm? "The nodes won't be there in a month."

As he and Holly were cleaning up after dinner, Holly was overcome with vertigo, catching herself against the kitchen counter as if she'd been clubbed from behind. He helped her to the living room couch. Nausea, chills, her head spinning. An hour later, she began to throw up. Would a doctor have seen a connection between this episode and her daughter's phone call earlier in the day? Was there one?

The next time Brett spoke to Leavitt, he told her there was maybe a forty percent chance it was Hodgkin's, originating in a new site. That left room to believe it wasn't cancer at all. But their daughter was discouraged—hanging in midair again, she said—oppressed with the ever-present back pain and impatient with them, the cheering parents.

"I could *feel* you resisting the impulse to call me these past couple of days," she told them, as though their unconditional concern for her, which she had seemed to seek and count on, she now found annoying.

Holly said, "Try to hope it's not . . ."

"Of course I hope I don't have cancer, Mother."

"What are you doing tonight?" he asked.

She was going to view a work of performance art at New Langton Arts, where Beth had acquired a prominent position.

Holly was in tears when they hung up.

Brett's fevers abated, then in early May began to trouble her again, occurring every few days, it seemed, and only at night. "I wake up damp." She continued to absorb herself with work, the intensely wrought, largely black-and-white charcoal drawings. When he asked her how the art was coming, she conveyed a sense of urgency. "I have a lot to do."

As he lay in bed each night waiting for sleep, when he awakened in the small hours, and then at dawn before he got up for the day, he found himself pleading passionately to the partial dark—please, please, please—for her to be all right. The interminable winter, a season of anxiety and grief, was over. Bluebirds had returned to the nesting box on the north lawn, phoebes were back in the barn, dogwood, tulips, narcissus in bloom, ground phlox flowering, the viburnum, crabapple, and lilac just beginning, the field green again, the hills that soft pale green of budding trees. A prolonged and profuse spring. Nathaniel was completing his freshman year of college, Jocelyn would graduate in June. He and Holly were catching up on debt and taxes. She continued to be busy and productive. His first novel, years in the making, was about to be published, a box of books due to arrive any day now. And Brett . . . No, he implored, please. Each time the phone rang, his pulse jumped and his neck stiffened.

Dad, it's Brett." And he knew. "It's cancer." The cluster of nodes in the back near her kidneys appeared slightly enlarged in the CAT scan. She had the impression that Leavitt didn't think they'd still be there. Now they were hoping a surgeon could reach the site with a needle for biopsy. The nature of the cancer had to be established before they proceeded with treatment—Leavitt had introduced the improbable but ghoulish thought that this could be a non-Hodgkin's lymphoma resulting from her prior therapy—and she would have to be staged again. The transplant now seemed most likely, but it was important that the disease be in retreat first, so she'd require some preliminary treatment, as yet undetermined. His daughter's voice was calm and controlled as she dealt out this information. After leaving the clinic she and Beth had been walking around for a couple of hours. It was almost exactly one year since his daughter had triumphantly completed the six-month course of chemotherapy.

"How's Beth?" he asked.

"She's great." She'd taken the day off to be with Brett.

Holly bustled into the kitchen with groceries. These first splendid weeks of spring, for the first time in months, she'd seemed positive and happy, as though she'd discovered a new source of strength.

"It's cancer," he said.

She fled to the other phone. "Brett!" she cried. "Oh Brett, I'm sorry."

When she heard her mother's tears, Brett began to cry. "The terror comes in waves," she said. "The third time! I can't believe it either, Mom."

"No!" he swore, frantic. "No!"

"When should we come out?" Holly asked.

"I don't know yet." They'd have to figure all that out when they understood just what was going to happen next. She had to go, she said, because she was on her way to see S.J.

He and Holly embraced in the kitchen. Beyond the window the gold-green spring evening assaulted him. The future arose blank, ominous. How would they manage this?

"Do they know what they're doing?" Holly asked.

"No. They do the best they can."

"What does it mean?"

"There is no meaning. You can be lucky, and if you aren't lucky, you suffer." It felt like punishment, but of course it wasn't that. Only random suffering. "Christ," he said, "is this what it's been about from the beginning, through all these years?" Then, in the next breath, he became resolved. They weren't going to brood and pine for the next several months. They weren't going to foster despair in one another. For Brett to go through the fire, she had to believe she would prevail, and so did they. Any other view was pointless. There was no alternative to a successful outcome. "The transplant procedure exists because it works. People go through it, and go on." Paul Tsongas, for God's sake, the former congressman from Massachusetts, was running for president.

When Jocelyn called to learn the results of the scan, her tone indicated that she wasn't worried. In a moment she was sobbing. He spoke to her again that night after she'd reached Brett.

"How was she?"

"She said she's sad and confused. She needs to know that people love her. Her therapist told her not to deny her grief but to let it out.

Not to hate her body but to remember that her soul and creativity and self don't have cancer. Brett said that helped. She wants me to go out there when she's in the hospital," Joce said, "and I want to go."

Nathaniel's response, like everyone else's, was disbelief. That semester he was taking the course that Brett had taken years before, The Biology of Cancer, and he talked about a man in his sixties, a cancer patient for many years, who had recently addressed the class. "He looked like he was in his forties," Nathaniel said.

"It might be a good idea to give Brett a call."

"Do you think she wants to hear from me?" The moment he stated his reluctance, the answer was clear. "No, I want to talk to her." For his twentieth birthday, earlier in the month, Brett had sent him one of her oil pastel drawings. The image was of a naked man standing up to his waist in a sea, raising a naked woman on his shoulders as she attempted to reach for an anchor that swung through a starry sky. In an otherwise black-and-white picture, the anchor and the sea were the same sea green color. "I'll definitely call," he said.

Despite the pep talk he'd given Holly, he felt, as the night wore on, that everything was out of control, he was out of control. He couldn't bear to think of his daughter in her apartment in that remote city with her impossible thoughts. Her body had been telling her something was wrong for many months. Everyone, even her doctors, it seemed to Brett, had been in denial, wishing to believe another recurrence couldn't be. Before going to bed, he called San Francisco. Beth answered.

"She's having a snooze," she said pleasantly.

"Just tell her I called to say good night."

Dad . . . if it came back again . . . I can't help these thoughts . . . I don't think I could go through this any longer. I don't think I could do it.

You won't have to go through it again.

. . .

They'd hoped to get adequate tissue samples with two needle biopsies, but they didn't hit pay dirt, Brett said, until the fourth attempt. The pain was reminiscent of a bone-marrow biopsy. As ever, Beth was with her, though witnessing the procedure made her a little woozy. The two pathologists on hand to examine the tissue seemed to shake their heads over the slides at one point, and she'd heard one of them say, "We have a lot of lymphoma cells here." Brett said, "I have a very bad feeling about it." She added, "If they do the transplant, that's it. That's it," she repeated emphatically.

Her doctors soon informed her that the cancer was definitely Hodgkin's, not some other lymphoma.

"I'm relieved," he said. "Aren't you?" Hodgkin's, crucially, was treatable.

"Yes," she said impatiently.

But according to Leavitt, as he tried to account for this new emergence of disease, the Hodgkin's they'd now identified below the diaphragm appeared to be biologically different, more slow-growing, than Brett's previous disease; the disease in her chest, he recalled, had nearly doubled in size in one month. Chemotherapy was most effective against rapidly dividing cancer cells, and Leavitt speculated that the new cells, possibly present all along, inchoate, incipient, might have survived the six cycles of treatment. With hindsight he speculated that it might have been beneficial to do radiation therapy below the diaphragm as well as above. Now, for example, Brett appeared to be free of cancer above the diaphragm.

"This disease!" she exclaimed in frustration.

The plan now, Leavitt assumed, was to precede the transplant with a six-week course of radiation therapy. But the Tumor Board would make the final recommendation.

Given what Leavitt had described, mightn't radiation be the exclusive treatment necessary? he wondered. Certainly radiation would entail immeasurably less suffering, less risk, and in the event that it wasn't successful they'd still have the transplant as a backup. Was that a reasonable view of the situation? Brett's chemotherapy had addressed the more aggressive cancer cells. Her earlier radiation treatments had eliminated disease above the diaphragm. Now radiation to the site of the recurrence might well be conclusive. Before submitting to the hell of the bone-marrow transplant, wasn't it worth a try?

"I don't want to discuss this right now," she said. "I've got to get out of the house." She'd spent the day waiting for Leavitt's phone call, which had only left her exasperated and pissed off. She had things to do; that night she was expecting six friends for dinner.

The next day he called George Canellos at Dana Farber to discuss the question of Brett's best option. "Could radiation alone conceivably succeed?"

Canellos said, "There have been such cases." If there didn't appear to be cancer above the diaphragm and they could target the site of disease, it was worth the chance. "At least," he said, "it would buy more time." If extensive radiation was necessary, he would go directly to the transplant rather than jeopardize the bone marrow with less decisive therapy.

When he recounted his conversation with Canellos to Brett, she wasn't impressed. She'd had enough. "I don't want to live waiting for my disease to recur," she said, "being constantly monitored, hoping for the best." She wanted to do it and be done with it. "My psychological state has to be factored into the equation." In any case, they were still waiting—each day they waited—to hear from the Tumor Board. Hastily she changed the topic, and her tone suddenly brightened. "Yesterday Beth and I signed the forms to make ourselves domestic partners. We went to dinner to celebrate."

"You mean you got married?"

"Sort of."

"I want grandchildren," he said.

"I read the piece from the *Times* that Mom sent me," she said then.

The article was written by a young man with testicular cancer who had been through a bone-marrow transplant. It hadn't been successful, the young man was living with cancer, but Holly had found the story inspiring nonetheless. Their daughter saw the young man's struggle—like Hodgkin's, testicular cancer typically had a ninety percent cure rate—as very similar to her own.

"He seemed like an exceptional guy, didn't he?"

Brett thought the tone of the writing was one of resignation. "He's accepted his death," she said.

Was resignation what he'd heard in her relative calm lately—at the end of her rope, beyond anger, prepared to endure the final trial and suffer the consequences?

"It seemed like his metastases didn't respond to treatment," he said. "There have always been plausible explanations for why your cancer recurred, and it has always responded."

"Yeah," she said halfheartedly.

Two days later the Tumor Board was unanimous in deciding that the transplant was unavoidable. No one wanted to take responsibility for doing less.

"How do you feel?" he asked.

"I'm not there yet. Oh, I loved the lilies," she said. He and Holly had sent flowers to the newly domestic partners.

They both heard the impatience in her voice. After a pause Holly asked, "Brett, how do you feel about these telephone conversations with us?"

Frankly, she said, she found it a strain talking to them lately. They were usually helpful and supportive, but the upbeat, you-can-do-it routine wasn't much help to her. She often hung up feeling they'd missed each another, which only made her feel more alone. "I don't need you to be positive and encouraging all the time or to dominate the conversation or tell me what I must be feeling. It isn't calming, you know, when you talk at me. I just need you to listen. When I talk to Joce she just listens and cries—she's pure emotion—and I get the feeling she loves me." Already, she said, she felt better getting this out.

"I understand," he said. Insistent hopefulness was bound to ring hollow, but maybe they needed to do it for themselves. When he found her feeling low or discouraged, his impulse was to try to bolster her up. They couldn't bear to hang up feeling she was down. "But I know what you mean," he said, which, he realized by the time they hung up today, was a perfect example—this insistence of his, this explaining, this reasoning, this defensiveness—of what she was talking about.

They were both stung. Despite their best intentions, they hadn't been a comfort to her in this latest catastrophe, they'd added to the strain.

"I never know what to say to Brett," Holly said. "When I try to say something, it always seems the wrong thing."

"Most of her comments were directed at me, not you." He didn't know when to stop analyzing, he didn't know when to shut up. The domestic partner arrangement was an effort to grow away from them, to have her own family. She had declared her independence years before, of course—she was twenty-six—but now they needed to give her space just when the distance felt wrong.

But he knew it was more complicated than that. Failing to connect with them left her more alone, yes, and yet that sense of aloneness also came from leaving them behind, losing them, finding herself on a path where they couldn't follow. The separation sprang from loss. To fail to hear her fear and pain—what was really happening—over the din of his own encouragements and protests, was to forsake her, the exact opposite of what he meant. Despite all his mental rigor and cocksure empathy, he'd evidently been failing his daughter as desperately as his mother, for entirely different reasons, had failed his father. It was a tremendous lesson. If he could learn it.

Brett's interview with Charles Linker, who would be her presiding doctor during the bone-marrow transplant, was not encouraging. His manner was utterly frank, she said, yet remote. He had advocated the transplant at the time of the first recurrence, he informed her, following the six cycles of chemo. Apparently this latest relapse didn't surprise him. She introduced Canellos's advice into the discussion. The renowned oncologist from Dana Farber was a conservative from the old school, in Linker's view; he hadn't kept pace with the technology. If Brett were to stop with radiation and forgo the transplant, Linker told her, he was absolutely sure that her disease would come back. The chance of another recurrence would be one hundred percent. And at that point the disease would be completely resistant to treatment.

When he, the vigilant parent, continued to raise hypothetical questions, Brett replied, "I don't need doubt. I need to believe this is going to work and commit to going through it."

She went on to describe the long, harrowing process Linker had outlined for her. She'd never again go through anything like what they had in store for her, he said. The risks were ultimate. The greatest pain, for which she'd receive morphine on demand, would probably be mouth sores and a gray-purple rash, the result of the skin's "burning" under the assault of the overwhelming chemotherapy. The disfiguring rash could last for months, long after she'd left the hospital. "It looks like death," Brett said. "I've seen it, but I didn't know what it was." She added, "I can deal with the rash." Not only would she lose her hair, the chemical blast would eliminate her fingernails too. She would be fed intravenously, unable to eat because of oral and intestinal sores. Following her weeks of radiation, she'd get two weeks' rest, then enter the transplant ward. While chemo was the preferred preliminary therapy, they were willing to trade the knowledge they might gain from that—how her disease reacted to the chemicals—for reduced toxicity. Throughout their meeting, Linker seemed rather glum. At the end of it Brett asked him what her chances were if she got through the hospitalization. Linker said fifty-fifty. But that seemed pretty good compared to the alternative: no chance. If everything went ideally she could expect to be out of the hospital in eight weeks. She was quite composed relating the information: she could do this. By the time they hung up, he felt they'd had a good talk. The tension of their previous conversation seemed completely gone.

With Andrew Leavitt, though, he continued his interrogation concerning the transplant. They had treated Brett's disease optimistically, Leavitt said; now it was time to strike with all they had. The fact that it had initially recurred within months, and then again in a new site one year later, following six months of chemotherapy, left them no choice. Brett's "B" symptoms—fevers, night sweats—were an additional negative factor. Furthermore, as Brett's radiation oncologist had informed her, they were concerned about an area of the spine that might contain something besides marrow. Other specialists at the clinic didn't wonder why Brett was being recommended for a transplant; they wondered why it hadn't been done six months before. Leavitt's answer, he said, was that Brett's lungs couldn't have taken it then. The toxicity of the bleomycin had been severe. While her lungs had recently tested out adequately, they remained his greatest concern. The dire intensity of chemo during the transplant would be hazardous.

The idea that Leavitt and his superiors might have recommended a transplant six months earlier had it not been for Brett's fragile lungs—this was the first he'd heard of it. Even if the others had urged the transplant then, he couldn't imagine that he or Brett, following the six months she'd endured, would have agreed with them. She'd done the maximum treatment, and as early as the fourth cycle the disease appeared vanquished. Yet Charles Linker's confident and urgent assessment of Brett's situation chilled him. What did Linker know that had made him argue for a transplant a year before? What had been so clear to him even then? It was as though they'd never been entitled to be hopeful, to believe in Brett's struggle. If it had been ingenuous to take faith in the six cycles of chemotherapy, as Linker implied, why now believe in the transplant? Because, he thought, there was no alternative. His daughter would go through it, she'd do what she had to do—again!—and she was right: she didn't need doubt. Recently, on the phone, she'd stated to a family friend what she had never spoken to her parents: "I don't want to die." Like a revelatory line of startlingly original poetry, the words astounded him—that his child had come to such an utterance.

They were determined to celebrate Jocelyn's graduation from college, but all such ordinary rites of passage had lost their luster. Brett was unable to come east for the occasion—marching off to radiation each day, locked into the depressing hospital routine once more. Her treatments often left her tired and nauseated. Yet at other times—like the gutsy day she went out and bought herself a new leather jacket—she could sound wonderful. Though they wanted to be with her now, he and Holly had decided it would be more important to be there for the duration of the transplant. They needed the month of June to make arrangements for the temporary move. By early July, the first step— radiation—was over. When they spoke the next day, she'd just re- turned from another CAT scan of her whole body. She'd also seen S.J., and that night she was going to treat herself to a massage.

"How are you?" he asked. Now that radiation was over, he meant, and the event that had seemed unthinkable for so long was imminent.

"I have sort of hysterical fits of crying when I anticipate the trans- plant, then I go on with whatever."

"What are you most afraid of?" he asked.

She knew the answer. "I'm afraid of what I'll become afterwards, what I'll learn or find out—like the knowledge, the losses, I had to face when I found out I had cancer." She paused. "I'm not afraid of dying, I tell my friends, but of living like this. The anxiety, the abnormality. Now it's hard to feel hope, to believe and be positive, and I feel guilty that I'm not doing enough, fighting hard enough." Before he could pro- test, she added, "Compared to who? That's what S.J. asked me. She says I have other people to do that for me now—to hope and believe."

"You do."

"I try to keep from withdrawing." Recently, she had this uncharacteristic tendency to retreat from her friends, she confided, because she felt so cut off, so unlike them. "I'm trying to reach out to them more, to be with them." Sometimes she forgot about the cancer—fleetingly—then it crashed in on her again. "I think of the normal life span or whatever you call it—seventy years or something. That seems incredibly long to me. People talk about life being too short, but to me it's too long. I can't imagine going on like this. The tests, machines, needles—it's so hard, it wears you down. I'm afraid of my life going on like this. I can't stand the waiting."

"But this is going to end," he said, "it's going to pass. Listen, maybe you'll make some positive discoveries when you've come through the transplant. Maybe you'll be happy," he was bold to suggest. "I anticipate being happier in September than I am now because it will be over, and we'll have every reason to believe the cancer is over. Maybe it's your happiness that will surprise you."

Was she listening?

"You'll have to learn to have confidence again. The future is unknown for all of us," he said, trying, trying. . . . "You have to believe in the day, to be happy in the day. This whole year, as the months passed, you were worn down by secondary incidents, until finally you seemed to lose confidence, and didn't believe you were well."

"I know that."

"The transplant will be different in that respect. There isn't anything else. That's scary but also a kind of relief," he said. "I think it's important that you haven't been depressed through all this." He meant defeated, destroyed.

"No, I feel vital." Each day she tried to go on with her journal, her art. "I feel awake, superawake, but that makes me feel fragile, too."

"I believe the transplant is going to work, and all this will pass. What happens in twenty years isn't important now. No one knows. You could be free of the disease right now." The course of radiation could have been decisive, as in Canellos's scenario. "That's plausible."

"I've been telling Beth that."

"But you have to do the transplant."

"I can't wait until you get here." Her family. "I really need you here."

"We'll be there in a week, in the flesh."

She had another painful bone-marrow biopsy scheduled. The one she'd endured a month earlier had been unnecessary. They needed a biopsy fourteen days prior to entering the hospital. "I feel some pride each time I get through one of those," she said.

Her sadness, the outrageous idea that her young life seemed to her to have gone on too long—the weight of her words felt like darkness coming down on him.

On Friday, following the biopsy, she sounded tired but okay. She and Beth were off to Lake Tahoe for a brief respite before the plunge.

They were due to arrive in San Francisco on July 10. The pretransplant meeting between them and the UCSF staff was scheduled for the eleventh. He handed the phone to Jocelyn. For some time, half an hour, he and Holly could hear her wholeheartedly laughing in the kitchen, shrieking. Joce was the smitten audience and her big sister was the irresistible show—that had always been the nature of their relationship.

"What can Brett be saying to her?" Holly asked.

The rather austere "designer" apartment at 111 Buena Vista Avenue East, which he'd come upon through a bed-and-breakfast organization in San Francisco, was tasteful: tall-ceilinged, white-walled, light-filled. At a glance, their random choice turned out to be lucky. The tall windows in the living room looked out on a wonderful view that reached to the bay and the mounded modest hills beyond. That horizon would be vital, he saw. There was an efficiency kitchen, a comfortable master bedroom with bath, and a guest room for Jocelyn. He could work, possibly, at the small glass-topped desk in the bedroom—he'd brought his typewriter—and Holly could use the dining table during the day. The place was a manageable walk from the medical center and only minutes, through Buena Vista Park, to Brett's apartment on Central Avenue. They could live here, was the feeling, although the move, like everything about this trip to San Francisco, felt like a risky experiment, like trying on someone else's life to see if it fit.

The next morning the five of them, Brett and Beth, Jocelyn, he and Holly—Nathaniel was spending the summer in Colorado—met with the staff. Brett had asked Andrew Leavitt, casually dressed in off-duty clothes, to sit in, although from this point on he would no longer be involved in her case. Dr. Linker explained, as he had to Brett, that a Hickman catheter, a more elaborate device than the subcutaneous port, would be implanted in her chest under general anesthesia. Everything she received intravenously—chemotherapy, nutritional substances, saline solution, blood products, antibiotics, her own bone marrow—would go through that line directly into the vena cava. There would be five days of chemotherapy, various drugs administered for a total of eight hours each day. The regimen was designed to be as toxic as a patient could tolerate. Years before, while they were trying to figure out just what those limits were, patients had suffered more than they did now. Under the controlled circumstances of the transplant, the drugs would be used in amounts greater than anything she'd experienced yet, but the ill effects wouldn't be any worse and possibly not as bad. During the intensive chemotherapy Brett would have a urinary catheter inserted to rinse her bladder constantly with saline solution, so as to prevent damage. After a two-day rest, her preserved marrow would be given back to her, injected through the Hickman line. The obnoxious aspect of the marrow infusion for the patient was mostly a result of the preservative it had been stored in. There would follow a period of total exhaustion. The first difficult side effect would be the mouth sores, a condition reflecting what was happening to her entire digestive tract as a result of the chemo. Her weight would be maintained with TPN— Total Parenteral Nutrition—including intralipids, fats. Just when the

110

mouth pain began to subside, she'd develop the rash. She'd lose her hair, and so on. While Brett was neutropenic, immunosupressed, her marrow completely destroyed, she would be vulnerable to infections of all kinds, so she'd receive regular infusions of antibiotics and gamma globulin. Until her transplanted marrow engrafted and began to produce adequate numbers of blood cells, she'd receive blood and platelet transfusions as needed. She'd receive the growth hormone GCSF to stimulate the production of white cells. By the time her blood counts were normal and stable, she'd be waiting to go home, but she would be released only when she was eating normally, holding food without throwing up. Traumatized by the chemo, her insides would have to learn to digest food again. Ideally, all this could happen in six to eight weeks.

They sat listening patiently, nodding as though this bizarre scheme seemed reasonable enough to them. He interrupted Linker's summary with questions. The family inquisitor. The doctor reviewed the dangers. Brett's pulmonary test showed that she had seventy percent of normal lung function, which put her lungs at risk. The chemo could also cause irreversible liver damage. The marrow might fail to engraft. People died during bone-marrow transplants. Because the program was considered experimental, Brett would be asked to sign documents releasing the hospital and staff from liability in the event of catastrophe. But according to Linker, there was only a five percent chance that any of these hazards would occur. He believed they would cope with whatever happened and Brett would get through the period of hospitalization. The greatest concern, overwhelming all other considerations, was the risk that the disease would not be permanently gone.

They nodded. Of course that was the overwhelming risk. This might not work. Linker sat in the center of the room, with his colleagues seated at various distances around him. Brett sat on a couch directly facing the doctor, flanked by her mother, Beth, and Jocelyn, while he sat to Linker's left. Brett looked fairly radiant just then, he thought, a slant of sunlight illuminating her red-gold coloring. Dressed up for the meeting in linen pants, a silk blouse, and her good shoes, she might have been an applicant interviewing for admission to medical school. The responsible oldest child.

"We're worried," Linker said, sounding a new note in the proceeding, electrifying the air of the room. "Brett's recent bone-marrow biopsy revealed scarring in the marrow on one side," he informed them. Unless it was the result of radiation, the scarring could reflect the presence of disease.

To rupture the suffocating stunned silence he asked Linker, "What do you think it is?"

"I think it's Hodgkin's disease in the bone marrow." It had never been there before.

She had been bravely listening to what was soon to befall her—*her,* not anyone else here—steeling herself, resolved to do what she needed to do. Now, as though Linker's words were insupportable leaden weights, she broke down. Holly put her arm around her and Brett leaned against her mother's shoulder. Jocelyn struggled to stifle tears. This was not the time or place to ask them to take in such news. They'd believed they already knew the worst, they'd faced it. They were here, the family, as a body of support, to face what was ahead. To spring this crushing detail on them now undermined their will—he could feel that happening in the room—and dashed their resolve. This new twist would have been more manageable, their morning here more positive, if they'd known about it going into the meeting.

Linker plowed ahead. "This development makes the hope of achieving a cure worrisome," he said. Furthermore, the disease also seemed to have recurred in an area that had previously received radiation. As for the nodes in Brett's back, the CAT scan indicated a small reduction in size, but it was often hard to decipher the impact of radiation. These factors, combined with the fact that Brett's recurrences had been relatively rapid following standard maximum treatment, all added up to a discouraging picture. Linker had put her chances following the transplant at fifty-fifty. Now he'd venture that her chance for a cure was twenty percent.

They listened, shaken, yet endeavoring in this official context to conceal their emotion, their audacious confidence evaporating. Was Brett expected to proceed with so little hope, march passively to slaughter? They'd come here seeking encouragement, he realized, not despair.

So the question became, Linker went on, given all the risk and pain involved, was the transplant still worth it?

What was his daughter thinking? It was *her* body, *her* marrow, *her* life they were talking about.

They were worried, Linker repeated, but in his view there was no alternative. If Brett didn't do the transplant, they would pursue outpatient chemo again, and he would not feel at all optimistic about that.

A silence. It was all entirely too bleak suddenly. Anxious to counter Linker's assessment, impatient with the numbers game, he told the others, "What happens to Brett happens one hundred percent. From the beginning she always had wonderful odds, but those odds never panned out. It doesn't matter what the odds are." The crucial thing was that they regarded her as a likely candidate for the procedure. There were patients who didn't qualify. "We have to be positive and resolute," he said, those formulaic words. The transplant had to work—the truth was it would or it wouldn't—and the numbers didn't make any difference. "It's time we got lucky around here," he said. "Brett is long overdue."

Linker seemed to be regarding him with pursed lips, as though the bearded man in the tweed jacket puzzled him. But Brett was nodding as if she agreed this needed to be said. She had already recovered her composure. Jocelyn's tears had stopped. Beth stared at the middle distance as though peering into a crystal ball. Almost spontaneously, each of them mentally scrambled—you could see it in their faces—to accommodate Linker's grim announcement. *There was no alternative.* By the time the meeting ended and everyone stood and shook hands, the mood, weirdly, was practically cheerful.

. . .

That evening they made dinner for Brett and Beth and three friends. Ellen Lougee, also a Smith graduate, was an aspiring painter and a rock climber who worked for the U.S. Geological Survey. Amy Huber, who had come to San Francisco after Harvard, was a counselor at a clinic for battered women. Although they'd known Brett hardly a year, they had become important friends. Eve, a powerful reminder to him of Brett's life before Hodgkin's disease, was the last to arrive, as vivid and intense as ever. "I was afraid to come," she confided just inside the door. She had a job now teaching art to city kids, and she liked it. The gathering rapidly accelerated into a lively party.

After dinner, while everyone remained seated at the round glass-topped table, Brett began to talk about her life. "I have a lot to walk, and talk, and draw," she said. "I have a lot to do. And I want to do it. I desire to live." She talked about the love of her friends and her family, the people here, and how important that was to her. "Tonight has re-minded me what pleasure life is—what *pleasure*—and I want to expe-rience that. I'm so strong," she asserted, "I'm so strong. I feel so alive, so intensely alive. I feel hopeful."

Brett was holding Ellen's hand on her right and Amy's hand on her left as she spoke, sitting very straight, smiling, emboldened just now by her own words. Later he would find that it was difficult to recall much of what she'd said, or even how long she'd talked, he was so completely involved, so taken over by the moment, instead of observ-ing, collecting it.

At one point she spoke her name. "Rebecca Brett Hobbie. That's who I am. This person. Who is living." What bothered her most at the conference earlier that day, she told them, was the way those people sat there calmly discussing her life or death, calmly assigning numbers to her future, all that as though . . . "My life! Brett Hobbie. One thing I know for certain, the cancer can't destroy my imagination. I know that."

Her friends each held one of her hands in both of theirs like a surprising found object, he thought, looking from those hands to his daughter's face as she continued to talk it out, all she wanted to tell them.

"I'm just like you," she said emphatically, smiling, as though this terribly important and obvious truth could be forgotten or overlooked. It was an appeal to them. "I'm just like you. That's why I'm glad you're here. I want to be like you again—to be well again—and I will be."

They received her pronouncement of hope and belief as a gift that helped alleviate their fear for her.

While their guests began cleaning up the dishes, the family formed a close circle in the living room, holding one another tight. Their warm bodies, their breathing, their moist faces, the scent of hair. They were like one thing, primal, animal.

Holly said, "Nathaniel is missing this." He had called earlier that evening and spoken to Brett, and regretted not being there.

"There will be other times."

That weekend, with Brett as their guide as usual, they walked for hours through the city, they toured the Castro and walked along the outer bay from the Sea Cliff neighborhood to the beach at the end of Golden Gate Park. Still pale and thin from the weeks of radiation, Brett had no trouble vigorously ascending San Francisco's steep hills. It wasn't summer here. The bright days were cool, and at night cold fog drifted in and remained until midmorning. As he and Brett walked back to her apartment that Friday night, the dense whirling fog, its smell and raw dampness, reminded them of the Maine coast. She clung to his arm and chided him for not bringing a warm jacket from New England, as she'd suggested. On Sunday evening she and Beth arrived at 111 Buena Vista all dressed up for the evening. Brett had gotten a buzz cut, as she called it, that afternoon, which suited her remarkably well. She looked lovely in the moss-green dress of bold leaf forms her grandmother had made her, dark purple tights, the new stylish brown leather jacket, the sort you'd intend to have forever. It had been a day of last things for Brett—temporarily—her last day on the outside, her last long walk, last meal. She was in very good spirits. He proposed a toast to the end of her long struggle with Hodgkin's disease. Raising her wine glass, Brett said, "To this night."

They all climbed the fire escape to the roof at one point, and he snapped her picture standing in wind framed by the vast horizon of San Francisco. She stood with her hands in the pockets of her jacket, her legs slightly parted, smiling, as though the scene behind her, this city she'd come to, had been conquered.

5

MARROW

Dense fog cascaded over the eucalyptus trees on the steep hill outside his daughter's hospital window. Her experience in San Francisco, he thought. She had yet to simply live here. The long-ago diagnosis of Hodgkin's in November of 1988—he clearly recalled sitting by her hospital bed following the splenectomy in Boston—had come to this. It was July 1991. As she began to regain consciousness following the Hickman operation, he had to wipe the solemnity off his face, look alive.

"Hi."

Her primary nurse, Mary Cranley, promptly connected Brett's newly implanted catheter and flushed the line with heparin to prevent clotting. Tethered, shackled. Linker, stopping by to welcome his new patient, predicted she'd "snooze" through the five days of chemo. Holly and Jocelyn returned from a walk. Toward evening, reluctantly, they left her in the climate-controlled room. 1122 Long. This first night Beth would stay with her.

As they descended Parnassus, a sturdy young woman with glinting red hair in a silky bob was athletically marching up the hill. The three of them—he, Holly, Jocelyn—did a double take so obvious to the woman that she smiled, possibly flattered, as she passed. The woman looked startlingly like Brett—her build and coloring, her hair, even the features of her face—about the time Brett had graduated from Smith.

"I can't believe that," Jocelyn said.

Eve corroborated the existence of such a person. She had also seen this apparition hiking up Parnassus as if she had the world on a string.

The first day she was fairly snowed under. The second day he unplugged her IV monitors, tied on her face mask, and she attempted a brief walk around the corridor, holding up the tubing from her urinary catheter while he pushed her IV pole, hung with plastic bags and bottles. It was vital for her to get up and move as much as possible. Blood clots and, especially in Brett's case, pneumonia were major hazards. A long hallway encircled a central block of offices, utility rooms, and the nurses' station, with the patients' rooms facing outdoors on two sides. The elevators were at one end of the floor and there were meeting rooms at the other. The third day of the chemo infusion a new anti-nausea drug allowed her to remain alert without being sick, and she circled the floor five times. Twelve times around, someone had calculated, was about a mile.

"Aren't I having a good day?" she smiled. Her relief—she hadn't exploded or imploded; maybe she could do this—was almost happiness.

By the time she completed the five days of chemotherapy, no drugs could repress her nausea, long hours of sickness that culminated in wrenching fits of vomiting, which produced an odorless green bile. Her urine was an unreal red. Brett appeared to pay no attention to the disturbing colors. She was stoic. Lloyd Damon was the doctor on duty that first weekend, a tall blond man who seemed to suffer from pink-eye. Using a flashlight, he examined Brett's mouth for the impact of the chemotherapy. Her response so far was normal. "We hope the chemo has done what it was intended to do," he told her. Lying there blasted, looking at him as if he'd been driving the truck that ran over her, she nodded.

More than once this day, out of the blue, she said, "I love you, Dad," and he eventually realized she was making the assertion as though to set the record straight while she still had the chance, in the spirit of last words. He was reminded of that afternoon in her Central Avenue apartment following the first recurrence.

Midafternoon, breaking a silence with sudden emotion, she said, "Dad, I'm so afraid."

"Of what?" he asked, squeezing out a facecloth soaked in ice water, placing it across her brow. It was a real question. What exactly? Tell me.

"I'm afraid I won't make it through this. I'm so sensitive to everything. I react in ways that other people don't." She added, "I feel so helpless."

"You're doing all you can do. Everything has happened according to schedule. There haven't been any surprises here so far. You're doing well." He had no doubt whatever that she would come through her time in the hospital. "I know that," he said, "I'm not worried about that."

He wasn't worried.

They talked, he bathed her face with the cold cloth, this moment of fear passed. "I'm not lying here frightened all day long," she said, as if to reassure him. "It comes in waves." She was anxious about the bone-marrow transfusion tomorrow, though. Very anxious. That wizardry was scheduled for eight.

He awoke at two in a sweat, a clammy dampness covering his naked body from head to toe. The same unsettling sensation had spooked him for two nights the week before. He'd never experienced anything like this, his body out of sync, mysteriously pursuing its own agenda. Dampness between his toes, behind his knees, in the crooks of his elbows. His wife, asleep beside him in a flannel nightgown, was cool and dry. His pulse raced. Was this what had ominously tormented his daughter's sleep intermittently for the past three years? He imagined her anticipating the upcoming be-all-and-end-all event. *I have no doubt that you'll come through.* When he told her that, he was telling the truth. That afternoon the busy hermetic world of 11 Long had seemed to be safely and efficiently, even cheerfully, humming along. The movement of doctors and nurses and numerous others contributed to the illusion. Behind closed doors, people were fighting for their lives. As during the previous week when he'd awakened in this state, he was unable to get back to sleep.

Brett was sitting up in bed, agitated, when he and Holly arrived shortly before eight. There was already a machine going in the room, gently rocking a flat, traylike container of warm water big enough to roast a turkey, which would thaw Brett's frozen bone marrow. A dish of sliced oranges sat on the nightstand. Like everyone else who entered the room, he and Holly immediately scrubbed their hands.

Brett was especially concerned that painful vomiting would interrupt the procedure, she wouldn't get through it, something would go wrong. "My throat feels like glass," she said. From the days of retching she'd endured already.

They showered her with encouragement. What else?

"Fuck this," she swore.

Things happened quickly. The floor nurse, Carol Viele, entered with Brett's frozen marrow, harvested in 1989 following her first course of treatment. Charles Linker, his tie tucked into his shirtfront and his sleeves rolled back on his strong arms—as if he were on his way to shoot some baskets—arrived to execute the infusion. Of the numerous intravenous substances the patient received around the clock, the only one the doctor personally administered was the marrow, lending the moment a ceremonial aspect. His daughter's marrow was contained in eight large square plastic bags. Blood was what made the vital substance appear red. Carol read Brett's name off each bag; evidently that was protocol. One plastic bag filled two large syringes seven or eight inches long and an inch in diameter. Sixteen in all.

"The worst thing is the strong taste of the preservative," the doctor said. "Something like garlic, they say." The oranges were intended to combat the odor.

Carol filled the syringes, thawing one bag at a time, and handed them to Linker, who attached them to the Hickman catheter entering Brett's chest and pressed the marrow into her bloodstream. It would eventually find its way home, he assured them, where it would begin to grow and produce the variety of blood cells that sustained life. Brett sat as though listening to her soul, inaudible to the rest of them, waiting for some uncontrollable disaster to begin, trying not to hold her breath. Holly had taken her hands, while he continued bathing her forehead with cold facecloths. The nurses referred to the event as a second birth. Giving birth, under difficult circumstances, might have been what was happening here. Yet the procedure appeared to be going well. Brett wasn't getting sick, for one thing.

"We're cruising," said Linker, depressing one syringe after the other without a hitch. The audacious act didn't seem arrogant or blasphemous or crazy. It seemed plausible. Linker volunteered the story of visiting his ten-year-old daughter at camp over the weekend, and he, the other father here, found himself recalling Brett at ten. Oshkosh overalls, long red braids, her totally unguarded smile, her seriousness, her wholehearted happiness. That was the year they'd moved into an eighteenth-century house on a town common in western Massachusetts, in October, their three children up to their necks in autumn leaves from the maple trees out front. Among the snapshots that Brett had taped to a wall near her hospital bed, there was one that represented her at about ten, in fact—a summer in Maine. Watching Linker depress the blood-red syringe containing her irreplaceable marrow, holding the cool cloth against her brow, he thought, This is that ecstatic girl.

The fearful infusion was over by nine. Minutes later, sitting on the toilet, Brett reached for her mother, suddenly overcome with the enormity of what had just transpired. Second birth. "I'm sad," she said. "I'm sad."

Almost immediately she composed herself. She hadn't been sick, she hadn't become flushed, as predicted. The abdominal cramps that had come toward the end of the infusion had already begun to abate. She'd done it.

"The chemo is over," he said, "the marrow infusion is over." Although it was Brett's ninth day in the hospital, the day of the infusion was designated Day Zero of the transplant. Tomorrow would be Day 1. "I have a good feeling about it."

She squeezed his arm. "Now I just have to endure," she said.

Brett was started on three different antimicrobials to stem the development of infection, viral, bacterial, or fungal. The skin on her back, especially where she'd received radiation, was burned intensely, blisteringly red, suggesting the extent to which her body had been saturated with chemicals. She had dreams about never eating again, starvation dreams, she called them. The odorless convulsive vomiting, which began to produce a thick, gagging mucus, persisted. The sweetish garlicky odor of the preserved marrow hung in the room. This was the smell, they realized now, that periodically permeated the corridor, emanating from one room or another. A relaxation therapist, Pam, asked her to describe a moment in paradise. Brett's version was a Greek island, white flourlike sand, orange blossoms perfuming the air, the sound of the sea lapping the shore and the sides of fishing boats. She was at a café, a table with its feet in the sand, she said, drinking lemon water, with the poet Olga Broumas. In cadenced, formulaic speech, Pam evoked the scene, hoping to transport the patient there, and Brett was smiling contentedly by the time Pam was done, open to whatever might help.

She received her first infusion of irradiated, CMV-negative platelets, which had to be maintained above 20,000. A normal individual might have ten times that number. Her mother's platelets gave her an excellent bump, from 15,000 to 78,000, but the very next day they were down again. Only he and Holly, her brother Gary, who flew up from San Diego three times to be a donor, and Eve turned out to be platelet possibilities for Brett. Jocelyn was plagued by a persistent sore throat— she often wore a mask in the room—which prevented her from donating. A half-dozen friends turned out to have developed antibodies to the CMV virus, which would be hazardous to someone with a severely suppressed immune system, who was CMV-1 negative. One friend was anemic. Nathaniel was unable to donate when he showed up because in recent years he'd been to Mexico, where he might have been exposed to malaria.

Day 5, Sunday, the hospital almost eerily silent in contrast to workdays, she seemed to exist in an altered state, a nadir of weariness. Her eyes were closed, her mouth open. She ran her hand over her head, the buzz-cut hair, as though bewildered.

The nights were more frightening than the days, she explained. She particularly wanted someone there at night. He had not soothed his father's brow with a cool cloth, he thought, he had never stayed with him through the ominous night. He hadn't known enough then, six months earlier. Now he knew. Looking at his daughter, he thought, *How is she going to get back to herself from this?* Her numbing lassitude was as frightening to him as anything that had occurred. He was relieved when Holly turned up with Jocelyn, releasing him for a while.

At a respectable pace, he jogged down the panhandle into Golden Gate Park. This had become his routine four or five days a week, a forty-minute loop that took him across vast green lawns, past palm trees, sequoia, flowing water, and throngs of people. Each time he came here he was reminded of the Sunday afternoon he and Brett and Eve watched the mating dance of rollerskaters in the small asphalt arena, the occasion of his daughter's first recurrence. Her shock and pain then, which soon gave way to acceptance and determination, seemed remote. *It can't get any worse.* The park teemed with beautiful women and beautiful men. Health was the key. His splendid daughter was confined to the transplant ward in the hospital on its hill, a ravaged version of her former self. *I'm just like you.* It's temporary, he told himself, running, stupidly running, his frantic habit, the familiar pain between his shoulder blades again, avoiding the beauty and pull of human faces, men and women, his life here completely repressed by his daughter's ordeal. Come on, Brett, come on, this is temporary. He felt heartbroken. You did what you had to do, you carried on, all that—he was out here, he was one of them—but the truth was inside you—this heartbreak—like an ineradicable disease.

Nathaniel called from Colorado. Returning from a mountain outing in Utah with his friend Meghan, he'd lost control of her car on sand and gone into the guardrail. The car was totaled. No one was hurt. They'd have to pay the deductible. Meghan was probably going to get more money than she could have sold it for, so she wasn't too bummed out.

"Jesus Christ! You're lucky you weren't killed."

"I guess so."

"Goddamn it!" A few minutes later he allowed, "Thank God no one was hurt." His son was due to arrive in San Francisco by train in a week.

The scary fatigue lifted as mysteriously—to them, the ignorant bystanders—as it had descended. Dilaudid was substituted for morphine, an automatic drip, which made her less sick. Brett resumed walking the corridor, where one or two other patients at a time shuffled along with laden IV poles like forlorn pilgrims on a treadmill. The most dedicated and vigorous just then was a young man from Hawaii, who had received a transplant for acute leukemia. Doggedly making their rounds of the floor, he and Brett nodded to each other; they didn't stop and talk. Patients had almost no contact with one another, embroiled in their own battles behind closed doors, at different stages, physically and psychologically, of the process. Most were too sick to attend the support sessions held once a week in the solarium at the end of the hall. With the paralyzing fatigue mostly passed and her nausea reduced, at least for the moment, she told him she was no longer frightened that she wouldn't survive the hospitalization.

Sitting with her as she intermittently dozed, he would read, sometimes aloud. Just then he toyed with the miniature Zen rock garden— the gardener placed the rocks, raked the sand in patterns—which they'd brought into the room for a diversion. When he looked up, he found she'd awakened and was watching him.

"Does this remind you of your father?" she asked.

"Yes, but only in the most general way. I feel like I've been here recently, and yet everything is different."

She understood.

"I miss him, I want him to know this is happening to you." Part of the new loneliness was the repeated realization that the absent person didn't know what happened next in life. "I wish he was alive for himself, of course, and so he could share what you're going through."

"Yes," she said, "I wanted him to see me through."

"He suffered, not uncourageously. He knew he was going to die, and he finally just did it, alone. He went to bed and died."

Nausea, culminating in harsh, bloody vomiting, continued to be the worst thing. The mouth pain, when it came, wasn't as bad as she'd expected. Her already shorn hair began coming out in clumps, leaving what she referred to as puzzle-shaped bare patches, so she had her head shaved again with an electric shaver. Cards arrived from friends and relatives almost daily, and most of them went up on her elaborately decorated wall. He and Holly and Jocelyn, singly or in pairs, came by for some hours every day. Beth, who had a job to go to each day, came by at night and often remained until morning.

Amy, Ellen, and Eve also took turns with Beth and Holly staying overnight in the hospital. The odd bulky chair they'd carted up to Floor 11 converted to a narrow bed, and they'd also brought in a small futon.

Day 8, her seventeenth day on 11 Long, Linker had good news to report. There was evidence that her white cells had begun to grow back, the grafting somewhat ahead of schedule thanks to regular injections of GCSF. Uncharacteristically, Charles Linker waved his arms with enthusiasm. "I never doubted it," he said, "but it's good to see." That day Brett circled the floor eight times, a record for her, but it wore her out and left her vomiting at the end. A little good news didn't go far. He mopped her face and neck with the cloth. Relax. Relax. Her petite, soft-spoken Japanese-American nurse, Karen, arrived with Benadryl and his platelets. Their lemon color was a healthy sign, she said. The milkier look of some platelets was fat. Brett wouldn't have cared.

She began to have dreams about drinking, greedily gulping bottles of cold liquid. Television advertisements about soda and juice and beer and sparkling water drove her crazy, she said. As her mouth started to heal it was unbearably dry. Her main discomfort then became the chemo burn on her backside. A grayish rash in her armpits and groin didn't seem to trouble her much. By Day 10 her white count, though barely on the boards, showed that the marrow was decidedly grafting. Vigorously, she walked her laps in the corridor. She wasn't sick all day. Squeezing cold water over her head and face with the facecloth, letting it rain down on her, she smiled—an authentic smile!—a sight he hadn't seen for days. He put on a tape of solo guitar music. As it played, she sat in bed and wrote a letter to a person in Cambridge she had never met. Mary Burger, the friend of a friend from college, had lost a lung to recurrent Hodgkin's disease. She and Brett shared that bond and an interest in literature, art, the world of women. In a short time, through letters and photographs and phone calls, they'd cultivated a relationship.

"I've never seen anyone at this stage of the transplant keeping up her correspondence," Brett's nurse told him. "She must have quite a will."

When Jocelyn appeared wearing new shoes, Brett said, "I love those, Joce. I love them." By Day 10 she was back—that was the feeling.

Linker seemed more relaxed and sociable than usual. They were extremely pleased with Brett's response so far, he said. The threat of infection was passed, he believed. The potential toxicity to lungs and liver hadn't occurred, and her mouth was healing nicely. Although the rash would worsen for a while, it would not develop in new areas. Their anxiety, he confided more clearly than before, was that her system wouldn't tolerate the massive chemo following all she'd received previously. She'd tolerated it well. Remarkably, her face had escaped unscathed, perhaps because of the constant application of the cold facecloths. In a week, he predicted, she'd be feeling much better.

That afternoon, walking the corridor, they entered the large conference room at the end of the hall. The wall of windows here looked out on a grand view: the dense green park, the city, the glimmering bay, and the Golden Gate Bridge. People—small, indistinguishable figures from their perspective—hurried along Parnassus below them, contending with the wind. "I want to be out there," his daughter said. "I want to be out there."

Back in her room, as Mary Cranley rigged up Eve's platelets, Brett picked up the phone and made a dinner reservation for her parents and her sister at one of her favorite restaurants. Jamaican. They had to go out and have fun, she said. It was Saturday night.

She'd brought pictures to remind her of her larger life and taped them to the wall opposite her bed. There was a photograph of the Connecticut river near which their old house had stood, a road of ancient sugar maples in Conway, their present home in its field of red clover. He was surprised at first that she'd included snapshots of herself as a child. In each of them she was the older sister, helping her brother climb a jagged rock in Maine or manning the oars in her grandfather's dory or riding Jocelyn on the handlebars of her bicycle. Two pieces of her recent art hung on the wall, mounted behind glass: a brilliant yellow field with a horizon of dark trees—"I need to see horizons," she said—and the striking image of a naked woman standing with folded arms, an endless estuary of gleaming water meandering behind. From the wall above the desk in her apartment she'd taken the large reproduction of a contemporary painting: an open window that looked out on nothing but blue sky. He contributed a poster of a stream cascading through lush green woods and a close-up photograph of granite rocks rolled smooth by the ocean that reminded them of a beach in Maine. Nathaniel composed a panorama of the Rockies from photographs he'd taken that summer. And there were the cards, strung, draping, just below the ceiling. At least one wall of this high-tech institutional room was colorful, engaging, individual, and evolving. It should be mandatory, he thought, for patients to make the blank wall they faced a window that connected them to their real lives.

At first Brett listened to tapes of natural sounds like rain and ocean surf, to poets reading their work, to music. Those things were only useful when she was feeling pretty good. She'd brought several books of poetry—Octavio Paz, Pablo Neruda, James Wright, Olga Broumas—but she found she was unable to read. Absolutely unable to read. Writing to people, however, made her feel good. If it was a good day, she occasionally watched television—I wanted it to be about pitbulls, she said the day *Oprah* featured transvestites. Most of the time, however, day after day, hour after hour, she was struggling with some discomfort, another medication, a new stage of the process. *Now I just have to endure.* There was walking and a rest from walking. Days of nausea, days when she was snowed under. When she turned her head to the right there was the window: fogged-in days, and days when the sun came out. Every day was a day of waiting—to feel better or to feel worse, waiting for the day to end or the day to begin, waiting for the nurse, waiting for the doctor, waiting for results, changes, developments, news of how she was doing. Waiting for Beth, waiting for her father, her mother, her sister, waiting for another face, an unexpected visitor. There were endless days, lost days.

On Day 14, her twenty-third day of hospitalization, she tried her first sip of water. Soon she was munching ice and then she attempted apple juice, healing on the inside. Her back still burned, the skin coming off in layers. The whites of her eyes were slightly yellowed, a temporary manifestation of the chemo's stress on her liver. She began to sit in her chair, the blue chair, rather than in bed, she walked more, and she started lung exercises with an incentive spirometer, a plastic inhaling device. In Linker's view she was ninety-five percent through the transplant, all major dangers past. She could start thinking about leaving the hospital once she got the bags off the IV tree, once she began to eat and move her bowels.

Nathaniel arrived from Colorado—to camp on the living room floor—looking fit and sturdy. His presence gave everyone an added lift.

But on Friday of that encouraging fourth week she awakened with pain that began in her armpit and shoulder and soon settled in her chest and back. She couldn't take a breath without severe discomfort. An EKG showed no evidence of a heart problem. The doctors speculated that it was a pulmonary embolus and started her on a course of heparin. While on heparin she'd require more frequent platelet transfusions due to the increased risk of hazardous bleeding. In an instant he felt his back go rigid, his anxiety surfacing—a pulmonary embolus could be suddenly fatal. Brett submitted to the stress of a Ventilation-Perfusion scan, which indicated that an embolus was highly unlikely, after all, but the incident, occurring just when they were gaining confidence, brought home to them the perilousness of her position.

Linker came by in the afternoon to say that everything continued to look well, they weren't worried. Possibly she could go home in ten days. He was off for his summer vacation and wouldn't be back until after Labor Day, when he would see Brett at the clinic across the street. They all parted with handshakes, pleasure-to-meet-you sort of thing. Have a safe trip back to Massachusetts, he told the parents. Initially, they were surprised, especially Brett, that the doctor would leave his patient in midstream. What if she needed him?

"That's fantasy," Brett said impatiently of Linker's ten-day prediction. She felt a long way from eating, for one thing.

The next day they circled the dreary corridor, its gray tiled floor, at a stubborn pace. Another Saturday! 11 Long was quiet again, a place sealed off; outside the large windows the day was clear and blue. Seated on the bed back in her room, as he plugged in all her apparatus again, her central line dangling between her legs like a grotesque umbilical cord, Brett suddenly broke down.

"I wish I did this last year. I want to be well."

He embraced her. They had been entitled to believe six cycles would be successful. How could she have done this last year?

"They were against the transplant then because your lungs couldn't have done it. Did you know that?" He needed to disabuse her of the idea that her chances had significantly gone down because of a bad judgment call—that what she was going through now might have already been behind her.

"I hadn't heard that before."

Andrew Leavitt's surprise social call in the afternoon, his fairly ebullient presence—T-shirt, jeans, sneakers—brightened the day considerably. He had looked at her chart, just out of curiosity, and didn't believe her present pain was a serious setback. He encouraged her to take Dilaudid to get comfortable so that she could practice her lung exercises, keep the air sacs open to prevent infection. Amiably he chatted about California's wine country and his son, a toddler. As they talked, it came out that Leavitt and his wife had only been in San Francisco for the past three years.

"As long as I have," Brett said, seated in her hospital bed. The fall he began as a fellow at UCSF was the fall he had diagnosed Brett, another newcomer to the Coast, with Hodgkin's disease—as if they had come to this city, doctor and patient, destined to meet. In her second year of treatment she'd learned that his wife was the daughter of Kenneth Rexroth, another amazing coincidence to Brett's mind.

The moment Andy left the room she began laboriously inhaling and exhaling on the plastic lung exerciser. The rise of the ball in the clear cylinder was hardly inspiring. After each good puff, she had to pause.

When he left, she was sitting up in bed writing a card, a thoughtful, hopeful, probably amusing card, to Janice, her aunt, who had sent her supportive notes almost daily.

Sunday morning, her thirty-fifth day of hospitalization, Day 26, she called to report that she'd spent the night sitting erect in the bed, unable to breathe. A terrible night, and she was gasping over the phone just then. They didn't know why. One doctor thought he heard "crackling." They'd taken an X-ray.

"I was doing so well," she said, hurt, discouraged.

By afternoon they learned that something was now visible in the X-ray, but whether it was a fungal infection, pneumonitis, or possibly bleeding as a result of heparin and Brett's constant cough wasn't clear. There was dried blood on her teeth from coughing. The good feeling about how she'd been doing seemed dashed. This treachery of lungs, breath. That night he lay awake, shaken, praying to the dim ceiling for the sudden setback to pass, haunted by his father.

He was with her on Monday when they performed a bronchoscopy in an effort to establish what was occurring. Another crude invasion of her body.

"We prefer people to leave the room," one doctor told him.

The man in charge said, "You're fine right there at the head of the bed; that's a good place."

The long black lighted scope was inserted down her throat and into her lungs, accompanied by a local anesthetic. There were two eyepieces so the specialists could confer over what they were seeing simultaneously, although what they saw didn't seem at all clear to them. A saline solution was injected into her lungs through the tube and flushed out, providing samples of lung fluid to be cultured. He kept a cold facecloth on her head, held her hand, and throughout the procedure talked to her, close to her face, of Conway, autumn, which was in the offing, how well she was tolerating this latest damned nuisance, how proud he was of her.

"Squeeze my hand if you're doing all right."

She squeezed. She was patient and cooperative. Within ten minutes they withdrew the black tube.

"That's as smooth as it goes," the technician said. A course of erythromycin was prescribed in case infection was present.

Now the wait to see if anything grew out of the lung cultures.

"How are you?" he asked the next morning over the phone.

"Just bloated and deaf." The antibiotic had caused a temporary decline in hearing.

She was unable to walk, to practice the breathing exercises, or to eat. A setback.

Jocelyn had returned to the East Coast to find an apartment and take up life in New York City. She had been with her sister some part of each day for six weeks. With school beginning soon, Nathaniel, who had spent fifteen days here, returned to Conway, where he intended to start painting the house, a huge undertaking for one person. All of them felt the pressure to return to normal life and, in so doing, possibly, to spring Brett from her increasing sense of imprisonment.

Nothing developed in the cultures. Inclined to dismiss infection as the cause, they attributed her difficulties to bleeding brought on by a combination of heparin, low platelets, and intense coughing and exacerbated by water retention. That was encouraging, although Brett was now oppressively bloated from the constant, long-term infusion of liquids. And the remedy for that seemed to bring on burning diarrhea. There was another pill that might control *that*. The constant juggling of medications and side effects represented trade-offs arrived at by trial and error. He and Holly wheeled their daughter to another floor for a pulmonary-function test. In a state of exhaustion, Brett gave it her best.

The next day, the lung scare seemed to have passed. She was no longer wheezing. Holly set off for the hospital at eleven with a pot of homemade soup. He worked at his desk, as usual, and then ran through the park. The fog had dispersed, the day was sunny, cool, breezy. He put on a tie today, as if to mark some occasion, and walked up Haight Street, which still made him feel he was in a foreign country. A young woman wrapped in a blanket sat on the sidewalk against a building, sucking her thumb, while the crowd streamed around her. He arrived at the hospital at two-thirty, entering through the emergency area, as usual, and walked to the farthest elevators. Room 1122 was directly across from the nurses' station. His daughter was always inside, turning to the door as it opened.

"Hi."

He washed his hands thoroughly at the sink just inside the room.

"How are you?"

"Pretty good." She'd enjoyed her mother's soup and half a pear. She had to eat, exercise, and get the hell out of there.

They circled the hall a half-dozen times, still rather disconnected from anyone else here. Hard labor on the transplant ward wasn't a group activity. The first-rate nurses who had cared for Brett—Irene, Karen, Lin—greeted them. A tall black woman, Sandy, accompanied by an older man today, smiled as they passed her. Family members, presumably, conferred outside the room next to Brett's, where a young man suffering from brain cancer was critically ill. He had a wife and two small children, they'd learned. His most constant visitor was his sister.

Julie, the physical therapist, worked on Brett's back for an hour, releasing tension along the length of her spine.

"What's the worst thing been?" he asked his daughter. The chemo, the retching, the mouth sores, her skin, the pain in her chest and back?

"The worst thing has been breathing—my lungs." There was terrible fear involved in not getting a breath. But it was all hard. "I've been in this room a long time," she said. "I've got to get out."

It was Friday, although the day of the week had no meaning for him here. He stopped at the Real Food Deli on Stanyan Street and bought a baguette. On Haight, thronged with young people to whom Friday did have meaning, he rented two movies. His scotch tasted good tonight. The panorama of the white city beyond the tall windows was dazzling in the evening light. It might have been Greece, he thought, the sparkling distant bay glinting like the Mediterranean. Unlike his daughter, he'd never been to Greece. Of course, he didn't know much more about San Francisco, even after a month and a half. The narrow swath between 111 Buena Vista East and the summit of Parnassus, that was the city to him, and his experience within that range had been as circumscribed as it was draining. That evening, he and Holly dared to believe the end of her internment was at last in sight. The lung scare hadn't proved disastrous. A lighthearted Woody Allen movie amused them. For the second feature he'd brought home an awful X-rated movie, a rare diversion for them, featuring raw fucking and sucking so mechanically desperate it looked like it hurt. You had to laugh, and yet the dumbbell show primed the pump—that was the point—and this night turned out to be the first time sex had felt right between them since they'd come to San Francisco.

That night Brett suffered a renewed period of strangled breathing. Christ! The following afternoon Damon reported that her pulmonary-function test, which indicated she could exhale but couldn't inhale, had finally persuaded them that she did have a pneumonia, after all, that she'd been quite sick, in fact. Fortunately, the infection had been responding to the precautionary antibiotic she'd been taking, and her lungs appeared to be improving. Damon hoped that this new complication could be resolved in two weeks.

Two more weeks?

"All right," he said, the adamant parent, "it's better to have a clear explanation. The pneumonia is responding, it will pass. Now we know."

Grimly, seated in her chair, Brett nodded. The horizontal yellow lines across the center of her eyes had disappeared. Now the whites of her eyes were distressed by broken blood vessels. Grimly, she struggled to her feet to walk the corridor again. The flimsy blue and white bathrobe over the johnny, the inmate's uniform.

From the wide windows in the conference room they looked down on Parnassus, the park, the receding cityscape. "I forget what it's like out there," she said. "I can hardly remember the places I used to go in the city."

"You'll be out there again."

Back in Room 1122, Brett's therapist, S.J., called for the first time in two weeks. She'd been away on her vacation. Another day Brett would have been thrilled to hear from her. "I was doing so well," she said, "but I've had a setback. Pneumonia. And now it's really getting long." She hated imparting her disappointing news. When she hung up the phone she couldn't repress her emotion any longer.

"Go ahead and cry if you want to." He put his arms around her as she sat in the blue chair by the hospital bed.

"I can hardly remember what it's like to be normal ... I don't know when I'll feel normal again ... It just goes on ... I was doing well, and now this, one thing after another. What will the next thing be?"

. . .

The IV tree: Septra (to prevent pneumoystis), acyclovir (antiviral), doxycycline (antifungal), heparin, Dilaudid, magnesium, potassium, gamma globulin, intralipids, TPN, saline solution. She needed irradiated CMV-negative platelets and units of red cells regularly. There was Decadron and Ativan for nausea. Lasix. GCSF injections.

She felt bloated. Her abdomen was black and blue. She was bald. Her ankles and feet were swollen, her back ached, which made walking hard. Breathing hurt, the hacking cough hurt. Eating was a dare. What came out of her body, the color and sight and smell of it, was unnatural. Her body had become the laboratory for some far-fetched experiment.

He opened the narrow closet in her room. "There are my clothes," she said, as though she'd spotted a sail on the horizon, moving out of sight.

Seated in the chair, dozing, she opened her eyes with a start. "I just had a flashback of running at Northfield Mount Herman before soccer practice. It was so vivid."

On Monday, Brett's forty-fourth day in the hospital, the pulmonary specialists weren't at all certain it was pneumonia, after all, but they would continue to treat her for that, just in case. In the afternoon an echocardiogram didn't reveal anything. He watched her heart beating on the screen, a detached image, which didn't move him. The worst doctors, he saw, focused on the detached image—the myriad of detached images—rather than the person.

By Tuesday her white count was normal, she was eating almost normally, and they began to reduce her IV load, discontinuing the intralipids, taking her off doxycycline, tapering down on TPN. She no longer needed Dilaudid. Lloyd Damon appeared downright delighted with her condition. "I heard him tell a bunch of residents," Brett said, "'We don't know exactly why, but she's getting better.'" Brett furrowed her brow. "Very scientific."

They began to prepare her for her imminent leave-taking, possibly the next Monday, the doctors thought. Despite her white count, she would still lack fully functioning B-cells and T-cells, including T-helper cells, leaving her very susceptible to viral infections and dependent on prophylactic medications. Septra, acyclovir, IV gamma globulin. For three months or so she'd have to be very careful. No raw fruits or vegetables outside her own home, where they could be thoroughly washed. Her diet was unrestricted, although her taste buds had been changed and it might take some time for them to return to normal. Her immunity against diseases like mumps, measles, and chicken pox was, of course, gone, so she had to be careful around small children. She'd have to practice safe sex, no exchange of body fluids, for she could be carrying the hepatitis virus, which is transmitted sexually. Stay away from crowded places, such as movie theaters. Stay out of wilderness areas like woods, where fungi dwell. Even earth, dirt, could be worrisome. Wash hands frequently. She would leave the hospital with her Hickman catheter because she'd continue to require platelet transfusions and gamma globulin. She'd learn to clean and care for the line, which was a port of entry for dangerous infection. For a while her life as an outpatient would take up much of her time. She couldn't leave the hospital until she was able to get from Friday to Monday without requiring platelets, for the clinic wasn't open on weekends. Yet almost unexpectedly, that day seemed within grasp.

"I'm never coming back to this place," Brett said.

. . .

By the end of the seventh week, her white cell count was greater than the combined counts of all the other patients on Floor 11. She continued to taper off various drugs and to substitute oral medications for their intravenous forms. By August 30, a Friday, the IV stand had been almost completely dismantled. Her calorie count was posted outside her door. The doctors were unable to say just what had occurred with her lungs; she had improved, that was the important thing. In the afternoon she received more healthy platelets from Eve. If she held on to them over the weekend, she'd be out of there. The anticipation was dizzying.

The very next day, however, it was clear her platelets weren't going to hold. She'd been receiving too much heparin, her blood was too thin. It would be hazardous for her to leave the hospital until the blood levels were right. She had bumped her foot somehow, evidently, and it was dramatically swollen and bruised, so that she hobbled now as she attempted to walk her rounds in the hallway. A fresh discouragement.

After all she'd been through, her mother asked, how could she let a sore foot bother her? Holly was afraid Brett was losing her fight.

"You don't think I'm doing all I can?" Brett asked. "I'm a very positive person," she insisted. "Goddamn it."

The miserable foot had the power to disturb her because of all she'd been through. They were both in tears.

When he entered 1122 on Sunday afternoon, she greeted him with the results of her last X-ray. The specialists were concerned about two white patches in her lungs, clearly something new. The patches might reflect a fungal infection, the doctor had told her, scarring from a prior infection, a recall of radiation (pneumonitis), bleeding, or—and here, Brett said, the doctor had placed his hand on her shoulder—Hodgkin's.

"That's not a possibility," he replied to his daughter. The suggestion shocked him.

They'd scheduled a CAT scan for Tuesday.

A new resident, Debbie Shih—a pretty, petite young woman who might have been mistaken for a teenager—detected some wheezing when she listened to Brett's chest but didn't know what to make of it. They sat there, the three of them—for Holly had arrived—numb, like people in a bus station at two in the morning, waiting for a bus that wouldn't come. Then Brett got to her feet, the sore foot, to pace the hall. They stopped in the bright conference room. He opened a window and she stuck her arm into the air. "It's so nice out," she said wistfully.

Hope Rugo, another of Linker's colleagues, came by at the end of the day. A fungal infection didn't seem plausible—Brett didn't seem sick enough—but they would put her back on amphotericin. He brought up Hodgkin's disease.

"That's very unlikely," Rugo said. "It's too soon." As she was leaving the room she told Brett, "Just a few more days."

Brett said, "She didn't make it sound unlikely enough." The back of her shaved skull, mottled again with patches of stubble, looked small and vulnerable as she halfheartedly bent over her hospital dinner, propped on an elbow. How much more could be required of her?

They were too frightened, all over again, to be depressed. The ampho was toxic. A fungal infection would postpone everything interminably. They had to return to Massachusetts soon. They had to be working, they were out of money. It was September 1. They trudged back to the apartment drained, speechless. Holly had begun to think that their daughter wasn't going to get out of there.

Labor Day was a summer day in San Francisco. Brett and her mother were surprisingly relaxed, watching the U.S. Open, when he arrived at the hospital. Possibly, Rugo had told her, she could leave the hospital on Wednesday, if nothing new occurred. When they left her that evening, she and two girlfriends were headed down the hallway to view the sunset. Hobbling on her bad foot, wheeling the IV stand, Brett had them laughing about something.

The next day Debbie Shih informed them—as though she were referring to a movie she'd seen, some matter-of-fact gossip—that something had grown out of the lung culture after all, two weeks later. "TB," she said. Or an infection belonging to the family of organisms call mycobacteria. And the CAT scan Brett had had that morning showed more fluid outside the lung, at the base, than they'd seen in the X-ray. Repeating what she'd been told, without any apparent grasp of the impact this news might have on the patient, Shih went on to say that the ambiguous picture in the scan could be tuberculosis alone or Hodgkin's disease. Brett would now be put on a daily course of several TB medications.

His daughter sat as though she'd been bludgeoned from behind, her expression blank. "I can't do any more," she said, her voice breaking. "How do they expect someone to do this?"

"It's not Hodgkin's," he said. "That's not it. They can treat TB." Of course they knew nothing about tuberculosis or the implications for someone in Brett's condition. How had she contracted the disease in the controlled environment of the transplant ward?

This promising day had become one of the hardest, saddest days. When Brett roused herself again—"Let's walk"—her nurse caught up with her in the hallway with a face mask. She'd have to wear it whenever she left 1122. Visitors would have to wear masks inside the room. Everyone who had been with her lately would have to be tested for TB.

"How can I go home?" Brett asked. "How can I be at home?"

They sat through the long afternoon, waiting for Linker to appear, hoping for some clarification. Fresh from his vacation, the doctor was tanned and rested-looking. He hadn't expected them to still be here, he said. As he talked about the lung mystery, it became obvious that he hadn't been told yet about the TB discovery. This latest twist caused him to brighten considerably. TB was good news, insofar as it explained Brett's symptoms—the wheezing, cough, shortness of breath, fluid—and removed the unacceptable possibility of Hodgkin's. Brett couldn't leave the hospital while she was infectious, but the medications should take effect within a week. So maybe Friday. Brett fought back again. All right, she could do TB, too.

Wednesday she flushed her Hickman catheter herself for the first time, carefully injecting heparin while keeping the valve as sterile as possible, then she taped it closed. She stood, and with her arms held out, she turned in a full circle, unencumbered by plastic tubing. For the first time in fifty-two days she was not tethered to the IV pole. She smiled and freely walked around the room as if on parade.

"Can you believe it?"

That night, when he left the hospital, there was strong wind and dense fog at the top of Parnassus, like an approaching storm on the Maine coast, he thought. The street, with its dark towering buildings, was deserted. He was reminded of one of their first nights in San Francisco, back in July, when he'd walked Brett to her apartment following an evening at 111 Buena Vista East. She'd taken his arm as they plowed, heads down, against the wind. That memory seemed to belong to another year altogether.

Debbie Shih brought more news the following day. Instead of TB, Brett had a less common and indolent mycobacterial infection known as MAI, which was more familiar to AIDS patients and didn't respond as well to treatment. That's all she knew.

They listened without comment.

Seated in the blue chair, wearing her small, multicolored, jeweled skullcap from India, Brett wrote a letter to a friend. A Shawn Colvin tape was playing. One couldn't have imagined that she'd been repeatedly ill that morning, her vomit the color of prune juice. They spent the afternoon waiting for Linker, who didn't turn up until six.

"I would have preferred the infection to be TB," he said. "That would have accounted for all the symptoms." The MAI didn't do that as well. "My second choice would be a fungal infection, but we're going to treat for the MAI, which is all we've got to go on right now." If Brett's condition deteriorated they might put her back on an antifungal.

"What about Hodgkin's?" he asked.

"Only a fool would say Hodgkin's was impossible. Anything is possible." But it didn't look like Hodgkin's to him in the CAT scan, and it was unlikely Hodgkin's would present so soon in a new site. He touched Brett's brilliant cap. "You can go home tomorrow if you want to."

After the doctor left the room, she said, "So if I get better, I get better, and if I get worse, I get worse?"

"What else is new?"

Instead of returning via Haight Street, he walked up Frederick, past the pink stuccoed apartment building and the Japanese grocers, then over the top of Buena Vista Park and down the other side to their building, a forty-minute walk. Drained, one foot in front of the other.

"There's nothing left to her," his wife said. "She's being destroyed."

"Tomorrow. Linker said tomorrow."

When Brett vomited blood the next morning, Debbie Shih inserted a tube through her nose to her stomach and flushed it with saline solution to establish there was no active bleeding there. What might have seemed an almost trivial procedure two weeks earlier was now an insupportable indignity.

Richard Shaw, her friend from Massachusetts, and Holly were in Room 1122 when he arrived that afternoon. Brett sat on the bed in tears, but they were tears of rage.

"I'm never going to get out of here. I'm never going to get out."

Linker had just left the room. He caught up with the doctor at the nurses' station.

"Brett's going crazy in there. What's happening?"

"We don't know. It's frustrating." She'd been running a fever much of the day, and he was concerned she could now have a bacterial infection in the Hickman line. If she didn't respond to antibiotics within forty-eight hours, they'd know that wasn't the problem, and they'd switch back to treating her for a fungal infection. If that worked, they'd have to decide whether to discontinue the MAI drugs. The MAI might have been in a contaminated test tube, after all, rather than in the fluid from Brett's lungs. Linker was hoping this process of elimination would finally lead to some answers.

"I haven't seen her this upset. She's got to get out of here."

"Brett's doing all right," Linker said. "I'm not concerned with the number of days she's been here. The problem becomes more dangerous the longer it goes unresolved. I want to solve it."

He returned to Brett's room and explained to her what Linker evidently hadn't made clear moments before or what, in any case, she'd been unable to hear. It was the fever now that was keeping her in the hospital, and they had to get to the bottom of it. Linker was going after the line infection first because it was the more hazardous possibility.

Brett listened, and this grasp of the game plan seemed to calm her. She said, "Did he tell you I hate him?" Evidently the expression on her face, as Linker attempted to explain why she had to remain in the hospital longer, was poisonous.

She was informed that she had to vacate Room 1122; the transplant room was needed by an incoming patient. Carefully, he dismantled her wall of cards and posters and artwork. They'd assumed they would be taking it down in a mood of celebration. It wasn't like that. He helped the nurse move everything in the room, including the furniture, down the hall in the direction of the elevators. Her former room would be meticulously scoured. The new one, while less cluttered, with more light, felt like defeat. For the first time his daughter seemed to him not angry or sad or frightened but dispirited. *Forlorn.* The word resonated.

She sat passively on a small metal table the next day, while Shih, supervised by Terry Jahan, a fellow at UCSF, confidently inserted a large needle into her back just below the shoulder blade. They'd decided to draw the accumulated fluid from Brett's pleural cavity, hoping for some clue to her lung problem. Amber liquid, a liter of it, flowed from his daughter's chest through a flexible tube into a large clear bottle.

"Are you okay?"

She nodded. She wasn't talking.

Monday Brett was eating, walking, taking her medications, but she had nothing to say. They'd started her on the antifungal amphotericin and today her fever was gone, but that didn't cheer her up. When he spoke with her on the phone at nine that night, more confusion had arisen. Jahan had assumed the fever was not the result of a line infection because she hadn't responded to vancomycin, an antibacterial, within twenty-four hours. He'd prescribed the amphotericin. But Hope Rugo had just told Brett it must have been the vancomycin that brought the fever down, that she must have a bacterial line infection, because a fungal infection wouldn't have responded to the ampho so readily. Rugo was putting her back on vanco. When Brett said she hoped she'd be out by the end of the week, the doctor would only say, "I hope so, too."

"I feel trapped." She went to pieces. "I'm trapped. No one can tell me what's going on. The constant physical insults, these procedures— you're constantly being assaulted, but you can't react," she cried, "and so you turn numb. You get stabbed in the back, but you can't react. It's cumulative, it keeps building up and building up and you just have to take it. These complications are holding me up, they're using up my precious time," she cried. "I feel my life is very finite now. I'm afraid I won't have time to enjoy anything before the cancer comes back. These secondary problems are imprisoning me here. I'm losing myself."

"Brett," he said. "Brett."

"You're the object of all this trial-and-error bullshit, you're just an object, and you lose sense of yourself. I'm losing myself traipsing around the fucking corridor, the same horrible corridor every day, in these horrible fucking hospital garments. I don't know who I am."

"We're at the end of this now," he said. "It's only since you began to feel that it was over that the frustration has become intolerable. The Hodgkin's has to be gone," he told her. "As long as it's gone everything else is manageable. Your fever is under control now. We'll know more about the lung involvement soon." Rugo didn't tell her she was getting out, he suggested, because she didn't want to make any more false promises. "But you're almost there, Brett. You are." He felt like he was diving down, unable to hold his breath much longer, desperately reaching for the body drifting just beyond his reach. It was necessary most of all to listen, he knew that, but he couldn't leave her despair as the last word.

Brett continued to pour out her misery. When Beth entered the hospital room, she hung up.

In the morning she sounded as if everything were possible again, and her spirits continued to improve throughout the day when she managed fistfuls of medications without being sick. Her breakdown last night, she told him, was necessary to her sanity. The numbness she described had lifted.

As it turned out, Rugo's assessment of the situation had been accurate. Jahan had mistakenly abandoned the vanco for amphotericin after only twenty-four hours instead of the necessary forty-eight. They had now returned to the original plan, treating the presumed line infection, the cause of the fever. The mix-up would cost Brett another day, and she'd received an unwanted dose of ampho. She'd stay on vancomycin three more days, when it was hoped she'd leave the hospital.

The pneumonia was a separate issue. If MAI developed from the fluid they'd drained earlier in the week, the diagnosis would be confirmed. If it didn't turn up in the lab work, on the other hand, that wouldn't mean Brett wasn't infected. In all his years on the transplant staff, Linker had never seen a case of MAI, and it puzzled him. They had no choice but to treat her for it—a long-term process. If her symptoms worsened, they'd have to consider the possibility of a fungal infection, after all, but you didn't put a patient on a toxic antibiotic requiring at least three weeks of intravenous treatment unless it was clearly necessary.

Three weeks? No, thank you.

They didn't know where they were from one day to the next. In no time, it seemed, another unexpected symptom could send Brett, and the rest of them, into a tailspin. Wednesday began for her with more pain, a dose of Dilaudid, nausea, but she got through the day without a major incident. By that evening she was herself again, joking on the phone to friends. Despite the prevailing uncertainties, leaving the hospital loomed again as a real possibility. Again, Friday was the day.

He borrowed Beth's small blue car, as he'd done regularly for the past two months, and he and Holly went grocery shopping in anticipation, giddy anticipation, of Brett's freedom from 11 Long. Later he dropped Holly, supplied with sponges and detergents and a good vacuum cleaner, at Brett's apartment. She intended to make the place safe for Brett's homecoming. Beth appreciated her help.

When he reached her room, Brett had just gotten out of the shower and looked pink. At this eleventh hour, Debbie Shih reported that there was no evidence of Hodgkin's in the pleural fluid. They'd been assuming that, of course; it was good to hear.

"If the fluid on Brett's right side becomes uncomfortable," Jahan suggested, "we can draw that off as well."

"We can do that at home," he said, "now that I've watched you do it."

Laughter.

Brett had received blood the night before and she was soon rigged up with a bag of platelets this morning. He rolled up posters, packed stuff away, organizing her belongings.

A pharmacist arrived and went over the host of medications she would go home with, a dozen different drugs, along with pain and nausea medications, to be taken in various combinations from morning to night, an onerous regimen. At Moffitt, directly across Parnassus, he waited in line at the pharmacy to get her numerous prescriptions filled. When he returned, Brett was wearing a new black tam—it was windy and cool outside—and her new red sweater, a gift from her mother, and she was pulling on her blue sweatpants.

"Clothes!" he said. "Clothes!"

She nodded, her lips compressed. No more horrible hospital garments. She looked pale, frailer somehow, in sturdy ordinary clothing. She moved rather cautiously, thoughtfully, taking her time. They packed her gear onto a cart. There was no fanfare. The hospitalization was over, that was the plan, but the struggle wasn't over. Far from it.

They didn't expect to see Charles Linker. He casually sauntered into the room just before they left. "Matching berets," he said. That's right, father and daughter were both wearing black berets. The belief was that the vancomycin had resolved the line infection, he told them, and the MAI meds would eventually address Brett's pneumonia.

She asked him to look at her feet. Sitting on the edge of the bed, Brett removed her unlaced sneakers. Both feet were swollen and mottled black and blue. All her steadfast walking.

Stooping to examine them, Linker seemed at a loss. "Your feet will be all right," he told her. He put his hand out. "Congratulations."

Brett whacked him a handshake. She'd see him at the clinic next week. Her first impression of him during their first interview months before—distant, cold, more scientist than doctor—had turned out not to be accurate. Linker was an impressive man. The whole family had grown fond of him.

She pushed the cart of her belongings, while he carried another armload of stuff. He could feel her holding it together as they descended on the elevator, packed in with strangers, bearing all her secret knowledge of places no one could imagine.

"Back down to earth," he said.

Then they were walking the corridor of Floor 1, not Floor 11, suddenly walking in a crowd of vigorous hurrying people, the first new place Brett had seen in nine weeks. She broke out in a big smile. This was becoming exciting. As they stepped outside, she looked at the sky, at trees, carefully taking things in, breathing the outdoor air through her flared nostrils.

"Whooo-hooo," she hooted, high-pitched, beautiful. Several hoots of celebration. Happy. It was September 13, 1991, a Friday, Day 52, if you were his daughter's oncologist, sixty-one days since she'd entered Long Hospital.

Driving down Cole Street, she hungrily absorbed the scene. "It's so *nice*," she said. Everyday life. The sight of people, awkward, amusing, busy people, excited her. It excited *him*.

They drove directly to 111 Buena Vista East. Just as they entered the apartment, Jocelyn happened to call from New York. He and Holly listened to Brett regaling her sister with the adventure she was just then experiencing: I'm free.

She had been released with a long-term lung disease, in pain. A renewed fever could dump her back in the hospital at a moment's notice. There was the harrowing array of medications, along with their inevitably nauseating side effects. There was a length of plastic tubing

protruding from her chest, and she faced an ongoing schedule of transfusions and checkups as an outpatient. The specter of cancer had not
been vanquished. For all that, his daughter was impressively relaxed
tonight. Everything delighted her.

"You're here," he repeated emphatically.

These past two months Beth had had little to do with them. They'd
had dinner once or twice, they'd frequently crossed paths on the street
en route to or from the hospital. His impression was that Beth was
stretched to the limit, holding down a full-time job and coping with
what her girlfriend was going through, as well as her own loneliness
and frustration and anxiety. Whatever comfort they might have been
to one another hadn't been something she needed to discover. Tonight,
though, Beth was thrilled when she arrived at their apartment, and
whatever misgivings he and Holly had felt about their relationship
with Brett's domestic partner evaporated. The love between these two
young women was real.

He'd gotten his hair cut on Haight Street and was returning to Buena
Vista East just before noon. His days in this place were numbered. It
was hard to believe they were finally leaving. He glanced across the
street, then glanced again, startled. He had not immediately recognized his daughter. She walked along the steep lawn that rose to the
densely wooded park. All bundled up—black beret, navy-blue
sweatpants, her waist-length maroon jacket. The spanking white running shoes they'd bought her the day before! She had many miles of
recuperative walking ahead of her and wanted a new pair of cushioned
shoes. She moved slowly, slightly stooped, clearly headed for their
apartment. The sight of her on the street, from a distance, twisted in
him painfully. Her bravery. What was it like being out here again,
viewing the life around her, with what she now knew?

I'm afraid of what I'll become afterwards.

"Hey!" He waved and ran across the street toward her. "Brett!"

Smiling, she waited for him to reach her.

That afternoon was cold, windy, with fog. They visited the de Young Museum of Far Eastern Art in the park, they strolled through the Japanese Tea Garden. Brett had to rest from time to time, but she was doing all right, she was having a pretty good day, apart from the cough, the constant cough. That afternoon she said, "I feel the cancer is gone, I have no problem with that. But I want to feel better."

Tuesday and again on Friday they accompanied her to the clinic, and amazingly, it seemed to him, Brett's counts continued to hold up. She required neither blood nor platelets. There was no change in her X-ray. As soon as next week, possibly—after one more infusion of gamma globulin—they could pull the Hickman catheter. Charles Linker was in a bullish mood.

The doctor thanked Holly, then him, for their help. "Next time we meet it will be to celebrate." He had never made such a bold statement to them before, and it seemed wildly unlike him. They shook hands, a second official parting. Really, this last visit to the medical center—their last visit—Brett's prognosis couldn't have been more encouraging.

Friday evening when they picked her up for dinner, she emerged from her apartment absolutely transformed. She wore wide pantaloons that Joce had made, a black silk blouse, her new leather jacket, the bright little ornamental cap on her head. She was wearing lipstick. Her posture was straight and her step energetic. She smiled, happy, as though she'd managed some unimaginable coup. And Beth, when they met her at the restaurant, Zuni's, was smitten all over again. She couldn't take her eyes off Brett. Their last night in San Francisco was a blessing, a going-away present that helped them feel better about leaving.

He sat in the dark, looking out at the night view through the tall living room windows. Holly was in bed. The stream of light was a bridge. The pool of blackness was the bay, which led to the ocean. He'd never live with such a cityscape spread before him again. He'd begun to take this vista for granted, even while it remained as unknown and mysterious as it had been two months earlier. Summer, that word, with its promise of pleasure, a breathing spell. This had been a season lived outside the pale, a summerless summer. He recalled the night when his daughter had held them all spellbound with her eloquence and passion. *What pleasure life is. . . . I feel so alive . . . I desire to live. . . .* He'd been slow to grasp the depth of her fear, she'd been so courageous. And she did it, he thought, she came through the fire. Now let her have her life, he pleaded, looking out at the immense spectacle of the shimmering city, set against the dark horizon.

They shared a shuttle to the airport with two fortysomething couples, who clambered on board with four sets of golf clubs, bound for Las Vegas. At seven in the morning, these people carried on as though they'd already tipped back a few drinks, pumped up about their holiday now under way. He and Holly sat there like baffled oddballs from another country, refugees from some embattled past.

His carry-on bag contained an abandoned typed manuscript, a five-hundred-page notebook filled with his hurried, cramped handwriting, and bills, numerous impossible bills from the place they were leaving and the place they were headed. They both dreaded getting back to their lives, the work and worry awaiting them in Massachusetts. They dreaded the phone's ringing the moment they walked into their house. And yet everything was possible, he reminded his wife, everything would be manageable one way or another if their oldest daughter—when the phone rang, when they took a breath and picked it up—was all right.

September 21. "The birches will just be turning," he said.

She seemed to see it, as she glanced at the dense massed clouds beyond the window of the plane. "Another fall."

6

PAIN

If they'd imagined their daughter would be set free once she'd survived the ultimate treatment, like a political prisoner at the end of a war, they were mistaken. Each subsequent visit to the clinic, both tedious and oppressive to her, was a descent into the underground where every patient's story, hopeful or despairing, now recalled an unhappy place she had been. Fatigue, exacerbated by persistent painful pleurisy, was frustrating. Nausea overcame her unexpectedly. Shortness of breath and the ravaging cough were taxing. She fell apart, she said, when she attempted to write in her journal for the first time. By early October, though, a mere two weeks after her release, she was working on her art again, she wanted to get herself an exercise bike, she said, and on several occasions she'd had people to dinner, including Mary Cranley, her primary nurse, who wanted to be a friend, it seemed.

"We eat as much garlic as we can," she wrote them, "and avoid large, coughing dogs that have been in the dirt or near small children. Last night we went to a Vietnamese restaurant that served pig noses. It wasn't *crowded* and the noses were thoroughly *cooked*. . . . Beth and I will probably drive up into the Sonoma orchards this weekend in search of apple cider donuts and dashes of color. She'll drive like a bat outta hell while I cough and hoot. We'll end up buying cheese. It's a nice change to walk around the little sleepy towns—brick buildings, porches, fat families that stare. . . . I can't wait to be home, taking slow strolls with Ben, sitting around the fire with all—the peaceable king-dom. San Francisco misses you. I do too." There was a small, almost abstract oil pastel enclosed, a seascape.

A few days later she called to report that she'd had the Hickman catheter removed. "Linker and I were looking into each other's eyes as he pulled it out of my chest." The tube seemed about a foot long. She had to lie down compressing the spot for an hour. No more blood transfusions. *Now it's really over.*

Except the following week there was a full-body CAT scan, and soon after that another bone-marrow biopsy: three months had passed since the infusion of her marrow. You wanted to just forget these dreaded follow-up procedures—*That's it!*—but you couldn't.

Toward the end of the month she and Beth flew to Massachusetts for a week. One month earlier no one would have imagined such a trip was possible for her.

"I'm here!"

Her first night back there was a full moon, which seemed pro-pitious.

There followed a stretch of mild, balmy days. The inflamed colum-nar maples along their private drive stood like torches on the field. The October light in Boyden's west pasture, surrounded by towering sugar maples, made them feel, the evening he and Brett walked out there, like they had stepped inside an illuminated pumpkin. She had not seen a New England autumn since she'd moved to San Francisco three years earlier, and she was as thrilled as a visitor who'd never been here before. One day she and Richard Shaw hiked from Field's hill across Parker's land to Fisher Meadow and down through the woods to the house. On Sunday, Mary Burger, a tall young woman with an air of serenity, drove out from Boston to seal the friendship that had evolved between them at a distance. The week was tarnished by two unexpected upsets. Jocelyn, who had been keenly anticipating this family celebration, was hospitalized in New York City with a severe case of tonsillitis. And Holly, the last night of Brett's visit, collapsed in the kitchen, struck down by a nauseating attack of vertigo, if that's what it was. Both events, which might have seemed minor another year, seemed ominous to him now.

The morning Brett was to return to the West Coast, she was distraught. New England felt inspiring to her—this gorgeous fall—and she didn't want to leave. She hated what San Francisco had come to represent, she said. The apartment, the streets, the steep climb up Parnassus, the dark, glassy facade of Moffitt, the fifth floor, the view from there—everything was about being sick. Returning to San Francisco meant returning to the results of her biopsy, it meant more tests. She and Beth spent a last hour on Field's hill taking in the crisp autumn air, the colors of turning trees. The calm of the Herefords as they grazed in the green pasture made it seem that it was these dull beasts who understood what all this was about.

The next day she called from her apartment on Central Avenue, and she sounded good. She'd been intensely plugging away at her desk all morning. Linker had called while she was out of town and left a message on her answering machine: the bone-marrow biopsy was normal.

He felt a rush of joy.

"It worked," she said. The series of drawings she was so fiercely focused on was entitled "The Future." "I become obsessed. I can't drag myself away from it."

In early November, as if evil had come to live in their house, he thought, unable to repress his panic, Nathaniel discovered a lump on the back of his neck. Siblings of Hodgkin's patients were at risk for the disease—they knew that. It can't be, was one thought—yet it was no longer possible for them to trust their intuitions. The doctor at the university clinic suggested waiting a week or two to see if the swollen node would resolve itself. Naive! Time was of the essence. His son was examined on Wednesday, the node was removed on Friday.

Nathaniel refused to be alarmed, he went about his business, but he was subdued, and as days passed while they waited for the results of the biopsy, he confided that he'd had one bad night thinking about all his older sister had been through.

The answer took a week to come, but when it came it was good: benign. They didn't feel ridiculous for pouncing on the now-innocent lump; they were relieved.

He called George Canellos at Dana Farber, whom he'd contacted earlier in the week, to let him know the outcome of the biopsy.

"How is your daughter?" the doctor asked.

He succinctly recounted her most recent history with Hodgkin's disease. There was a long recuperation ahead of her, of course, but she was strong and already appeared to be doing well. They were hopeful.

"The transplant very well may have done it," Canellos agreed.

In their phone conversations lately, as Brett talked about her friends, her work, a trip with Beth to Point Reyes, the weather there, she sounded like her old self, her smart, funny self. In mid-November she made her plans for Christmas. She'd fly to Boston to visit Mary Burger on December 13, a Friday, then continue on to Conway until the end of the month. She already had her ticket.

It worked!

The Tuesday before Thanksgiving, that evening, Brett called just after they'd gone to bed. The night before she'd started running a fever and ended up in the emergency room soon after nine, not to return until two in the morning. She'd left a message for her doctors, but they hadn't gotten back to her yet. The week before, she'd been struck with excruciating hip pain, something new, but X-rays had been unable to decipher the cause. That intense pain was still present, and the pre-scribed anti-inflammatories didn't touch it.

He hardly knew how to respond. Inexplicable fevers just before Thanksgiving. Another awful trip to the emergency room—the cold gray entrance, the hurried, overworked staff, the downcast, disheveled patients—how insupportable for her. He lay in bed holding his wife from behind. Her breasts were small, fragile pouches of flesh. Recent tests for estrogen had revealed she was deep into menopause; she hoped hormone-replacement therapy would give her a lift. Stress over their daughter's plight had dried her up as a woman—that's how it seemed to him tonight. The lavish breasts each of their children had nursed at—brought to this! He thought, Why are we born?

Brett spent the holiday with half a dozen friends. She and Beth were intermittently panicky, she said. They had their weepy moments, then carried on. She was angry that no one from the clinic had gotten back to her yet. It was sunny and blue there.

"Are you going for a walk?" he asked.

"I'm going for a cough."

Linker ordered another bone-marrow biopsy. The day of that procedure sleet and freezing rain rained down all day in Conway, transforming their long drive into a treacherous, impassable sheet of ice. He attempted to work, but his mind kept returning to the scene of his daughter's misery, submitting to more pain at the hands of Dr. Terry Jahan. He had never been with her during a bone-marrow biopsy; he didn't know what that was like.

She called the next day. "Terry said, 'If it's cancer, do you want to be treated on the East Coast or here.' I burst into tears."

Her blood work was discouraging, her platelets and white count dropping, which could mean the marrow was being invaded. Next week they were going to do another MRI.

"What are you thinking?" he asked her.

"Beth and I have been living with this so constantly for three weeks, so scared, that nothing shocks me now. The question of where to be treated, I can't answer that." She didn't know if she could be persuaded to pursue more chemotherapy, for instance. "I don't want to be sick all the time."

"We've given conventional medicine a chance," he said. "You've given it a magnificent chance. Maybe we should try something else now."

That sentence, his feeble attempt to say something, made her briefly tearful.

"I'm coming home for Christmas either way," she said with defiance. The fourth consecutive Christmas she was contending with this dread. Mostly she wanted to be free from pain. Today she was going to an acupuncturist, seeking relief, anything, for her hip and leg.

"I'm going to remain hopeful," he said.

"So am I. Linker said we have a scary set of circumstances here; it's worrisome—those were his words—but he's going to keep his fingers crossed."

When they hung up the phone he and Holly could no longer repress the anguish they'd been postponing for weeks, refusing to accept what they couldn't bear. She's going to die. The unthinkable sentence, a hateful and forbidden sequence of words, seemed to press on his skull and fill his chest. "I need her," he pleaded. "I need her."

When all this began, years before, he believed his daughter trusted him, as though nothing unendurable could befall her while he was there to insist upon that. "Everything you have done for me," she wrote him the first year. "I will be there for you." After his solo visit to San Francisco following the first recurrence, she'd written, "Thank you for being there. You take the loneliness away." You're going to be all right. That wasn't coming true. The impossible could happen. Protector!

In the past few days Holly's face seemed to have collapsed. She looked ravaged, she couldn't speak. He thought, We're being destroyed.

They weren't expecting her call the next morning.

"I feel like I'm going to die," she cried. "In my mind and in my body. I can't take any more. I feel terrible all the time." Today she didn't want to get out of bed, she was alone, she couldn't get hold of anyone. This was the voice of her despair, awakening in San Francisco surrounded by terrors.

He and Holly tried to summon words of comfort. They had to live each day as it came, for example, one day at a time—that familiar bumper sticker—as they'd been doing all along.

Brett said, "But my days aren't that good." She hadn't been getting out lately, she hadn't been walking because of her pain. It was sunny there, another beautiful day, but she was confined to the apartment. "I feel like an old person." She'd lost ten pounds since October, when she was in New England. There was blood in her sputum, which probably meant low platelets.

"If you could get to another place," he said, "mentally, I mean, if . . ." Capitulating to the kind of jargon he abhorred. He meant, if she could only grant herself some peace, some . . .

"There isn't another place. This is it." S.J., her therapist, helped her understand that these moments were part of the process, they were inevitable and necessary, and yet her blackest thoughts were only thoughts. Good thoughts could be just as powerful.

He didn't ask, What process?

"I was having a nightmare. I was in graduate school and I began having fevers at night. Friends were encouraging me to do my work and I couldn't make them understand that it didn't matter. You were encouraging me. I was working on a paper for graduate school or something, but I knew it didn't matter because I wasn't going to make it. I woke up feeling damp, terrified, and so I called you." There was a silence. "I don't expect you to say anything. I just had to call. I was feeling alone."

They wanted her home, he said, they wanted her in Conway, where they could be with her. In a week, whatever happened, she'd be here.

Brett was uncertain. "I live in San Francisco," she said. Tomorrow she would call the clinic to get the results of the biopsy.

"Don't be alone when you make that call," he cautioned.

"I won't be." That afternoon she was planning to go to Beth's gallery, New Langton Arts, for an auction. She'd been contacting her friends, hoping to get them together for dinner Sunday night, and so far everyone was coming. "Potluck," she said.

They drove to Northampton to see if tests would discover the cause of Holly's mysterious episodes of collapse. Was it Ménière's syndrome? A tumor? He did the grocery shopping. Eight loaves of bread from Normand's festive, fragrant bakery. Everywhere this Friday in town there were signs of the impending season of joy. There had been snow and rain, and, returning, they only made it halfway up their icy road. They left the car where it was stuck. At one, he left a message for Linker, asking the doctor to return his call. As the day progressed without word from Brett, it seemed more certain that the worst had occurred. Good news would have prompted her to call them immediately. Two months of suffering in the hospital hadn't bought her two months of freedom!

Holly said, "I wish I could collect myself."

By nine he could no longer persuade himself to give his daughter space, to wait longer. It was not a phone call he wanted to make.

In fact, she hadn't heard from the clinic yet. "Linker's a jerk," she said. "Can't he imagine what I'm going through?" She and Beth were going to get themselves something to eat and watch a movie.

So it was past eleven when she called back. "Terry Jahan apologized for reaching me so late. The preliminary evaluation of the marrow shows no Hodgkin's."

"Thank God." But Jahan's report couldn't dispel the anxiety that had been building. "It's been a grueling day," he said.

"I guess."

Two days later the pain in her hip, descending into her leg, was so bad she couldn't walk. Fevers had tormented her at night again. Her breathing was poor, her exhaustion total. "I feel worse than I did when I left the hospital," she said. "Beth is so tired of it." Tomorrow: the dark tube of another onerous MRI. Tonight, however, thirteen friends were expected to turn up bearing various culinary delights. She would have to receive them reclining on the couch, she said, but the party was still on. Definitely.

They attended Christmas vespers at Smith College with a close friend and her six-year-old daughter. All these young women singing praises with open mouths and, from the sight of them in their white blouses, pure hearts—innocents!—while his daughter, her sturdy body racked . . . A few years before, she had been one of them: everything ahead of her. The moment the service ended, he fled the hall, this crowd of holiday well-wishers, holding tight to the child's hand. She went along with him, hurrying by his side, as if she understood his need to get away from there.

Awakening in the small hours, he was startled by a muffled sound, which disturbed him more the instant he identified it. Turned away from him, cradling her sorrow like an infant, his wife stifled shuddering sobs.

Tuesday they learned that nothing had turned up in the extensive tests Holly had undergone the week before: no Ménière's syndrome, no brain tumor.

Brett finally reached them that evening. Terry Jahan had just informed her that the MRI was clear. "I'd be ecstatic," she said, "if I didn't feel so bad." Her fevers and chills persisted, the pain persisted. Walking up the hill to her apartment, her heart thumped frighteningly. She couldn't imagine coming home on Friday, although she was still determined nothing would stop her. He seized on the hopeful results of the MRI and the biopsy. Her difficult breathing could be attributed to the TB, couldn't it? Possibly a bone infection, resulting from a bone-marrow biopsy, could account for her pain and fevers.

"Whatever your suffering now," he said, "everything will be manageable, provided the cancer is gone."

When she called the next day she was pissed, following another long, frustrating stint at the clinic, and wanted to make it quick. She and Beth were on their way out to dinner. She needed a blood transfusion. They'd also lined her up for a gallium scan—to evaluate her hip bone—and a CAT scan, and she had an appointment at the pain clinic. She had changed her airline ticket so that now she was scheduled to fly home on Wednesday, the eighteenth. She was coming home no matter what, period. Her Sunday night dinner turned out to be quite a success, by the way. Her friends had been calling to say what a good time they'd had.

Her forceful, impatient tone came as a relief to him. He'd been going around like a clenched fist, his shoulders rigid. He needed to get his breath.

Friday morning, the day she'd originally intended to fly home, she told them that Beth and their friend Suzy had carried her to the car the night before, bound for the emergency room. Her pain had become excruciating. With drugs it had eventually subsided, she was back home, but she couldn't bear anticipating its return. Otherwise she'd been injected with gallium for the scan on Monday. On the bright side, she said, she and Beth had found a new apartment they were happy about. While the large apartment on Central was great, they'd been sharing it with two other women, also from the East Coast, ever since Edgar had left after the first year, and they were eager to have a place of their own.

He was working at his desk that afternoon when the phone went off again. "Talk to me," she said, "just talk to me." Pain was smothering her; she couldn't breathe normally.

"Describe the pain," he said, frightened for her, thinking her own talk might distract her.

"In the hip, at the joint...radiating around my buttock," she gasped. "Into my groin...down to my knee." The intensity of a bone-marrow biopsy, she told him. It had been going on for half an hour, growing worse with each moment. She'd taken Dilaudid without effect. Beth was on her way home. "I can't be in this much pain. Talk to me."

He talked, saying nothing that he recalled, until Beth, undoubtedly tearing recklessly through the city in her small blue car, arrived. Beth called them later to say that Brett had been admitted to the hospital. The good thing was that Jahan had now seen the monstrousness of the pain Brett had been telling him about.

"Thanks for being there."

"She's worth it," Beth said.

H̲ere I am on Floor 11. Room 14." It was nine o'clock in the morning out there.

I'm never coming back to this place.

"I hate it," she said, but she was evidently so doped up she sounded almost mellow. "Fly out here and get me some lunch. I want company." There was the obnoxious calendar on the blank wall: Today Is December 14.

"Are all your beloved nurses around?"

"You bet. Pinkeye is on for the weekend." They wouldn't be able to evaluate her until Monday. "It's mild and raining here," she said. "It feels like spring."

She left the hospital Sunday, hoping oral medication could maintain some level of comfort now that the heavy IV drugs had broken the pain, but by that evening she was back on 11 Long again, having spent the afternoon stretched across her bed in agony, she said, chewing her pillow. "I can't do this anymore. I can't be in intense pain or drugged all the time."

"No, you can't go on this way," he said. "They've got to discover the cause and start dealing with it." He raised the possibility of a bone infection again.

"The doctors discount that."

"We don't know what's happening yet," he said. "They don't know. The MRI didn't see a tumor compressing anything."

The latest bone-marrow sample had turned out to be unreliable, however. Reluctant to penetrate the actual site of her pain, Jahan had extracted marrow only from her good side. Brett was suffering as never before, that much was clear—something devastating was occurring rapidly. He had imagined her walking away from the whole wretched hospital routine if the transplant failed, going on *as she pleased,* living out the rest of her life as she wished. Such an expectation, he saw now, was ludicrously naive. You had to suffer, you had to end up in the hospital in paralyzing pain.

The phone rang again at about nine that evening. "I just wanted to say good night," she said. The drugs had finally given her some relief. Beth was with her. She'd do the gallium scan in the morning, and the CAT scan in the afternoon. Damon told her they needed yet another bone-marrow biopsy. Her fever was a hundred and two. Yet just now she felt calm. "You may have to come out here." She meant for Christmas. *May.* She hadn't yet given up on getting home. "I realize I'm really a happy person," she said, "if I can be without pain."

They're keeping something from me," she confided the following day when he called her hospital room. A doctor had come by to tell her they hoped to design a recipe of medications to control her pain. "I asked him, Don't you want to examine me? He said, No, I think we know what's occurring. There was something in the MRI." A nurse had left Brett's record in the room, and Beth had read Damon's most recent comment. "The pain is certainly recurrence, that's what he'd written." She uttered the words without emotion. "I didn't tell you last night because I was so drugged up." She added, "They'll have to find some way to manage the pain because I can't stay in the hospital. I have to go home." She was very angry, but there was nothing to blame. She was all cried out, she said. She wanted to be free of pain.

"I was so hopeful, Brett. Listen . . . we'll be there soon." Overcome, he handed the phone to Holly. *Don't you want to examine me?* Her determination! She had been hopeful, too, as recently as that question, unable to believe in the end of life.

He thought, She knows.

Nathaniel entered the kitchen. "Dad?"

"Brett's cancer has recurred." Clasping his son, he said, "She's going to die."

Holly replaced the receiver. "My Brett."

The three of them clung together in the warm kitchen like mortals cast out of paradise, pathetic, uncomprehending, damned.

Brett called again at midday to say she wouldn't be talking to a doctor until six or so. "So relax."

Evening: a lovely storybook snowfall on a cold, still night. How she would love to see this, he thought, which led now to a stupefying question: Would she ever see such a snowfall again?

She called at nine-thirty.

"A young Chinese-American doctor, a woman, came into the room and said, Has anyone told you about the gallium scan? It showed a lot of stuff in the hip where your pain is, which is probably recurrence. Just like that, cold as ice." This was the first anyone there had spoken to her directly about what appeared to be going on. The woman was planning to perform three bone-marrow biopsies in the morning, hoping to get enough material to make a positive diagnosis. Brett wasn't sure such a physically small person was up to the task of penetrating her bones.

"I'm going to remain hopeful."

"Oh, Dad," she said.

He was trying to make arrangements for them to fly out Thursday, he told her, the day after tomorrow.

"Can I get back to you on that?" Brett said. "This is a hard time for Beth and me." Beth was returning to Massachusetts for the holiday, despite the circumstances. She hadn't seen her sister in two years, Brett explained, she needed a break. But until Beth left they wanted to have as much time together as possible.

"We want what you want," he said.

These phone numbers he'd put behind him—the clinic, Charles Linker, 11 Long, Mary Cranley, their B and B, a travel service—he needed them again.

Toward midnight he walked down their road in the new snow. Along the domed field, past the stout stone wall, over the frozen brook bordered by white birch. The glinting fields, already uniformly contoured, gave off light. The beautiful first snow.

I wish I could take her back," Holly said. "I wish I could take her inside me."

The petite young doctor did fine, Brett said.

"Do you want us to come out Friday or Saturday?" he asked. It was the eighteenth, the second date on which she'd planned to fly home.

Following a pause she said, "I just had a fantasy of coming home." Jahan had told her if they got the pain under control that would be possible, although the most effective treatment for her pain was bound to be radiation therapy, which would reduce the disease. Recurrence had evidently become a foregone conclusion.

They stumbled onto the question of where Brett was to live now. He'd already contacted a hospice program in their neck of the woods.

"What's hospice?" she asked. A word everyone knew, but what was it exactly?

He briefly described the role and goals of the organization. "You can't take any more aggressive treatment," he said.

"No."

He brought up the advantages to everyone of her returning to New England.

Brett contended there were greater resources in San Francisco for someone in her predicament. "I think I'm a long way from living in bed."

"Of course."

"This is where I've struggled for three years. I've done all the work here with Beth. I have important friends here. Leaving them would be tearing."

Beth would be with her wherever she was. Eve would be the most difficult loss; Eve would have to visit. And while she'd miss S.J., she could expect to find another excellent therapist. Otherwise, most significantly, there was Amy and Ellen in San Francisco. But Mary Burger was here, in Boston, along with other friends. And there was her family, there was Jocelyn and Nathaniel.

"It's not as simple as choosing between Ellen and Mary Burger."

"No, of course not. This isn't a debate. It's your decision. Naturally, your mother and I want you to be here."

"It sounds like you're trivializing my friendships. These people are important to me."

They represented her life, he realized—her own life. Leaving San Francisco would be a profound relinquishment.

"What's coming up is unknown," she said. "Beth and I have been thinking we want to take the new apartment." She added, "If I was married with a kid there'd be no question of my coming home."

"I understand that. I respect your relationship with Beth."

Suddenly the discussion shocked him. How absurd, even cruel, to burden her with a question that couldn't possibly be resolved then and there. It was his own need and desperation talking. "I think this," he said. "You should go on living in San Francisco until you know what you want. Maybe you'll find you want to come back here. Or you'll discover San Francisco is exactly where you want to be. You have to go on living as you wish. We'll accept whatever becomes clear to you and do the best we can."

"All right."

Debating where she should live the rest of her life, he thought, amazed, one day after they'd learned what they were facing. Just as they'd always discussed everything together—endlessly—every decision, large and small, practically from the time she could talk. Jesus, she must have been sick of it.

They spoke again that night right after Jahan had informed her that they hoped to administer between two and six weeks of radiation, depending on how well her counts handled it and whether the disease responded. She had signed papers that afternoon assigning Beth power of attorney.

"Beth knows my wishes best," she said.

"That makes sense."

"Naturally, she wouldn't do anything without consulting you."

"I know. Brett . . ."

Jocelyn, who had returned for the holiday that afternoon, took the phone, and Nathaniel went to a phone in another room.

"No," Jocelyn sobbed. "Not you. I need to be with you." Then she cried, "How long are you going to live for?"

"A long time" was Brett's answer, Jocelyn told them later.

Brett said she knew it was scary and horrible, but she wanted Jocelyn and the rest of the family to talk about her dying because it helped her. "It's hard, you know," Joce said, "talking about it for the first time."

He and Holly sat in the dining room listening to Jocelyn's end of the conversation, dumbstruck. Their three children on the phone together concerning the end of life. Brett's life.

At two in the morning he awoke again to the primal sound of his wife's tears. She was clutching him from behind. Her heart was like a fist rapidly knocking against his back.

Wounded animals, he thought.

. . .

Charles Linker reached him the next day. He was ninety percent sure Brett was experiencing a recurrence of Hodgkin's, he said, but they couldn't irradiate until they had clear evidence. They hoped the biopsies would provide that. If not, Brett might require surgery to establish the presence of disease.

"Would you say the transplant was worth it at this point?" he asked.

In Linker's view the transplant had given her the past several months, maybe more.

Worth it? he thought. There had been no choice. Brett couldn't have faced the end of her life knowing there was something more she could have done that might have made the difference. She couldn't have lived with that.

"You were all wonderful here this summer," Linker said. Everyone had done everything possible. Now her care would be largely a matter of troubleshooting. "We can't cure her, and so we won't administer therapy to attempt that. The goal is to maintain her life with as little pain as possible for as long as possible."

The unspoken speculation was deafening to him. He asked, "How long can she live?"

Linker hesitated as though he hadn't expected the question. "People in worse shape than Brett is have lived for more than a year. Time is difficult. There are too many unknowns. On the outside, Brett could live for a year. More likely six to nine months, but it's impossible to be precise."

He raised the question of where his daughter should be. Was access to a medical facility like UCSF necessary in order to provide her with the best quality of life?

"I don't see Brett packing her bags and leaving San Francisco," he said. The most important thing now wasn't the sophistication of the medical center but the person in charge of her care. "You can find wonderful doctors everywhere. On the other hand," Linker said, "there are oncologists at the best places in the world who are assholes."

He hastily walked out into the cold air as darkness was falling. Past the stone wall he turned up into the woods. Ben, animated by an unusual outing, bounded ahead into the black hemlocks. Six to nine months meant between June and September. How could this be? He hiked up to Fisher Meadow, walking hard, drawing the cold air sharply into his lungs, and continued another mile into Parker's woods before turning back. The moon was full; the sloping field of snow gleamed silvery. The old maples, gnarled, racked, enduring, stood like the souls of trees, he thought. That was a sentence from the novel he'd been working on since November. How could he maintain his interest in that undertaking—or any other—now that everything had changed? At the southwest corner of the Fisher pasture, as he was returning, the tree trunks were tall black columns, and in the amazing moonlight they cast their long shadows on the brilliant snow. He stopped. It was as though he had entered one of her miraculous charcoal drawings, stepped into her vision. This was the sort of night that belonged to her—the world with her name written on it.

Brett!

She's going to die. How could this be?

It was.

How would they do this? Who could tell them how you did this? His father's absence unexpectedly beset him. It seemed impossible that all this could happen—his daughter could die!—without his father's knowledge. To Brett it must have seemed impossible that her life could unravel—death could happen—*with* her parents' knowledge.

Holly was on the phone to her when he entered the bright kitchen. They'd failed to find Hodgkin's in the biopsy samples, Damon had told her. Surgery would be necessary to obtain concrete evidence of disease before radiation therapy could progress. She'd vomited the moment he left the room, Brett said. Was she to be subjected to more medical misery even now? She sounded more discouraged than ever before.

"We'll be there tomorrow," he told her. "Tomorrow."

Incensed, he called Linker's number and left a message on his voice mail, urging him, as commandingly as seemed effective, to intervene and allow radiation therapy without preliminary surgery.

It broke him up to tell other people about it for the first time, to say the words, as if by imparting what had always been out of the question he contributed to the unalterable reality of it. I don't know what to say, friends told him. If there's anything I can do. *Anything*. The day of their journey to San Francisco he seemed to observe the world—the highway landscape, the airport, the interior of the plane, other people—through a veil, obscured. He saw parts of people—the smile of the airline attendant, the hands of the waiter in a coffee shop—without seeing the whole person, as removed by grief as a terrorist was distanced by base intentions. The most mundane transactions, his ticket, his luggage, taxed his powers of concentration.

They rode into the familiar semitropical scene—green trees, profuse flowers, the warm sun—on a wave of sorrow. Brett's city. The drive from the airport—he and Holly looking out opposite windows of the shuttle, silent as prisoners—felt like penance. For what?

The apartment at 111 Buena Vista East wasn't available this holiday season, but he'd managed to locate a B and B on Delmar, just a couple of blocks above Central Avenue. When he called Brett's apartment, Eve answered. They were arranging Brett's art in a portfolio, she said. A spear in his side.

"We're on our way over."

They made the brief walk in silence. He was trying to imagine her, meeting her eyes. As for the first time. They climbed the steep single flight of steps to her door. Fluted pillars. The landing was a mosaic. *Now I have this wonderful apartment. . . .*

Unexpectedly, it was Brett who answered the door. She was supported by an aluminum cane.

Holly embraced her, and the emotion she'd been repressing this entire day of travel came to the surface. "My Brett."

She said, "Andy Leavitt just called. I'll just be a minute."

Eve had left the apartment before they got there, not wishing to be present at this moment between Brett and the parents, he assumed.

They stood in their daughter's room, now exclusively her studio, which connected to the bedroom she shared with Beth. The room hurt, like a vision of a lost world.

"I love Andy," Brett said, rejoining them. "He's going to snoop around, he said. He wants to meet me for lunch next week."

"Good."

"I know he'll always do his best," she said. "That's his nature."

Her dense new red hair, very much its original color, had grown in tight to her skull. Her Joan of Arc hair, she called it. In the aftermath of the transplant, her complexion was almost tawny, with numerous freckles, not unhealthy-looking but lacking her youthful pink freshness. She was dressed up for their arrival in new black corduroy pants and a jacketlike cranberry-red sweater. The bright running shoes on her feet, still like new, were untied. She moved about the apartment in evident discomfort, hobbling on the cane. Her weight had gone down, and the full-cut trousers hung off her hips. The cane startled him; no one had yet mentioned it.

"I almost have my portfolio done," she said. "I could finish it in five minutes." Clearly, she wanted to complete what she'd begun with Eve.

"All right, we'll go down the street for a few minutes. We'll be back soon."

On Haight Street, swarming this Friday before Christmas, they bought wine and cheese, and he browsed for books of poetry at The Booksmith. By the time they returned to the apartment, Beth was home from work. They sat in the living room, where small Christmas lights had been strung along the walls near the ceiling. Brett reclined on the couch as her pain, this pain they'd only heard about until now, steadily worsened.

"Linker told me there was a ninety percent certainty it was Hodgkin's," he said. "That leaves ten percent. There's still hope."

"There's always hope," Brett said. She was taking morphine and Dilaudid in alternating doses, orally. "The drugs make you calmer," she said. "Otherwise I'd be nervous."

They talked about Nathaniel and Jocelyn and her boyfriend, Michael, and about their plans for Christmas, holding down the fort in Conway. They went down the list of people, friends and relatives, who sent their love. The horrendous pain, which they could hardly imagine at a distance, continued to come down on her now, debilitating, paralyzing. She grimaced as he and Holly half carried her to the bedroom, where she hoped to be more comfortable. Seated around her on the bed, they hastily consumed the dinner of roast chicken and vegetables that Holly had thrown together.

"I hope I'll be free of pain so I can keep working," Brett said. She'd purchased a handsome portfolio, and now she slowly turned the large pages in silence while they looked at the remarkable number of new pieces she'd completed since leaving the hospital three months before. In recent days she'd been unable to function at all, and if she took enough medication to make the pain tolerable, she wasn't herself. "For Christmas I want a drafting table. And I want us to get a tree."

Tonight, although the new truth was implicit in everything they said, no one brought up the subject of death, of dying. The two young women talked excitedly about moving into the new apartment, their own place, as soon as Beth returned from Massachusetts. They'd already signed up plenty of friends to help. "It's going to be so great."

Toward nine, Beth said, "Go get some sleep. You both look exhausted."

He awoke in the small hours in the strange low-ceilinged room, frightened. Brett! She couldn't possibly go on this way, the pain worsening, drugged. Something had to be done. He reached for Holly. They lay awake without talking as the first gray daylight revealed the modest rented room. This year they'd wanted so much to be together, all together, in Conway, where they belonged. They lay there staring at the ceiling until they heard the strange sounds of people awakening above them: footsteps, a toilet, running water, a dog let out. Now, he thought, today. They'd do whatever was required of them. The thought of his daughter awakening, her consciousness this morning, jerked him upright.

B rett was dressed when they got to her apartment in the morning— the red sweater, black cords, Nikes—but any movement at all was difficult. The night she'd endured was legible in her eyes, the set of her mouth. Beth had gone to work worn out, she said. Holly, who needed to act, who wanted to be busy, went to the kitchen and immediately began concocting chicken soup with the canned broth and fresh vegetables they'd purchased at the grocery store on Frederick Street. He sat on the bed, where Brett was propped up against pillows, her legs stretched out in front of her. She smiled resignedly. Whatever defenses he'd mustered the day before went to pieces as he faced her this morning—*She's going to die*—and he felt pressure in his throat, heat coming into his face, his grief bursting. She shook her head, watching him, her lips compressed, resisting the impulse, then she gave way too.

"What are you thinking?" he asked.

"Everything I love is here." Her blue eyes, large in her face, had the look of suffering. "I don't want to leave."

They wept in each other's arms.

"I don't want to make you cry, Brett."

"I cry all the time." She added, "My sadness is so large. Sometimes I cry uncontrollably without any thoughts in my head at all. Your tears make me feel less alone."

"You aren't alone," he insisted. Then, "I can't protect you or help you."

"I thought the transplant would give me more time, just a little more time."

"You haven't had one break. You fought so hard," he told her. "You did everything they asked you to do. You were gallant."

"It's been a journey of losses. The loss of my body, my strong athletic body. The loss of trust. Now I feel like I'm losing my sense of self."

The profusion of tears amazed him, as if he'd tapped into some unsuspected reservoir within him. He said, "We can't cry all day."

"Yes, we can."

He talked about how young he was when she was born, all those years of his youth with a little girl, and the difference that had made to both of them, the extraordinary relationship they had forged, growing together, in a sense.

She nodded.

Outrageously, he was still young.

"Have I been a good father?" It wasn't a question that had been on his mind or that he'd thought to ask. It was his emotion talking.

"Do you feel you haven't been a good father?"

"No, but I don't know what you think."

"You're great, Dad," she told him.

That's not what he meant—to put her in that position, to elicit her approval.

"I wish I could know you longer," she said. "I'd like to see you get old."

Don't say such things. Please don't.

Holly entered the room and climbed onto the bed, and the three of them bawled, holding each other. They were the original family. The memory of two kids facing each other on Commonwealth Avenue as though stung by reality for the first time—I'm pregnant—was vivid to him.

"We didn't do everything right, but we always loved you completely."

Their daughter said, "I always felt lucky."

The intensity subsided, the phone rang, Holly returned to the kitchen.

Fearing she'd run short on Dilaudid if the acute pain struck again, she called 11 Long, as the clinic was closed on weekends, and arranged to have a prescription written by the attending doctor. Midafternoon he made the tryingly familiar hike to the medical center at the summit of Parnassus Street. Eleven Long, as he stepped into the silent gray corridor, with its odor of embattled illness, was like returning to a scene of unspeakable practices. They'd all carried on each day with steadfast resolve, as believing as members of a cult.

He was relieved that there was no one he knew well at the nurses' station. The doctor in charge this weekend was the one they'd had the least contact with during the summer. He wrote out a prescription in one of the small meeting rooms. "It's rare for Hodgkin's to get into the bone," he said, "but it can. It chews at the edge of the bone" was his way of putting it. "It's the worst pain. Tell her to use the drugs." He seemed confident that radiation therapy would eventually alleviate the pain. Handing him the slip of paper, the doctor said, "I'm sorry."

He returned to the apartment to find Brett writhing on her bed and Holly, in distress, bending over her. What they'd seen the day before had been only a glimpse of the pain that was visible now.

"It's like a saw. Worse than a marrow biopsy." She feared that it could last, as before, for hours. "It's too much for one person," she cried.

Mercifully, the acute pain passed within an hour, but the episode had penetrated her defenses and tumbled her into her bottomless sadness.

"I wanted to live in the country and have babies. A family. There's so much I wanted."

"I know."

Crying out, as from an arrow of deeper hurt, she said, "Beth will be alone. I don't want to leave Beth."

"You're never going to leave anyone." He held her. "When I think of you not being here, I don't want to live." He needed to talk. His wife's unhappiness seemed beyond words.

"You have to, Dad. People love you and need you."

Mary Burger had sent Brett an article from a reputable periodical about a woman who had inexplicably cured herself of HIV. "People do these things," her friend wrote. "I believe in you." Recalling Mary's letter, he said, "You must live every day as fully as possible and not give up."

"I never give up," she said. "I want to be . . . thirtysomething."

The three of them lay on the bed together until Beth came home from work. They wished the girlfriends a wonderful holiday dinner together—Beth was flying to Massachusetts the next day—and left.

More than other streets in the neighborhood, Masonic seemed to inspire in its residents a competitive show of exterior Christmas decorating, and the display made them miss home, the ritual of their own candlelit tree. Tomorrow he'd have to find a tree for Brett's apartment. Walking briskly uphill, they overtook two young women loaded down with bundles, animatedly talking and laughing, happy.

Holly shook her head. "She never just lived here," she said, in tears again. "She never enjoyed just being young here."

They went to the Ironwood Café on Cole Street, where they'd sometimes dined during the summer. This Saturday night the restaurant was busy and festive. The moment they returned to the room on Delmar the phone rang.

"Brett's pain returned twice," Beth said. "It was out of control. Torture. We're on 11 Long." Fortunately, Brett was admitted directly to the floor without going through emergency.

Brett came onto the phone. "Hi."

"Let them snow you under for the next day," he said. "You don't have to suffer. Hopefully there'll be relief on Monday with radiation."

Wearily she said, "They can't get the IV in."

All his hopes and anxieties had come to a single prayer: Don't let her suffer. Please don't suffer.

Whatever the ultimate outcome of the transplant, he'd assumed they'd put 11 Long behind them. It wasn't so. When they arrived at nine-thirty the next morning, Brett was in the throes of another siege of break-through pain that heavy doses of intravenous narcotics couldn't contain. Her face was tortured. She moaned, writhing, clutching her hip.

"I can't be in this pain," she wept. "I can't do this."

Holly held her head.

"Get someone in here," he told the three bewildered young residents who stood there, pointlessly, as if their job were to bravely face up to the distraught person on the bed. "Something has to be done."

Alarm quickened the features of the doctor's face the moment he entered the room. Brett's extremity, her twisting on the bed oblivious to his presence, was more than he had expected. He hustled the residents out of there.

There were three options, he said. Brett could receive radiation, but substantial marrow would be destroyed, requiring frequent blood transfusions that might necessitate indefinite hospitalization. Her white count might never come up again, leaving her vulnerable to dangerous infections. Steroids were a second possibility to reduce the tumor and alleviate the pain, but steroids raised the danger of inflaming her already fragile lungs. The third alternative was an intrathecal catheter placed in Brett's lower spine to administer morphine directly to the pain. That would require constant hospitalization, however, to maintain platelets sufficient to prevent bleeding and hematoma, leading to paralysis. In fact, paralysis was a significant risk.

Brett's pain, her visible agony, continued unabated while a nurse loaded her with morphine. She appeared to hardly follow what the doctor was saying, but when he was through sketching the alternatives, she said between her teeth, "It sounds like three different ways to die." She added, "I don't want the steroids started. It's my body." She'd already been through hell with her lungs.

They decided to wait until tomorrow, when Linker and others could put their heads together.

"I'm losing perspective," Brett said. Her eyes stared, dazed. "It's so tiring."

They were witnessing her destruction, he thought, as he and Holly helplessly sat there, leaning over her. Their daughter wasn't going to get any time, decent time. Everything had become more terrifying yet. She hadn't had a break since 1988. It was almost 1992.

Looking up from the knotted pillow, she cried angrily, "I don't want to suffer. I don't want to die in the hospital."

"You aren't going to be in the hospital," he said. "They'll come up with a plan."

"My options," she swore. "I want the option to die." She added, "I know you can't understand or accept that."

"I can understand," he said. "I love you. Whatever you want, I'll understand it."

Quietly, she said, "That means everything to me."

By one the awful pain had backed off. Brett remained alert. She needed red cells, the miserable routine of transfusions beginning again, hooked up to the damned IV pole. She had no accessible veins to speak of, and following the morning she'd been through, the insertion of the IV was another minor torment. "I can't do this anymore," she stated, squeezing his hand as the nurse probed.

"Who do you most want with you? Who gives you the most comfort?" he asked.

"Beth," she said. "We've done this together for years. I've watched her go from feeling weak and helpless to being strong and decisive."

He'd driven Beth to the airport at five-thirty that morning; she was just then en route to the East Coast. Brett hoped she'd have a good holiday.

Holly stretched out on the hospital bed with her daughter and stroked her hair. Relieved of pain, Brett looked calm, her complexion clear and smooth. He ran his hand over the top of her head, the close nap of new hair. *Steiff.*

"Your hair feels wonderful."

"I'm always doing that," she said. "I love the way it feels."

He and Holly walked from the hospital to Golden Gate Park. A lovely sunny Sunday afternoon. They were zombies from hell stepping into Shangri-la.

"I'm never going to be happy again," Holly said. "I just want to go away, far away. I feel outside life."

No words of encouragement came to him.

By that evening Brett was still relatively comfortable, but she could feel the pain returning. She was now receiving a constant IV dose of morphine per hour, and she had a pump that could deliver a bolus every ten minutes as needed. He began hitting the pump repeatedly to keep the encroaching pain at bay. Once the pain took hold, it had become clear, there was no penetrating it.

Now, at the end of this harrowing day, Brett was impressively relaxed as she sat in the hospital bed. "Beth will live to be ninety," she said, and the thought made her smile. "Her body is like a sapling. Her pulse is thirty. I don't feel it's my body anymore. It's had so much— again and again. I think of Than." Nathaniel. "He's so strong and loving." Touching her heart, she added, "My male self." She wanted her brother and sister to come out soon, she said.

Randomly, she began to recount memories of childhood while Holly lay on the bed with her and he sat in a chair nearby. Tidepools at Grindstone Neck in Maine. Zucker's Island, at the mouth of Corea Harbor, where she had to bring her violin to accompany the owner of the small island on his cello. The mossy woods of scrub pine and low bushes smelled like berries. She recalled rowing the heavy, rocking dory and the day her grandmother called the Coast Guard. Surprisingly, she then seized on her other grandparent's old place in Connecticut, sleeping in his boyhood room, descending the staircase in her pajamas on Christmas morning. She leapt ahead to their rambling eighteenth-century house in Hadley, the site really of her growing up—their fierce Saturday-afternoon soccer games on the common in the rejuvenating fall.

With sudden emotion she said, "I used to know where you were by the smell of your pipe. Then I'd run." Touching her thin thighs, atrophied now from lack of exercise, so changed, she said, "I used to run. I didn't realize how much my identity was connected with my strength. I feel like I've had several lives. Childhood was one life. And high school. The violin was another life. All the different things my body did—could do—then."

The awful pain was there, hovering, threatening.

"If only it wasn't pain," she said. "If they said I had cancer, but there wasn't pain, then I could just go do some things I want to do—that I have to do." She insisted, "I can't be in the hospital."

"They're going to get on top of the pain. You're not going to be in the hospital."

"I want you here when I get sick," she said. "I don't know when."

How would they do this? he thought. The doctor they'd seen that morning had told him he didn't think their daughter had six months to live.

"We'll be here whenever you want us with you," Holly said.

By ten, with his wife tucked into the portable bed and his daughter's condition apparently stable, he left, reminding Brett's nurse to continue hitting the morphine pump regularly.

My *sadness is so large.*
It's too much for one person.

. . .

He let himself into the apartment on Central Avenue and turned off the recently installed alarm system as Brett had instructed him. They would stay at her place while Beth and the roommates were away. The long hallway of the apartment was dark and cold: the place felt lonely, haunted, the forsaken setting of disappointed hopes.

Everything I love is here.

He took a beer from the refrigerator and sat at Brett's large white desk, crowded with photos, postcards, papers, small objects, signs and symbols of her inner life. He took a black sketch pad from one of the shelves underneath. He didn't know whether the book contained sketches, plans for drawings, or words. It was a journal of the months preceding the transplant, the spring of 1991. He shouldn't do this, he knew; opening the book felt wrong. Yet he might never know what her journals expressed, and he wanted to know everything he could know, hungry for insights into her heart and mind. He couldn't bring himself to begin at the beginning, however, as though such a frontal assault on her privacy would be more shameless than a casual riffling through. As much as he wanted to know *everything,* he was also afraid to face his daughter's naked, most personal pain. He browsed, leafing from back to front, his thumb releasing several pages at a time. The journal was almost exclusively preoccupied with cancer, death, and dying. A cry of unrelieved anguish, which spoke of the unbearable fevers, the inevitable approach of disease again. Terror. There was her anger at Leavitt for not telling her right away. There was her frustration with the persistent back pain that everyone refused to acknowledge for what it turned out to be. His daughter's prose was passionate, tough, alive with her sorrow and foreboding. She spoke of Eve's long hair sticking to her cheeks as they cried. There were poetic passages, which made her ask, "Why do I write this sentimental bullshit? Because it's there." She spoke of suicide, an option that she'd raised with both Beth and her therapist but that she'd never mentioned to anyone in her family. S.J. had told her, "Our business is to keep you alive." Her suffering was no surprise, but the raw measure of her pain and her unblinking expression of it shocked him. Once she knew what was ahead that spring, his daughter wrote, "I'll go through the transplant, and come out and die." He didn't believe she'd submitted to that ordeal with so little hope. The pages were scrawled, the writing furiously hurried, fueled by rampant feelings, a spontaneous unburdening.

Flipping through, overcome by his daughter's anguish all over again, he read, "He is insufferable. I don't want to see my father. Today he drank some chalky stuff for tests and talked about being dehumanized. . . . He says he has back pain like mine all the time. He doesn't know what pain is. How could such an idiot comfort me? I give up." Another passage a few pages along: "I want to yell at my father. His sickening pep rallies. He never wants anyone to teach, he'll never hear me. . . . He'll never understand anything." Now he was alert to references to himself. "He's always narrating his story and never living." He read, "I don't want to see my parents. I'm sick of their stupid voices."

The notebook ended with two pages written after she'd left the transplant ward in September. She summarized the awful sequence of major events in the most general terms; she referred to Beth and to her brother and sister. There was no mention of her parents. To a stranger coming upon the passage it would have seemed the parents, who had been present day and night, had not been there at all.

But the tale of *his* trip to the hospital for a GI series was intended to make her laugh, he thought defensively. When he spoke of *his* chronic back pain, he meant to encourage her to believe that her back pain was an ordinary ailment, not cancer. Yet the distance he'd felt between them the preceding spring was clearer now. While they desperately wanted to believe the cancer was over, their daughter knew it wasn't, and their persistent encouragement, separating them from her anguish, had left her that much more alone. A journey of losses. The parents she'd relied on—they were lost to her, too. Struggling to comfort and reassure her, he'd failed repeatedly, as though abandoning her. We fail, he thought, and can't help failing, despite our pain, our love, despite our determination not to fail. He imagined her getting off the phone with him, outraged by some inadvertent stupidity of his, disillusioned, and also terrified. In her greatest need, her parents had become a burden. *Their stupid voices.* He was hurt by her rebuke, bewildered at first, but perhaps he understood. That night, lying on her bed, he didn't sleep.

He arrived at the hospital, relieving Holly, at nine, eager to speak to Linker. Brett slept the morning away, still heavily sedated, while he wrote in *his* journal—a five-by-seven-inch spiral notebook he'd packed for the trip. She was awake, witty, and amusing when Mary Burger called from Massachusetts in the afternoon. "I'm sitting here in my UCSF evening wear," she said. Later, she became upset briefly, then explained, "I forgot that Beth wasn't here." Linker finally turned up at two-thirty.

Brett had had her IV narcotics turned off for hours so she'd be wide awake for the discussion. Calmly and intelligently, she answered his questions concerning the weekend, succinctly describing her symptoms. Mary Cranley, off duty today, had come by to visit and was seated in a chair by the window.

They'd decided to address Brett's hip pain with radiation and steroids, Linker informed them. He wasn't worried about her lungs. The goal was to alleviate the pain and get Brett out of the hospital.

"Following radiation," he said, "you'll probably have to come to the clinic twice a week for transfusions." That seemed fairly acceptable, didn't it?

Brett was sitting up in bed, facing him. Struggling to repress her emotion—here was the question no one was expected to utter—she asked, "How long will the radiation give me?"

Linker responded as though Brett were questioning the value of radiation. He was convinced the therapy would enhance her quality of life, et cetera. "You're not dying right now. There's nothing immediately life-threatening going on." Then he told her, "Optimistically, a year. It could be six to nine months."

Brett broke down, and impulsively, mindlessly, as he would have rushed to forestall the tears of a small child who'd taken a minor fall, he said, "Don't cry!"

"What if someone just told you that?"

"I'd be devastated," he said. "I'm frightened."

Surely she'd imagined more time, or she'd imagined the timetable was less definite, less clear, leaving room for the unexpected, for luck. *I want to live to be thirtysomething.*

As he bent over his daughter, holding her, Linker placed a hand on his back. "I'd like to see if we can get started on the radiation today," he said, and withdrew.

While Mary was with her, he wanted to return to the apartment for Holly. On the sidewalk, walking rapidly, oblivious to the people around him, he wept.

At four they went down to radiation. Down, he thought. She'd been here before. Even now, it wasn't over. Looking lost, his daughter sat in the wheelchair waiting for the next assault, trapped in this hospital, this process, this pain, this body. She vomited into a plastic basin in her lap, repelled. In the next moment, she was composed again. "I was suddenly overwhelmed," she explained.

She had to lie perfectly still on the radiation table while they marked her body, outlining the field of radiation, and the technician set up her case on the computer. This seemed interminable. Brett was stoic. He and Holly watched her on a black-and-white monitor in the computer room as she lay flat on her back, alone in the blank room, awaiting the treatment. Her beautiful body, he thought.

The radiation oncologist pointed out the area in Brett's right hip that they would focus on. Her pain was caused by swelling within the bone and by disease invading the bone from the inside. The sciatic nerve also appeared to be involved. The danger was that the bone could fracture, causing increased pain and bleeding, and that made radiation all the more imperative.

In the evening the three of them lay on the hospital bed together, holding hands.

"You come for Christmas and I'm in the hospital," Brett said.

For the time being, the pain appeared under control and Brett was calm. Her nurse tonight, Irene, was also a friend. "Do you think you'll be okay if we go get some sleep?" he asked. It was ten o'clock.

"Of course," Brett said.

He was awakened by the phone only an hour later.

"Dad, I'm having a bad time."

"Do you want me to pull my pants on and get over there?"

"Yes."

Within fifteen minutes he reached her room, and Irene, who'd been with her, quietly exited. He took her in his arms and her grief came in a torrent, her body shuddering with sobs.

"Everything is lost ... I want Beth. I want to be with Beth ... I want to live in the country and have babies and a house ... I want to do my work. I want to live."

They held each other. He was afraid, he told her. How? he thought. How would they do this?

At last he said, "The goal is peace. You need to discover the way to do this. You will. We all have to learn how to do this." That sounded absurd—peace?—and yet how was she to go on in the time that was left?

"Eve believes your soul joins other souls, so you aren't alone." His daughter didn't have the consolation of such a belief. "I feel so alone. It's not the terminal prognosis," she said, "it's the number that hurts me. One year. I feel I'm shrinking. Everything is being taken. I feel such panic," she said, "like I'm not going to get time for anything. I need time."

Somehow they had to get beyond the panic. "I don't know how you do that, but that has to happen." Maybe there was a place . . .

"I can go there in my room," she said, "when I play music and draw. It would be more possible if there wasn't pain." After a moment she asked, "What would you do?"

He couldn't answer that. He imagined he'd go on living day to day just as he did then—doing his work. He believed her work, too, was a source of strength. One could be transported, absorbed.

"I know. I need to make things." Her vehement sadness welled up again. "There always used to be hope, a future. I could do what I needed to do because I was going to live."

He had no sense of the passage of time as they lay on the bed in partial darkness. As before, when the storm of their emotion abated, they entered a calm that hadn't seemed possible moments before. And it was as though the hospital room had disappeared; they were in a private chamber where any confidings were possible, where honesty was possible.

"For the past two years or so I know you've been angry—with me. It was obvious. I can imagine why, but I want to know."

"It's not too complicated." It had to do with dependency, she said. She'd always gotten the message that she needed to be more independent, but the dependency wasn't only hers. She was a kid, trapped in her parents' dependency. She needed them, but they, too, were unwilling to let go. They needed her to represent them, in a way. They were mutually dependent, but hers was the imperiled self.

"You always tried to make everything all right by knowing the answers," she told him, "explaining everything, being in control. And you kept doing that concerning my illness. You became more determined as you became more afraid. I'd come to this pain and grief, which you weren't acknowledging." Instead of just listening and telling her that he didn't know what she was going through or that he was sad, he'd pile words against her reality. "When I tried to say how terrified and stricken I felt, you'd say, I know exactly what you mean. And that made me invisible. Like my suffering wasn't just mine. But of course it was. I didn't need pep rallies. I needed compassion, silence. Why didn't you just cry on the phone?" She added, "But I've never rejected you or Mom. I've never stopped caring about you."

"We were so young," he said. "We didn't know anything. We wanted you to have everything. We were afraid to let you make a mistake, we were so anxious for you to succeed." As though they'd known what that, success, might represent.

"Cancer helped you see me as a separate person."

Could that possibly be true? He felt more connected to her than ever. He said, "You'll have to forgive me for who I am." We don't know what we're doing, he meant, even while we believe we're doing the best we can. We live in the dark.

"Of course I forgive you," she said.

They came back to where they'd begun hours before. They had to learn how to face what was before them, how to arrive at some peace. "If anyone can do it," he said, "you can. You have the resources, the inner life, you have the strength to do that."

She said, "I know."

Unable to locate a small tree, they settled for a balsam garland. But when they returned to the hospital with it in the afternoon, bearing, as well, a poinsettia that a friend had sent to the apartment and several small gifts, the pain, like a nightmare revisited, like a murderous intruder who wasn't gone after all, was beginning. Within ten minutes it became unendurable. Their daughter twisted on her bed, suppressing cries between her clenched teeth, kneading her pillow as if a torturer . . .

He sought Charles Linker in a nearby room, and Linker, with one glance at Brett's distress, raced to find Lin, Brett's nurse that day.

"I don't understand it," the doctor said in the hallway outside the room. "I don't know what's going on. We were congratulating ourselves about solving the hip problem."

"She can't go on like this," he said. "The other day she said she wanted the option to die."

That wasn't an option, Linker said; the law prevented that from being an option.

"Yesterday, for the first time, she was feeling well enough to begin thinking about her death."

Linker saw no recourse except to continue radiation.

Lin, who had been important to Brett during the transplant, had wide experience in the world, not just on the cancer ward. She'd been married once but now lived with a woman. She was a Buddhist. To them she had the energy and generosity of a Mother Teresa, and they felt an added measure of reassurance whenever she was on the floor. She loved Brett, she said, and she was prepared to take charge of her predicament. Pain used the drugs, she explained, and with Brett's pain there was practically no risk associated with dosages that most doctors were reluctant to authorize. By the time he returned to his daughter's room, the morphine Lin had given her had worked. Linker seemed to recognize Lin's significance on the floor.

They made a large wreath of the evergreen garland and hung it on the wall opposite the bed, then strung small white Christmas lights around the perimeter of the room, transforming the cool, antiseptic space. It was Christmas Eve. For their dinner he went out for Chinese food, which they ate hungrily in the modestly festive hospital room, the three of them quietly at home, relieved that the pain had stopped. He gave Brett one of the books he'd picked up on Haight Street, an early Christmas present, and he watched her as she turned the pages thoughtfully.

When Holly, speaking with Jocelyn on the phone, said, "No, it's not a happy Christmas this year," Brett indignantly corrected her from her bed. "I'm happy," she said emphatically. At that moment, free of pain.

He and Holly slept in reclining chairs lined up against the wall at the foot of Brett's bed.

Brett said, "We're like boat people."

. . .

Their morning in the room was warm and pleasant. There were gifts for Brett. A friend of Mary Burger's came by, and he and Holly left the hospital in the afternoon to walk through a residential neighborhood they'd discovered during the summer and then down to the park, which was very quiet today. Brett remained well all afternoon, and her mood, listening to music, sociably shooting the breeze, was cheerful. She began the transition from IV to oral pain medication, in the hope of leaving the hospital by Friday, the day after next.

Beth called that evening. "Do you miss me?" Brett asked her. Then, "What do you miss about me?"

That phrase was like a bell tolling. The thought he'd resisted all day, in so many words, came down on him: Brett's last Christmas.

He and Holly spent the morning shopping for the new apartment, looking through old furniture places for almost anything interesting. The search seemed futile, desperate, until they finally came upon a set of four English oak chairs at an antique shop on Waller Street.

When they got to the hospital, Brett had just finished radiation. They described what they'd found that morning, which led to more talk about the proposed move.

"It depresses me to talk about this." After a pause, she said, "I'm going to die."

"Brett." Her mother moved to the bed, reaching for her.

"I feel I have everything to do all at once."

"You can't do everything all at once."

"I know." In the next moment she had collected herself. "I'm going to love the apartment. I think I've had a lot, you know, but I've never had a home. My own."

She'd been free from pain since the day before Christmas, and they'd begun to believe the acute episodes were over, the combination of steroids and radiation having reduced the tumor. Brett had made the transition to an oral, time-released morphine. When she was awakened by pain in the middle of the night, she promptly took a large dose of a backup drug. The pain continued. Inspired by Lin's example, Mary Cranley injected sixty milligrams of morphine, Brett's allotment for four hours. The pain intensified. An additional twenty milligrams didn't touch it. Within an hour Brett was in agony; she was being smothered.

"I can't do this," she cried.

He and Holly, who had stayed the night again, hovered helplessly, trying to comfort her, waiting for the narcotic to take effect.

"My body's not big enough for this pain," she said. "I can't hold it." She moaned, stuffing the pillow into her mouth, her young face tormented.

Another hour passed.

"What is this?" she cried. "This is a hospital. I can't be in this kind of pain." She felt her hip would explode; it was on fire. Why was there no blood? "No one knows," she said. "No one knows."

Mary continued to administer morphine.

Hours passed without relief. Hours. Brett struggled like a deranged person to adjust her position, but could find no way to lie there. By daylight she despaired of her body, of medication's ability to control the pain. Her haunted eyes raced over the ceiling as if seeking an answer. "It's not working," she cried. "It's not working." She asked for the phone; she gave him a number and told him to dial it. Brett herself spoke to S.J., a succinct appeal. "She's on her way over," she said.

A sturdy woman in her forties with dark hair soon arrived, entering the room with authority. Brett described her therapist as a guide who helped her face questions and fears she was reluctant to express. S.J. could be there for her in a total way, she explained, without judgments or expectations, because she had no other relationship to her except in that moment. The woman promptly seated herself at the head of Brett's bed and took her hand. Speaking quietly, close to her face, she focused on taking Brett away from the pain, transporting her elsewhere, and Brett began to respond, filling in the details—a ship, the sea, phosphorescence, stars. Beth was there.

S.J. glanced up at them. "She has such a beautiful mind," she said.

Holly retreated to the corridor and wept on Lin's shoulder.

Gradually, the intensity of the pain lifted. They had been part of her suffering, he conjectured, unable to arrive from the outside as the therapist had done. It was Brett who knew what might help, who had rescued herself through S.J. They'd assumed that pain management had become an almost perfected art, that there was always some solution for pain in the controlled environment of a modern medical facility. They'd believed, with Lin and Charles Linker, that Brett had turned a corner and would be able to leave the hospital that day. Now she was on IV morphine again; she wasn't going anywhere.

S.J. stroked her hair. Heavily sedated, Brett lay on the bed like a person washed up on the shore.

"Thank you all for being here," she said. Soon she was sleeping.

When a nurse arrived midmorning with her container of pills, Brett, almost in a stupor, roused herself to take them. She didn't want to fall behind for the day. She got herself into the wheelchair to go down for her radiation treatment, which still offered the only hope of eventual relief.

"I've been coming here so long," she said, descending the ramp to the hospital's lowest level, the flimsy blue-and-white bathrobe over the wretched blue-and-white johnny, the thin synthetic slippers on her feet.

Stoically, with help, she eased herself onto the radiation table, and then they left her alone in the austere room with its high-tech apparatus.

"Today's episode of pain suggests a fracture has occurred," the radiation oncologist said. "Ordinarily, we would pin it, but we can't in Brett's case, because of low platelets. If that's what has happened, she won't get relief until the bone heals." That afternoon she'd have to submit to the arduous discomfort of a hip X-ray.

"If there is a fracture, her doctors are responsible for her suffering," he told the man. "They could have acted sooner."

When he reached out to smooth the deep vertical crease that rose from the inside of her right eyebrow, Brett said, "I want my face to show what I've been through."

Jocelyn and Nathaniel arrived from Massachusetts, and he and Holly backed off for a while. He would never know what transpired between the three of them as they faced one another, as for the first time, in the hospital room.

In the hallway he asked Lin, "Can Beth handle this?"

"It should be possible." She took his arm. "I understand. You're in an awful place. Brett is an adult, but she's also your child, and she's dying." The Buddhist cancer nurse gave him a long, strong hug, holding him hard against her enormous bosom.

Their movie in the hospital room that evening was *Truth or Dare,* Madonna on tour, and he was anxious that this show would trouble Brett, who was wild on the dance floor, loved nothing better than a night of dancing. She might not dance again. But when the movie ended, she announced, "I've had a very good day."

Nathaniel had been fighting a cold since he'd arrived in San Francisco, but it had finally leveled him, more like the flu, in fact, and so he was confined to Brett's apartment. Holly and Jocelyn dressed up as much as possible, and the three of them went to dinner at the Ironwood Café, which was filled to capacity, festive, the hostess boldly glamorous, he thought, with her bare shoulders. They raised a toast because what else could you do? Nathaniel sick in the strange apartment. Brett on 11 Long. He didn't know what to think. It was New Year's Eve.

192

He stayed with Brett that night. She awakened disturbed by a dream in which she was thrown from a roller coaster; the clicking sound of her IV monitor was like a roller coaster being hoisted to its launch. In the dream she was more like a *thing,* she explained, than a person—that's what was so frightening. He held her. Later, she was startled awake by yet another bad dream, her body like a tool, she said, a thing. Thankfully, the pain, the literal pain, didn't happen.

The first of January he and Holly went with Beth, who had returned to the Coast toward dawn, to look at the new apartment on Liberty Street. They wished to appear positive and upbeat about the prospect, this new beginning, but the sadness kept breaking in.

That evening, joining them for dinner, Beth put her face in her hands and wept. Earlier Brett had shared with her Linker's view of how much time she had to live.

"It's so hard to know what to do," Beth said.

You can't ever be alone," he said. "We can be here in a day, at a moment's notice. For now the hope is that you'll be able to pursue your life as you choose, that you'll have some time."

"I think I will, don't you?"

Nausea replaced pain as the major problem—Brett was swallowing too many drugs—and she began to question the move that she and Beth had planned.

"Before, it was *we* who were moving," she told him. "There was the shared excitement of fixing the place up, all that. But now I can't help. It will all be on Beth, and she can't do it alone. I wanted it so much, our own place, but . . ." So much had escalated out of control in the past week.

He'd been unable to imagine her living on, mortally ill, with two other roommates in the apartment on Central Avenue. That had been tolerable the preceding year, when the cancer was presumed over. Now, though, a move seemed even less possible than staying put. He agreed, more relieved than he let her see, that it would be pointlessly stressful to adapt to a new place. Her priority was to gain strength. Yet he knew giving up the apartment on Liberty meant giving up a last temporary hope. Under impossible circumstances, his daughter's good sense, the inescapable sense of responsibility that had always burdened her, prevailed. She saw the truth of the matter: the timing was wrong.

Beth was initially hurt by the decision, Brett reported after speaking to her, but it was the right decision, she said, for now.

The orthopedic people concluded that Brett's hip had not been fractured; she would be able to walk as soon as she regained confidence. Linker, determined to get her out of the hospital, began tapering Brett's medication to relieve her nausea.

Jocelyn and Nathaniel—he spent a final hour with his sister wearing a face mask—left San Francisco on Friday. Brett was scheduled to leave the hospital on Saturday, which was when he and Holly were flying back to Massachusetts. They spent that evening with her, of course, but it hadn't been a good day—the nausea persisting—and saying good-bye was that much more wrenching. The hope was that she would be able to visit Conway soon. They would talk tomorrow.

This time they shared the airport shuttle with two women who were off to Vail, toting their skis. Their excitement, their sane, good-natured enthusiasm for their upcoming adventure, seemed like madness.

He turned to the last pages of his notebook, to Holly's distinctive handwriting, so much neater, so much more legible, than his own.

Alone in Brett's apartment, Holly had dared to open one of her daughter's journals, surely in the same spirit he had—to be close to her, to know whatever could be known. The journal she had chosen was a pocket-size book of black leather with an opalescent stone set into the cover, a volume that one might be reluctant to put to everyday use, as if everyday thoughts and feelings hardly merited such a fancy binding. In fact, Brett had purchased the journal years before while vacationing on Cape Cod, he remembered, a special gift to herself, but she'd never written in it until that fall. The small book contained one long passage, dated November 26. Holly copied it onto the last two pages of his spiral notebook, which he'd left that day on his daughter's desk:

> I have been afraid to write, to be taken into the unsayable fears and memories and try to give it words or completion when there is none. As if by ceasing to record, I had somehow disappeared, died. I am falling into a loneliness and grieving I have not felt yet. It goes on and on in me. It has possessed me. I am haunted by images of death, of the way I will go, of people's lives going on without me. Horrible thoughts come over me suddenly and I have to struggle with them ... being put to sleep before surgery—that frightening spinning-away feeling and the faint voices still. I watch Beth as if she were alone a year from now (whenever) and that she continues. Crying only makes me cry more. I am a mess of angry, frustrated confusion. I want to tell Beth to leave me. I fade out, give up, let go. I have no orientation to the future, no desire, no door out of the cage. I wait cold still. I stare at things without seeing them. Sometimes crying feels like washing away, cleansing, when Beth holds me and I am pressed into her dark healthy body. I want to stay there forever, a kind of shelter, a way to survive. "In a dream you found a way to survive and you were full of joy." Last two nights shaking chills, freezing in a

cocoon of blankets, and then fever. My body is shriveling, empty, weak. It does nothing for me except misery and scares. "Do you think you're going to die?" S.J. says. "Yes." I need an exorcism. It is eating my sense of self. Nothing is left that I was, that I was proud of. Beth asks if I'm just going to sit around and wait to die. I have already died. I am afraid of relationships, of having things, of any kind of wish. I don't know where we go after death. It seems lonely without anyone you love there. I don't tell any of this to my parents. They will not tolerate despair, the pain that splits every thought into dark and light, the pain in my lungs and back and legs making me curl up, wince, limp. Night is a minefield. Rolling around, trying not to wake Beth, bone-sore, icy, burying myself under the blankets. Mary calls. "Hold on." My voice is different and so is hers. Quieter, careful again. I am losing, I am losing a friend, I am losing myself. I don't know where to look for help. I don't know how to endure the day. I am afraid to go outside into the windy blue day—to see what I might leave. What has happened? No passion, just bruises and headaches and this sadness like a world beneath my chin. All I know how to do is cry and not cry, cough and shake and not believe and crumble. S.J. tries to tell me these are just thoughts and that I can be equally affected by good thoughts. Where am I? In my head? I am alone and on fire.

"Why did you copy it down?"
"I wanted to keep it. I wanted her words."
November 26 was that Tuesday, two days before Thanksgiving, when Brett had first revealed to them the onset of fever.

7

HOME

Her third day back in the world Brett booked a flight to the East Coast for the following week despite her debilitated condition.

"So soon?" he asked.

"Yes." Knowing that the disease in her marrow could turn up with awful consequences elsewhere in her bones reinforced a general sense of urgency.

She and Beth also made arrangements to fly to paradise, in this case Kauai, the first week of February. Given the suffering a day could contain, February seemed far off. On Friday night Brett staged a romantic surprise for her girlfriend—a meal in a fancy restaurant, followed by an overnight on a houseboat. And Saturday, January 11, they threw a dinner party for her closest friends. When he phoned her that night, Eve and Ellen had just arrived and she sounded excited in an altogether "normal" way, which was wonderful, he thought, but the eagerness in her voice on this occasion—her twenty-seventh birthday—also hurt.

She called the following evening with her flight schedule.

"How was your party?"

"It was good. I became emotional when they sang 'Happy Birthday.' But I took one of S.J.'s suggestions. I asked everyone to tell me how they would remember me. Everyone was a mess."

"I can imagine."

Beth later described Brett's candor that evening. "This is probably my last birthday," she had told her friends.

On Tuesday she missed her flight because she was so damn sick. Hoping to alleviate her nausea, she'd dropped the morphine tablets for a patch, thinking the patch, as one doctor had suggested, would prevent withdrawal symptoms. But he'd been wrong, and what she was experiencing—intense cramping, burning diarrhea, general misery—was classic withdrawal. At risk for dehydration, she had to go back on the pills immediately. But there was a positive development. The roommates who rented the two smaller bedrooms in the apartment were leaving the first of the month and Ellen was moving in, so the place was going to feel like their own home after all.

The following day, back on pills, she rebooked her flight for Thursday, anxious she might not get back to Massachusetts at all if she didn't do it now.

"We'll fatten you up when you get here," he said.

"Yeah, I have to fit into my bathing suit for Hawaii."

Beth called early the next afternoon. "Brett's on the plane!"

She was the last to exit the aircraft at Bradley International—by wheelchair. That measure emphasized the dire contrast between this and the many hopeful homecomings there had been. The brown leather jacket was still like new; black corduroy pants, black suede shoes, her black beret. She was smiling.

"Hi."

An arctic air mass had invaded New England, so they'd brought a down jacket for her, a wool ski hat, wool mittens. They—the whole family was there—bundled her up and hustled her through the terminal to the car as if clandestinely ushering an escaped hostage to safety.

For all her transformations in the course of cancer treatment, Brett had never looked so thin and wan, so unwell, as she did now, following weeks of pain and sickness. Always altogether bigger and stronger than Jocelyn or her mother, she weighed less than either of them. Her lightness startled him when he lifted her in his arms, sweeping her off her feet, a lark, as she stood in the kitchen.

Brett's first night back, Richard Shaw came out to Conway, Nathaniel and Jocelyn and Michael were there, and the mood was upbeat, fun. After dinner, though, she sat in the black Windsor chair by the kitchen table as though the wind had been knocked out of her.

"I wish Beth was here, too. We've had such a hard time. Seeing Joce and Michael happy together, I wish we could be like that. We can't, and we won't be." She added, "I just get sad, I guess, when everyone talks about their plans."

Plans were almost exclusively what they'd been talking about all evening. Her sister's aspirations in New York City, her brother's intention to subsist off the land in some northern territory. The idea of everyone's life going on . . . without her.

He leaned toward her across the table. "What's going on now is living, not dying." She had to go on living.

"I know," she said, "but it's so hard."

That night she slept with Michael and Jocelyn until the man was forced out of the bed. No room.

Mary Burger visited for three days during the severe cold snap, and Brett's recuperation continued steadily. The two friends spent hours, day and night, before the massive Rumford hearth in the living room, talking and reading aloud to each other or stretched out on the floor as close to the fire as possible, as though they worshiped its vital warmth, the flames alive against the blackened back wall, playing over the timbered ceiling. After dinner, as they cleaned up the kitchen, old rock and roll—Dylan, Neil Young, Joan Armatrading, the Stones,

Aretha Franklin—resounded on their hill. One afternoon Brett and Mary drove to Northampton for a hot tub, and the last morning of Mary's visit they went to the valley for breakfast. Brett had been free of both pain and nausea for days. On the phone to her grandmother, laughing, she said, "I think I'm in remission."

One morning she visited Albey Reiner, whose Biology of Cancer course she'd taken as a student. It was a reassuring meeting. In Reiner's view she'd done all the "body work" she possibly could. Alternative therapies were out of the question. For Brett the most important avenues to pursue now were spiritual and psychological. He'd been involved with cancer patients for sixteen years, Reiner told her, and he'd witnessed so-called miracles—the inexplicable. The valley, he said, was a healing place. His calm and openness were comforting. She had begun to question the importance of remaining in San Francisco. Her meeting with Reiner made her feel she might be better off here, after all.

"It's so hard to decide," she said. Where to die.

That night he was awakened by disturbing sounds. Had Brett plunged into a bad moment? A nightmare? But it was the sound of laughter, not tears—the two sisters in bed together, talking and carrying on as in their more innocent, carefree life.

These were the days, one year before, when his father had been dying. That seemed like yesterday, and it also seemed long ago, so much had happened in between. The anniversary pointed up the failure all around; he didn't know if his father had died before or after midnight, the twenty-third of January or the twenty-fourth.

Brett said, "I had the notion that there could only be one death in the family right now, that he'd gone in my place."

He understood what she meant. He'd accepted the loss of his father, willingly accepted it, while it seemed his daughter would be spared.

. . .

The day she was scheduled to return to San Francisco, Brett decided to extend her stay another week. She didn't want to return until the two roommates had moved out, for one thing. And she was feeling so well, relatively speaking, she didn't want it to end. The weather grew milder and she ventured outside, climbing their uphill drive despite her ragged, persistent cough. She drove to the valley for groceries and other errands with her brother and sister or her mother. There were inspiring fires each night. Richard came out to read aloud with her and to administer expert massages. She spent long days in her mother's studio, laboring over new drawings in charcoal.

He and Holly were just finishing their meal in a Northampton restaurant when Brett and Mary, quite by chance, swept into the place, laughing, like a blast of fresh air. Her friend had driven out from Boston to be with her this last night of her visit. Dressed up for the evening, Brett approached their table absolutely beaming.

"Fancy meeting you here," she said.

Glimpsing her in the world, the sound of her occasional laughter as it carried to them across the room, felt like a blessing.

At midnight he heard her climb the stairs to the bathroom, racked with coughing. She must have just gotten home. A moment later she went back down to her room, still coughing, and closed the door. Exhausted, he imagined, making the most of the evening.

They were up at six-thirty to make her flight. Her stay here had exceeded everyone's expectations. She was returning stronger than seemed possible two weeks before.

"I wish I was just going to *visit* San Francisco," she said.

At the breakfast table she gave him a black-and-white charcoal drawing she'd done a few days earlier, a slightly belated present for his forty-eighth birthday. It depicted a small figure striding up a black hill under a dramatic wintry sky implying wind. Two disembodied hands were imposed over the dark hill, embracing the whole image of this figure in the landscape. Brett had written out part of a Mary Oliver poem on the back of the drawing:

> *I don't know exactly what a prayer is.*
> *I do know how to pay attention, how to fall down*
> *into the grass, how to kneel down in the grass,*
> *how to be idle and blessed, how to stroll through the fields,*
> *which is what I have been doing all day.*
> *Tell me, what else should I have done?*
> *Doesn't everything die at last, and too soon?*
> *Tell me, what is it you plan to do*
> *with your one wild and precious life?*

Below the poem she'd written, "I go through the fields with you always."

We're going to *paradise.*"

His fervent wish: Be all right! Forget everything else!

For ten days she didn't call, and they couldn't call her, because they didn't know where she was staying.

She sent a postcard inviting them to picture her and Beth "in rain ponchos, being sandwhipped and blown down this beach under hurricane skies and flying coconuts. We're as pale as ever (silk long underwear over bathing suits) and full of lichee nuts. . . . This is humpback mating season and the walls of this condo are very thin. . . ." As it turned out, the "garden island" was too much a tourist scene to suit Brett. No reality. She didn't recommend Hawaii. Their week happened to be cold, rainy, windy, only two days of sun, with heavy seas, but "it was our trip," she said. A temporary vision problem turned out to be caused by an antinausea patch she was wearing behind her ear. A bump in her chest, the only tactile evidence of Hodgkin's at present, caused temporary sadness on Kauai. As they talked, Ellen was moving into the apartment, which was great, but Brett felt a little awkward because, guess what, she'd decided to return to Massachusetts in April—spring in New England—and she knew Ellen was going to be bummed out to hear that. She'd already gotten into a miff with Beth, who couldn't quite grasp her wish to be closer to home. Anyway . . . there was a couch being stuffed through the door at that moment, she said excitedly. "We have oriental rugs now." It was Valentine's Day.

The next day, though, she sounded disheartened, and he knew that his conversation with her didn't help. "Now the official prognosis would seem to forgo hope, as if you could face what lies ahead without it," he wrote her.

> Our sense of hope has little to do with what happens, yet it is crucial to our well-being. If I feel hopeful today, it means the day is more possible, there's more light. I want to hope that it will be a good day for you and you will take it into tomorrow—that each day, rather than being frightened or discouraged, you will be hopeful for this and the next day, determined to live each day as fully as possible. . . . Panic comes from living in the unknown, the unknowable, instead of the day itself. You have been hurt and saddened when you hear people talking about their plans. No one lives in their plans, they only live in the day made more tolerable and full because of the plans it contains. Your day must also be enriched and enlivened by plans, but more graspable, immediate ones. . . . Taking control is a matter of doing what is possible hour by hour, day by day. . . . Each of us must continue doing what is possible in the face of what is beyond our control. The thing happening . . . I awake at night fearful that it is really so. . . . There can be hope and peace in the day, each day. We must strive for that.

He was reluctant to send the letter, concerned that its tone or language or sentiment would only exasperate her. *Insufferable!* His reluctance was something new, and it troubled him. Hoping to comfort and advise, he longed to be advised himself. Reassuringly, she called to thank him for the letter the day she received it. A blood transfusion had given her a pretty good lift. "Beth says I should have one every day." She'd just finished a piece of art for her brother. Tonight she was going out for a massage. She and Beth were planning a weekend in Mendocino with Eve. Oh, she'd told Ellen about her plan to return to Massachusetts, and Ellen understood. She'd do the same thing herself, Ellen said.

Afternoons in late February he and Holly drove to Northampton to check out apartments where their daughter and Beth might live. The task proved stressful, even depressing. Places that might have been more than adequate under ordinary circumstances wouldn't do now. They were seeking a space where the unimaginable could be lived, a place uniquely suited for impossible eventualities. Finally, on New South Street, in the Old School Commons, a school building that had been converted to apartments and condos within the last decade, they found a spacious, light-filled apartment of tall windows and ceilings, which faced east and south, with a view of the Holyoke range. There were trees out the windows, the distant view, the lively town at your fingertips; there were the peaceful grounds of Smith, with its lawns and gardens and its pond, a block away. Paradise Pond.

When she next called, frustrated by debilitating nausea, he was bluffly encouraging. She'd soon be back here, she'd get involved in the *healing* community. Recklessly he said, "It's not over until it's over."

"I know that, you asshole." A rough affection in her voice. She simply wanted to feel well enough to function. Throwing up was such a drag. "It's ruining my life," she said.

Another night, she sounded fine. "Good night, angel," she told him.

The years of long-distance phone calls—desperate, jubilant, anguished—were winding down.

. . .

San Francisco was the great adventure she'd gone to with Eve, the real beginning. *There's so much I wanted.* Her smart, funny, excited first postcards detailed lists of discoveries. The overwhelming discovery was cancer. Each year she embarked on the adventure anew, only to suffer another defeat. And now to leave, he thought, the disease, not her, prevailing.

Yet Brett sounded composed, even cheerful, these days when they talked.

She had her last meeting with S.J. Brett couldn't imagine her therapist not being there for her, she said, but S.J. told her she would be there in the end, no matter what.

On Friday she said good-bye to people at the clinic. "It was emotional. Terry's eyes welled up when he hugged me good-bye." Charles Linker told her she'd done the work, not him. He assured her that she'd be in good hands in New England, he wished her well, then he shook her hand—you know. As he was walking away, Brett went after him. "Give me a hug," she demanded. "Come here," he said, and he held her in a long, hard embrace—felt like minutes, she said, hard. The descent from the fifth floor in the elevator, the slate-floored entrance, the glass doors, the stairs, the food vendors at the curb, Long Hospital across the street. He could imagine. Good-bye to the world of her would-be cure. Once remote and intimidating, the famed clinic had also inspired hope and belief—until it gradually became all too familiar, hateful at times, dreaded, and finally of no further use to her. He could imagine: walking away after three years, descending Parnassus for the last time. Or could he?

When he called her on Sunday, the big 67 Central Avenue Tag Sale was in progress. It was raining there, so the sale was taking place in her large room. "We're selling *everything*," she said—her desk, her electric razor, coffee mugs, various clothes, everything they couldn't take or no longer wanted—for practically nothing. Selling off her life in San Francisco. Eve bought the bookcases and some of Brett's personal items. "I think she's building a shrine to me." Eve had been a little crazy lately, she said, dropping in unexpectedly to announce, "This is it!" Busy today, Brett sounded ... happy. "I'm in the public eye." She described the weird assortment of people, audible to him in the muffled background, coming in to look over their stuff. "You'd hate it," she told him. Mary Cranley had come by to help, and Amy, and Brett's childhood friend Lisa Bernard. By the end of the day, the wonderful apartment would be practically empty. Her good-bye with Andrew Leavitt was the only thing left to do. She'd made a charcoal drawing for him, she said, very much like the one she'd given her father for his birthday. "I'm sure I'll break down with Andy, too. Oh, well."

They met for two hours at Tasajhara, a bakery and coffee shop at the intersection of Cole and Parnassus. They talked about his work, she reported the next day, the frustrating rigidity of the medical community, the limitations of a system where a long-standing relationship with a patient could suddenly be severed. "He was sweet," she said. "He asked, How is it with you? Impossible to answer." He'd have her gift framed, he said. He didn't want to say good-bye, he told her, he'd write. They embraced, and then he was energetically off in his inimitable, bouncy sort of indomitable way, while she remained at the table in the window waiting for her friend Jean to give her a ride back to the apartment. He stopped and turned back to wave four times, she said, growing more distant each time, smaller, disappearing as he walked up Parnassus.

When they called her later that evening about her flight, she had a house full of people and was too distracted to talk. They were concocting a feast of Indian food. The last party. "You find out how many friends you have when you're leaving," she said.

They talked the next day to finalize various travel details. There would be a wheelchair at her connecting flight, he reminded her.

She was packed and ready, she said. "I want someone to take me for a last ride around San Francisco to see some of my favorite places."

Oh God, he thought. Boldly, if not ludicrously, he told her, "Say good-bye with a smile."

"I will."

"It's time to get out of there."

"Yup."

The night before, her friends had hoisted her over their heads on their upstretched arms, raising her to the ceiling, in farewell. "I felt so uplifted."

This is it! He and Holly were blown away by the sight of her walking into the airport terminal. Linen pants, the famous leather jacket over a silk blouse. The wholehearted smile.

"You look fantastic."

"It's the lipstick," Brett said.

She was thrilled with the apartment on New South Street, diagonally across the street from the enduring Academy of Music. She loved Northampton, her old town. Her high spirits her first day back—for good—surprised him. Now that she had tapered down on several drugs, her nausea at last seemed to have improved. She had some hip pain, elevated nodes in her lower abdomen, a lump in her chest, the ever-present dry, barking cough, but no crisis seemed imminent. She was doing as well as possible. The next morning, at the breakfast table in Conway, however, as though it had taken a day for the heartache to overtake her brave determination, she let her guard down. Her whole body hurt, her lungs were sore from coughing. "Some days I just feel sad." The late March sun imbued the room with shafts of light. He and Holly and Nathaniel came near her, mute, anxious. Once she composed herself, she said, "I cry once a day. It helps me."

"What's going on now? Do you think you're stable, or do you feel things worsening?"

"I feel things happening, I'm not as strong as I was in Kauai two months ago." Then, as if confiding the terrible truth, bereft, she said, "I can't believe I'm not going to get better."

In a moment he asked, "Is it more helpful to accept that or resist it?" How to be?

"No, I have to accept it—I can feel it happening. It's not a question of fighting to the end, like some people tell you, or of fully accepting, as Levine seems to say. It's always a combination of both things—each day you fight as hard as you can *and* you accept the reality. I've accepted it," she said. "That doesn't mean I'm not sad."

He'd recently finished reading Stephen Levine's *Who Dies?*, which Brett had recommended to him. In part, the book addressed the necessity of letting go of former ideas of self—the person defined by his or her career, possessions, physical beauty or strength, earthly goals and expectations—and opening to a more spacious awareness, a more basic relationship to life and death. It is our expectations of the way life is supposed to be, so often illusory, that are the source of so much suffering. If you are not this job, this dream, this body, who dies? Levine's quasi-mystical view struck him as easier said than done.

"The letting go Levine talks about," his daughter said, "of resistance, old models, concepts of self, isn't something you decide. It just happens because you know, because you have no choice. I never would have relinquished all I have, if . . ." She was letting go of the person she could no longer be.

"You've held on to more than you've let go of at this point," he said. But living had become profoundly moment to moment—that seemed clearer than ever.

She nodded. "You take each day and go through it."

"In a sense, everyone does the same thing, whether they realize it or not."

"I don't think about it all the time," she said.

Later that morning she blithely talked to her sister in New York

City. Richard came out for a walk in the afternoon. That evening, while the rest of them sat around the long table after dinner, Brett manned the stereo from the balcony overlooking the room, entertaining them with an ingenious stream-of-consciousness selection of favorite songs from years before. All the years.

She was more excited about meeting her new oncologist in Northampton, George Bowers, than someone anticipating a blind date. He and Holly had met him some weeks earlier, and Bowers had seemed somewhat short with them, typically busy perhaps, but he was youngish, in his forties, and he was the medical director for the area hospice program. Nothing glaring discouraged them about the man. Subsequently, he'd discussed Brett's case with her San Francisco doctors in preparation for her arrival.

While the Northampton hospital was bound to be a switch from UCSF, Brett's attitude was positive. It was the person now who mattered, not the facility. She didn't expect another Andrew Leavitt, just someone she could live with. "Is there a dirt floor?" she asked, smiling as she was leaving the house. "Let's go meet the guy."

When she returned, he saw she was trying to be cool, to conceal her feelings, but it was no good. Bowers had been abrupt, unwelcoming. Sitting back in his chair, forgoing any greeting, he had said, "What do you want me to do?" As if, instead of offering reassurance, the doctor expected the patient to take charge of her case. He wasn't interested in learning about her life, her medical history, or even her present condition. He knew all he needed to know. Coldly, it seemed to her, he asked, "What are you going to do if you wake up in pain?" Relating the visit to her parents, she became upset all over again. "He's going to be my doctor until I'm not here anymore." More than anything else, the man had seemed uptight and defensive. Ending the interview, he asked, "When do you want to see me again?" Brett said, "I shouldn't make that decision."

Their discussion was interrupted by Beth, calling from San Francisco. In a moment, Brett began hooting and hollering on the phone. "Do you realize?" she cried happily. Beth had just gotten notification that Brett was to receive over five thousand dollars in retroactive Supplemental Security Income. Until her hospice social worker had clued her in, she had never thought to file an SSI claim. The whole headache over George Bowers evaporated.

If Brett couldn't improve Bowers, they decided, she could always find another doctor. The next day she decided to sign up with Deborah Smith, the other oncologist at Cooley-Dickinson Hospital. When she called to inform Bowers, he was true to form. His last words to her were "I'll connect you to reception."

Brett got out boxes of memorabilia stashed in her closets and began sorting through them. An act of bravery she might have spared herself, he thought. One morning she read aloud to the rest of the family from a journal she'd kept in the ninth grade. The journal tended to focus on the trials and tribulations of friendship—remember Fred Treyes, Jim Neils, Tina, Priscilla! Someone was always jealous, betrayed, embarrassed. Even at fifteen she'd had an eye for detail and an ear for dialogue, and each of these kids—and their parents, their homes— was subject to rigorous scrutiny. For more than an hour, as they listened to her read, the harmless, uproarious past became vivid.

Over the next several days, sitting on her bed with piles of notebooks, papers, and pictures, she continued unearthing stuff that had been carefully packed away for years. "I was smart," she said, looking up from an old term paper as he entered her room. "Sorting through all this gives me the sense that I've had a long life. I've done a lot of things." She added, "I found the last letter you wrote me before the diagnosis." The card he'd written it on was a photograph of Edna St. Vincent Millay, one of the old Maine heroes of his daughter's girlhood. The letter was dated November 3, 1988. Then everything changed.

She'd found a notebook from the Biology of Cancer course. "I was doodling in the margins while he was discussing Hodgkin's disease." There were clippings from the local paper of Brett Hobbie on a bike-a-thon, age twelve probably, or intently playing the violin. Her round young face framed by long braids. Programs from concerts, Broadway shows. "I saved everything," she said. "It's lucky I realized mine was an important life." She showed him a snapshot of herself naked taken by Eve in Kentucky one summer: a lush, Rubenesque female. He lingered in the room and read letters he'd written to her at music camp. He'd always addressed her as an adult, he saw, precocious in her appreciation of the written word. When she was finished going through all the material, she put it back where she'd found it.

In San Francisco she'd been decisive about discarding possessions rather than preserving them. He was bothered that she'd sold a Christmas gift from her grandmother, for example, for practically nothing in her tag sale. To Brett, the lady's watch (chosen before Brett's prognosis was known) emphasized how out of touch her grandmother was with her, how removed from her reality. The wristwatch wasn't her, and she didn't want it. She'd also sold a memento her mother had sent her from England one year—a charming sort of knickknack. Holly was momentarily taken aback. "I couldn't fit it into my life," Brett stated flatly.

They were under pressure to get the apartment ready. At once exhausted and indefatigable, Holly bought a pine bookcase and painted it white; she refinished and upholstered a padded armchair with a summery blue-and-white-striped fabric. She and Brett went out and purchased a new bed, a lamp. Drapes were made for the unusually tall windows. There was a drawing table Brett could take from Conway, a rocking chair, a desk, and various other furnishings. Beth's parents, who had lived and taught in the area for years, also had furniture they could contribute to the cause. They began making trips to Northampton, the Volvo wagon packed tight with Brett's new life. The reality was always present, like a silent, unwanted visitor who might begin talking at any moment and completely dominate the evening, the next day, the rest of life.

Looking into her room on his way to bed, he found her sitting there as though she'd just received news that had stopped her cold.

"What are you thinking?" he asked.

"I don't know what I'm doing."

She had an interview with a self-proclaimed authority on living with cancer. Through her own struggle with recurrent breast cancer, now in remission, Terri Kerr had set herself up to advise others. Her style was bundle of energy, her mode confrontational. If you don't start doing something to turn this around, she told Brett, you're going to feel a lot worse. Terri wanted to open some doors in Brett's mind, she said. Brett wished to be inspired, but the woman mostly exasperated her and she decided not to return. She couldn't believe in arbitrary dietary restrictions; she wasn't going to swallow vitamins all day long; she wasn't going to Germany or Mexico in search of a miracle. More hard-core, heavy-duty therapy was out of the question. After all she'd been through, she couldn't believe IV vitamin C, coffee enemas, or live shark-fetus cells would make a difference. He agreed with her. Terri Kerr hadn't fought Brett's fight; she hadn't experienced a bone-marrow transplant; she hadn't been paralyzed for weeks by insane pain; she hadn't been told she had months to live. She couldn't imagine the doors that had already been opened in Brett's mind. She didn't know.

Beth arrived with Amy that night, and in the morning he drove to the Northampton apartment to drop off some final items. The young women were in a state of excitement with all that was happening, and he left as soon as he unloaded the car. The chill in the air this early April morning was invigorating rather than threatening; the sun promised a balmy day, promised spring. She'd made the move, she was in her place, she was here, living her life. All that. Yet as he drove north on the interstate, nothing felt right.

I don't know what I'm doing.

She'd been weaning herself from oral morphine for some time, reluctant to discontinue it completely. Now she'd finally dropped it from her list of medications and the chronic nausea had backed off, which made all the difference.

He reminded her of what the pain experts had said: she'd be on morphine for the rest of her life. Wrong! One prediction down.

She and Beth sounded thoroughly pleased with their new situation in Northampton. One week after moving in, however, when Holly stopped by the building, she found her daughter outside the front door, crumpled up in her wheelchair with abdominal pain. She'd been enduring this for three hours, and now Beth was taking her to the hospital. In an instant, they were cast into an abyss of anxiety. Was it beginning—three months out of Long Hospital? Not pain! By the end of the day Brett called to say she was fine—the pain had disappeared as mysteriously as it had struck. She would remain in the hospital overnight for observation. She was in a good mood and amused him with descriptions of the Cooley-Dickinson experience. Annals of small-town health care. She was never staying here again, she declared. The incident alarmed them: could her situation change so suddenly?

The following day it snowed all afternoon, amounting to a couple of inches that would melt with the next sunny day. Brett called late in the afternoon. The apartment was so beautiful in the snow, she said, hard to believe, the lovely snow coming down all around them in the large windows, magical, like being inside one of those glass balls that you tipped upside down. . . . They were hanging things on the walls. They both loved the place. She sounded wonderful, right there in Northampton. April snow. She hadn't seen a snowfall for years, he realized.

He looked out at it coming down in Conway: the last snow?

. . .

Easter, Brett was vivid in a boldly patterned shirt of black and yellow and red. There was the family, including Beth, plus several friends. It was a good day.

The following week she received a blood transfusion, which was always a double-edged experience. The procedure consigned her to an interminable day on the oncology floor and reminded her that, no matter how well she was feeling these days, the disease was present in her marrow. Transfusions also gave her an enormous lift, because she was usually dragging by the time she needed blood. That very night she and Beth and Edgar went dancing, she reported, and had a great time. All right! Keep dancing!

The red maples flowered, lilacs and apple trees in full bud. Bluebirds moved into the nesting box on the north lawn. Ruffed grouse drummed in the woods, beneath hemlock and poplar. He and Holly spent long hours outdoors, clearing and burning brush in the lower mowing, sending up smoke that said, We're nuts. They turned over the garden, uncovered the flower beds. Following the darkest winter of their lives, the light and air of the new season let the spirit up. Everything was alive.

"I'm feeling good," Brett said the last week in April, over the phone. "So Beth and I are going to Florence."

"Florence?" The town bordered Northampton to the west.

"Italy," she said by way of clarification. "Saturday. Dad, I'm so excited." She'd received her five thousand bucks from SSI, which would just about cover the trip.

She spent Friday afternoon, the first of May, in Conway, in a sense taking care of them, he thought. She brought him a recent volume of poetry, powerful to her, entitled *The Father,* a middle-aged daughter's account of her father's death from cancer. Events in an acceptable sequence, life—such as it was—as it ought to be. They walked down the long drive and back up through the gently sloping field. She couldn't climb the hill without stressful coughing, despite the bottle of water she always carried. They hadn't talked much about illness lately. Now they let the subject in. She could feel something happening in her back, the disease progressing. She couldn't seem to gain weight. Her platelets were really quite low.

"But I feel I can handle this," she said, referring to Italy. She'd pack her pain pills. They planned to be gone until the fourteenth.

"I hope it's great."

She sat in the garden, wearing her mother's moss-green brimmed hat, talking about her friends and casually browsing through a book while her parents worked in the long flower bed above the stone wall. They risked transplanting a peony from a neighboring bed, managed to botch the job thoroughly, and briefly squabbled about it, regretting the loss.

Brett looked up from her book impatiently. "Get over it," she told them.

Then she was gone, she could not be reached, and her absence now felt different than the Hawaiian trip had three months before.

A wood thrush sang in the evening woods, its clear, flutelike song almost unbearably evocative, the birdsong that most startled him each spring, as if hearing it again each year was like hearing it for the first time. As he stood on the stone terrace listening, his daughter was in Italy, where he couldn't picture her. Did the beauty there make her think of all the other extraordinary places she'd never know? Were there nightingales? The emotion that came over him was like a prelude to ultimate loss. He couldn't imagine this life without her in it.

Each time the visceral sensation of grief went through him it was as though he'd never felt it before.

They reached Logan Airport midafternoon, nervous about their daughter's return. A big letdown would inevitably attend the end of the adventure, he imagined. Fearful about her physical condition now, almost two weeks later, he was concerned that the trip might have spent her strength. Would Beth be wheeling her from the plane to the terminal, a pathetic drama enacted among other, more robust travelers? They watched the passengers file through. Where were they?

The two young women came striding from customs, Brett in a blue and white jersey, horizontal stripes, carrying her backpack and a bottle of Nivea, a big white smile on her tanned and freckled face. Just two ordinary young women, but to him they were valiant, heroic. From Boston to Northampton they excitedly described the trip—the best vacation they'd ever had, definitely—and he felt lucky that he and Holly were the first ones to hear about it. Florence, then ten days touring Tuscany, Beth behind the wheel of a little red car, usually staying in convents or monasteries. They'd encountered no other Americans in the countryside, it was so early in the season. The landscape and the ancient small towns always beautiful, the food always good. Brett ate like a Roman. Each day they hiked miles. Once they got past the anxiety of their first night out of the country, Brett felt well the whole time, the pain in her backside controlled by nothing more than Extra-Strength Tylenol. There was the flustered nun who insisted they take separate beds. The curious dark-eyed boy at the fountain, among other schoolchildren, who seemed to look into Brett's soul, smiling, when she glanced up from her journal, an almost sexual feeling, so that she fled as if she'd been found out. Vast cultivated sweeps of land bore cypresses on the luminous horizon. Women lay at the feet of David. Sun and blue sky every day. Their daring adventure was a triumph. Totally.

Two postcards followed their return, messages in her indomitable voice. The first, from Siena:

Morning in this rotunda—a parade of worshipers singing behind some relic of the Madonna as it's carried to a different cathedral, college boys in purple velvet capes and ostrich feathers . . . Beth scavenging pastries. Beer for breakfast, octopus for lunch, and then a siesta in our incredible room with a view and roly-poly nuns who adore Sweatpatch . . . angel at my table. In my T-shirt I've acquired the nickname Wishbone. The landscape is ravishing. The phlox and poppies and lilacs full-blown. I have the strange sensation of driving through my drawings or my imagination . . . My eyes are so full I can barely close them at night. Ciao, Brettino

The other card said:

I've decided to become a Franciscan monk—ring the bell, pick apricots, sing after a noon meal of rabbit, sparrow, wild fried flowers, vino, grappa, espresso . . . this hill town is a honey-colored labyrinth of archways and skinny alleys and towers and chapels and flute players, herbs growing in the stone walls, hidden gardens, nuns with video cameras, old men smaller than Beth smoking and shouting ciao at me, every cranny taken up with geraniums or the Virgin Mary or stray cats. We walk miles each day, drink plenty of olive oil, and sleep like stones. Florence was big and soaring and miraculous . . . I am having the time of my life and lighting candles and tasting fruits and hazelnuts. I feel light and full, surrounded by beauty, and please come here sometime. Love, Santa Bretta

Yes, they took lots of pictures. He adored the sight of his daughter in this ancient exotic setting, absorbing everything, pensive, happy. In many pictures she was bent over her notebook, oblivious to the doting photographer. In a crowded sidewalk café, in the midst of talk and laughter, she was the young woman seated at a table alone, busily frowning over her journal. Her short red hair, her thinness, the water bottle at her elbow, her total concentration, her obliviousness to the social buzz around her. Getting her experience on paper where it would be safe. Looking from her to the other faces in one of the photographs, the people surrounding her, he thought, They didn't know.

At the Old School apartment one evening he noticed a snapshot of his daughter and Beth affectionately horsing around in their new, sunny space.

"You look happy."

"We are happy," she said.

"Keep up the magic. Keep it going. Return to Italy if necessary."

She was able to attend the annual ceremony of the American Academy of Arts and Letters in New York, where he received an award for his novel *Boomfell*. To see him up on the stage, she said, felt the way it probably felt for him to watch her perform a violin concerto in the long ago: a rush. Back in February, when he'd been notified of the award, no one imagined she'd be up to going. Wearing the earthy-colored green dress with its bold leaf forms that her grandmother had made her, she looked lovely that day. But to witness this belated chapter of her father's life only just beginning, while her life . . . The absurdity made him ashamed.

Eve visited toward the end of May. She and Brett attempted one day at their Smith reunion but couldn't stick it out. In Conway, Eve joined him while he manned the charcoal grill.

"I'm amazed," she said. "She looks so fantastic. I thought she'd be in a wheelchair."

"I haven't seen her this well for a year," he said. Brett hadn't used the wheelchair since Italy.

"Four years." Every time Eve had been with her in the past four years, it seemed, Brett was always contending with something: ominous symptoms, awful treatments, pain, sickness. Something. In San

Francisco, friends were usually around at night, but she'd often been alone during the day. Too lonely. "The move back here is the best thing she could have done."

Another splendid day in a run of fair weather, he and Holly and Brett drove to Field's hill and walked home through green pastures and lambent woods. Brett walked slowly, but she covered the distance. Five months before, Lin, the Buddhist nurse, had given her three months to live. Wouldn't Linker, for one, have been amazed to see her strolling through these woods today?

The immense stand of old-fashioned purple lilacs in Boyden's west pasture, the only remaining evidence of a nineteenth-century homestead, was in ecstatic bloom against the towering backdrop of equally venerable sugar maples. Brett thrust her face into pendulous blossoms. Solemnly, with her eyes closed, she breathed in the fragrance, as though taking it deep inside her, and again, her brow furrowed with concentration, breathing in the scent that, more than any other, stood for spring.

Following another evening in Conway—Brett was Tex in her tall cowboy boots—he found Holly in the kitchen going to pieces.

"What is it? I thought everyone seemed good tonight." After dinner the whole group, eight in all, had walked down the long drive together harkening to the wood thrush, observing the evening light.

"Brett was here and everyone was enjoying themselves, but I didn't connect with her somehow and I feel terrible about it. These precious days with Brett, I feel them slipping by. It feels wrong and I can't make it right."

While their daughter was doing so well, they were all inclined to go with it, especially Brett—to celebrate the day—yet time was passing, yes, something was wrong and would never be right. He shared his wife's longing, her sense of inadequacy, and he didn't know what to do about it. As so often now, he awoke before dawn to the suffocated sound of muffled tears. There was no answer to their smothered suffering.

I've had too much socializing lately," she said. There had been a dinner party with old friends of Beth's. She'd been to the Wilson family homestead in Grafton, Vermont. Mary had visited all day Sunday. Brett came to Conway just to hang out and spent the day making tapes of old records, looking through the large box of family pictures, keeping to herself, not low but quiet, apart.

The first Friday in June she required a blood transfusion, and he spent the morning with her in a large, bright room on the fourth floor of Cooley-Dickinson. She was thinking she should make contact soon with people at Baystate Medical Center in Springfield.

"I hope you won't have to be in a hospital anywhere," he said.

She'd heard that hospice programs often couldn't really handle the end stage, she said. They didn't have the personnel or the money.

"While you're feeling well, while you have the strength, should we investigate other treatment possibilities?" Was there anything to do? He'd already called the Kelley/Gonzales program in New York, one of the more reputable alternatives, and learned they wouldn't accept a patient who had received a bone-marrow transplant.

Smiling, she said, "I don't plan to be sick for five years, anyway."

"It's wonderful that you've been feeling so well." He added, "I just don't want you to feel you've left some stone unturned, some—"

"I don't feel that way." She felt she had done, and was doing, all she could do. Her mood today was easygoing, positive.

It was two and a half hours before the nurse had the blood, some stranger's blood, dripping into Brett's arm. As he was going out to get coffee, he paused at the door. "Isn't this fun?" he said, recalling their long hospital experience in San Francisco.

"Oh, Dad."

In cut-off blue jeans, Richard stopped by to lounge on the hospital bed for an hour. The first bag of blood was empty by twelve-thirty, the transfusion progressing tediously but smoothly. Ever the vigilant father, he tracked down Brett's nurse with a question about the blood filter they were using, some small detail most people wouldn't question. His daughter said, "At UCSF there was a Hobbie support group for the doctors."

When Beth arrived, as if adhering to their old routine on 11 Long, he left.

That night, her batteries recharged, as she put it, Brett drove to Montreal for the weekend with Beth and Edgar.

Saturday evening in mid-June. Gin-and-tonics in the garden, where large pink oriental poppies and opulent peonies were beginning their brief season in bloom. Arm wrestling. A people pyramid for one snapshot, the men forming the base and Brett on top. She wore a pale-green sort of jumpsuit with blooming pants, borrowed from Beth, over a white silk blouse. There was a lot of picture taking, as though everyone felt something memorable was transpiring. He took one snapshot of Brett, a close-up, wearing her mother's mossy green brimmed hat on the back of her head. She smiled at the camera unguardedly. Wait, she said, take another picture. This was just between them, photographer and subject, father and daughter, no one else nearby, and this time she composed her face so her look, while neither severe nor sentimental nor sad, was deadpan, straight-on, a look that would say to whoever looked at the photograph: this picture was taken during the last summer of my life. I was living until I died, I was doing it. I was dying and I knew it. He snapped the picture, nodding as though to confirm, I got it.

The full moon, taking everyone by surprise, rose above the black woods, an astonishing presence. k. d. lang's wonderful voice—Brett had recently attended a concert—enlivened the patio. Save me, save me from you. . . . Beth and Brett, Michael and Jocelyn, danced on the lawn. Jocelyn suddenly went into a cute gymnastic mode, daring herself into cartwheels and back flips, stuff she hadn't done for years. Nathaniel effortlessly began walking on his hands, springing into flips and leaps. Michael joined the act with his feeble version of a cartwheel. The big moon, low on the horizon, was bright yellow. Look: fireflies in untold numbers hovered over the unmown hayfield, winking brightly, like a visitation. Inspired, Brett came antically running across the lawn and promptly scooted into a stiff-legged somersault. She was up and did it again. By the third time, Beth was in hysterics.

"You're so adorable," she cried, flat on her back, laughing. "You're so adorable. Oh, my God."

The Hobbling Brother and Sister Circus, Brett dubbed them. Suddenly, shed of her green pantaloons and white blouse, she gamboled across the lawn in her underwear, her skin pale in the moonlight. The rest quickly followed suit. The amazing moon over the dark woods, brilliant fireflies over the field, these half-naked dancing figures. He watched with Holly from the stone terrace. This beauty, this happiness, had the power to heal. Why couldn't such magic miraculously cure?

The imminence of death in their lives provoked a more demonstrative realization of commitment and love in their already close family, there was no doubt of that; but it wasn't as though the pain they lived with now let them out of who they were, or how they related to one another.

"Here he goes again," Brett said one evening in July about some remark he'd made. And in a moment, with raised voices, they were back to the issue of Brett's distancing herself under impossible circumstances, her complicated anger toward him. Here *we* go again! Jocelyn fled the room in tears, followed by Holly, then Michael. Something

Brett said about the so-called dynamics of their family made him blow his top. He exited the room, and she followed him. In the next moment they were clinging to each other in the barn, dismayed, but the emotion now wasn't about their father-daughter relationship; it was about the awful reality encroaching on his daughter's life. The friction between them had ignited their grief.

Back in the kitchen, Brett and her sister came together. "I'm going to die," Brett cried. "When you're feeling good, you can forget, but . . ."

"No, you're not," Jocelyn replied. They were both sobbing.

He put his arms around them, Holly joined the circle, and finally Nathaniel piled on, the five of them holding one another in the kitchen, their moist faces pressed together, a family about to be swamped, huddled against the cresting wave. It was so much like the moment they'd shared that night at 111 Buena Vista East prior to the transplant, except that occasion had been about hope and determination and coming through.

Accepting the respite of recent good months, they hadn't experienced quite such a moment together since Brett had returned to New England and especially since Italy. They hadn't talked about death and dying.

Later, on his way upstairs, he found Brett getting a glass of water in the kitchen. "Well, we got *something* done tonight," he said.

She nodded, smiling. "I hope we've accomplished something."

The next day, the Fourth, their gathering in Conway was a mindless bash.

The following week she spent eight hours at the hospital receiving three units of blood. He and Holly were with her during the last hour, then they dropped her at her apartment. Gabby Silver, a loyal friend from college, was visiting from New York. Jumping from the backseat of the car, Brett gave out a characteristic hoot. "I can feel the difference already," she said. In the morning she and Beth were off to Cambridge for the weekend.

"I'm barely holding on," Holly confided as they continued home. "Brett is creaming me."

With Beth and Edgar, she had the fortitude to attend an old friend's wedding and positively enjoy it. The bride's mother told her, "We think of you often."

One afternoon she went along to watch her father and Richard hit tennis balls and ended up getting into the game despite the blazing heat. The old form was there. "I guess you're just a natural athlete," Richard observed. Oh, you should have seen her with a soccer ball.

Visitors continued to make the pilgrimage to Northampton. Mary Cranley and Ellen had visited in June. Then Jocelyn Emerson from Smith, now a poet in the Iowa Writers Program; Brett's grandparents from Florida; Jean from San Francisco.

The first of August she and Beth went off on their long-planned weekend to Monhegan Island with Jocelyn and Michael. That in itself was a book, he thought, the last trip to the Maine coast.

As soon as they returned, Brett met with Alfred McKee, an oncologist at Baystate Medical Center, who had been recommended as a pain expert. Pain in her left hip, her back, and her groin had become constant. McKee deduced that the cancer in her hip was pressing on the main artery in her groin; there was also some sort of bladder involvement. Radiation, which was bound to decimate her white count further and make her more transfusion-dependent, was to be postponed as long as possible. Prednisone might also impact her white cells, as well as provoke the growth of MAI, but it still offered the best chance, he advised, of decreasing the disease with minimal side effects. Brett spoke to Terry Jahan in California, who thought steroids might be temporarily helpful if used cautiously.

"I guess they're worth a try for a while," she told her father.

He was glad there was something to be done.

"I'm not afraid of dying," Brett said. "I don't want pain."

. . .

Are you looking forward to this?" he asked, driving her out to another social afternoon in Conway. Her uncle and aunt from California, as well as her cousin and his new wife, had come to see her. Holly's older brother, Gary, had flown to San Francisco several times to donate platelets. They were grateful to him for that. And yet to Brett these people were basically strangers. Now they felt obliged to see her.

"Oh, sure," Brett said.

They were at the picnic table under the maple tree in the south yard. From the house he watched her energetically stride out the back door toward them. For the next few hours she gave an inspired performance. She drew out her cousin and his wife concerning their wedding, and their budding careers in architecture and design. She was curious about life in La Jolla, Gary's career in rockets. No one inquired about her life. She submitted to their camera. The last pictures they had of her would have been taken when she was a little girl. They knew they'd never see her again. Everyone meant well, of course, but he was relieved when Nathaniel finally drove Brett back to Northampton, returned her to her real life, where Beth, along with Mary Burger and Mary's friend, Marjorie, awaited her.

We were being tortured," Holly told him. "With primitive instruments like the ones Brett saw in Italy." Their daughter had visited a museum of Dark Age torture devices somewhere in Tuscany. "We were both in the same dismal chamber. There was a machine with a spike that went through the rectum until it struck a vital organ. That's what they did to us." She recounted disturbing dreams with a solemnity usually reserved for real events—as though what she saw in dreams had actually happened to her. Another morning, over coffee, she grimly reported, "We moved into a perfect little cottage, a charming, beautiful place, which hung out over a bottomless cliff."

. . .

This time last year Brett had been captive in the bone-marrow transplant. That siege seemed far more distant than only the summer before.

"Are you angry or bitter about going through that?" he asked. They were sitting at the table in Conway after dinner.

"No," she said. "And I'm happy that I'm not." Sometimes she found herself living the sort of moment she'd only desperately imagined during the transplant, and that made her sad. Like the tapes of falling rain she'd listened to in the hospital—she'd clung to that sound for dear life, to get through. Now, three thousand miles away, she listened to the rain at night in Northampton, she was here experiencing the real thing, but the sound of rain was no longer associated with hope, with being saved.

Losing the rain, he thought.

"But if I was told a second transplant would cure me," she said, "I wouldn't go through it again. I can't hope on one level, but I have hope. I've learned to seize the day. I feel I live fully each day."

"There was every reason to endure the transplant," he said. She couldn't have not done it. No one could undo what had occurred. "I'm glad you aren't angry about it."

"I am too."

There was the abhorrent thought that the disease had been present, dormant, indiscernible, in the marrow they'd extracted from her years before, dooming the transplant to failure, dooming the patient. While that seemed unlikely, there was no way to know. That risk had been less, the doctors would say, than the risks associated with using a donor's marrow.

"You were great through the whole thing," he said. "You came through magnificently."

In a moment Brett said, "Now I'm going to cry." But she held back her tears. "I have a lot of work to do."

Ever since Italy she'd been intent on getting out and enjoying everything possible while she was feeling good. Lately, the urgency to make her art, which had evolved from her struggle with cancer, as though you couldn't have one without the other, had reasserted itself. She would awaken excitedly in the middle of the night, Beth said, eager to discuss the next drawing she had in mind. She felt the future narrowing more than before. Manifestations of the disease could suddenly accelerate out of control. She'd called her radiation oncologist in San Francisco, who, advising her not to postpone treatment on the left hip too long, raised again the specter of an incapacitating fracture.

Her latest drawing in oil pastels: a frontal portrait of her naked chest in warm naturalistic color against a black background, a vivid black and yellow butterfly fastened to the skin between her full breasts with pins.

He picked her up at nine, a Sunday morning in the middle of August. Denim jacket, blue jeans, her knapsack, a new, smart haircut. It was raining steadily. What was she going to do in Provincetown with Mary in the rain? she wondered.

The steroids seemed to have reduced the swelling in her hip, but the pain, the bone pain, was worse. Maybe the cold, wet weather had something to do with it. Beth, she said, had been getting anxious as her symptoms grew worrisome. "Yesterday she wanted to make a video of me talking about my art and became upset when I didn't feel like it. She wants me to set my affairs in order, you know, while I can. Without rushing or leaving things unresolved."

In the close front seat of the car, sheets of rain coming down on them, they were in an intimate room. This topic—final arrangements—had not been broached between them.

"I might draw up a simple will," she said. She intended to have the hospice counselor help her with details.

He grunted his assent, unable for a moment to speak.

She wanted to leave specific things to special friends, she said. "I'm going to leave the art with you and Mom. It's a body of work and I want it kept together." She was exasperated that some of the early pieces were fading or discoloring slightly because of the fixative she'd used on them. "Goddamn it," she said. The work she left behind wasn't supposed to fade.

Talking with his daughter about her will as they drove toward Cambridge in the rain, he thought. They'd reached this pass.

"Then there are my journals," she said.

He had to say something, all right. Her friends were wonderful, they were absolutely essential to her, but they were young, they were going to go on with their lives. "Your things can't mean as much to them as they mean to us. Especially over time. Everything that's yours is important to us. . . ." He almost choked up saying this, the windshield wipers swishing back and forth, because this was about imagining her gone, the person beside him in the car no more. Only *things* left, things that stood for her.

"I know," she said. "I know that." Smiling at him, she reached out and touched the back of his neck. "You'll get the journals," she said.

Her touch made him feel he was the child here. How did she talk about this with such composure?

She asked to be remembered to her grandmother, his mother, whom he was going on to see in Brewster after dropping her in Cambridge.

"Obviously she can't deal with this," he said. "She doesn't know how to think about it. She can't help it." He wanted to assure Brett of her grandmother's love. For how must the woman's silence have appeared to his daughter?

Brett, who had long let go of unavailing relationships, nodded.

He hadn't felt as close to her all summer as he did then, driving east in the rain.

"I want to spend more time with you," he said. "Alone, I mean."

Getting together in a group to laugh and eat, even when it was just the family, was hardly enough. He didn't want to miss the opportunity to be with her; he didn't want to blow it.

"That sounds good to me," she said. He could take her out to dinner.

Downtown Cambridge was busy; almost everyone was young. They walked through a pleasant drizzle to the café where Brett had planned to meet her friend before they went on together to Provincetown. Because Mary was late they were able to enjoy for a half hour longer, over coffee, the mood they'd shared in the car, their small table a private enclosure walled off by other people, other voices.

"You look beautiful this morning," he told her.

She smiled. "My cheeks are a little puffy from the steroids."

He hoped his publisher would accept her design—it was the one she'd given him for his birthday, the small figure ascending the hill— for the jacket illustration of his new novel called *The Day*. They were going to do a mock-up and then decide.

"That would be great," Brett said.

When Mary arrived, the three of them walked over to Wordsworth's Bookstore to browse. Brett found three collections of poetry she could use, and he wanted to get them for her: Rilke, Wendell Berry, and Hayden Carruth. Then they separated. Walking toward his car, he turned back to glance at his daughter and her friend sauntering through the mist a block behind him. They all waved. He looked back again, he wanted to see her out here, on the sidewalk, and again her arm went up in that open-palmed gesture of hers: bye.

He and his mother, in her white pants and white cotton sweater, walked along the Mill Pond, a saltwater inlet where his father had fished for flounder, a favorite spot and the site where they had cast his ashes. That bright, clear February day they'd gone around the projecting hillock of land to the right as his father had always done. The weight of the blue box containing his remains seemed tremendous. They chose a spot just beyond a large boulder where the land turned out to open water. His wife, his mother, his sister, him. They said good-bye, ashes to ashes, earth to earth, rest in peace, and poured the dense white material, pulverized bone, into the cold water. One month later, in March, he returned to the Mill Pond toward evening. His father's cremains were not entirely dissolved or dispersed or washed away by the sea, as he'd expected they would be. They were right there, some portion of them, right there on the shore. Evidently the four of them had performed that last rite during high tide, so when the tide receded, the shell-like white fragments were exposed. God, Dad, had they botched that, too? With his hands and then with mussel shells he impetuously scraped the wet sandy area, scooping up the fragments, and cast them well out into the water. Dad! It would have taken a shovel to remove every sign. He scattered shells there to make the scar-ified spot look natural. Cold wind blew off the water. It was dusk. From the far side of the spit of land, he chose as large a rock as he could carry and placed it where the ashes had originally been deposited. This labor—he had to set the rock down three times getting it to the place—made him feel better. He knew the rock was temporary, but he wanted it there then. His wife was the only person who knew about this desperate hour at the Mill Pond.

Now, a year and a half later, there was no trace of anything, includ-ing the rock.

"I regret I didn't bury his ashes," his mother said, "and erect a stone, a place I could go to."

"I'm glad we did it here," he said. "I like coming here." And he liked the idea of ashes free in earth, so to speak, rather than contained.

"When I die I want a stone with both our names on it."

"I wish I'd known he was so near the end," he said. "I wish I'd been there."

"He wouldn't talk about dying. When that psychologist mentioned death, he said, I never want that son of bitch in here again."

He laughed, looking out at the beautiful serenity of the inlet with its tall grasses. He could hear his father saying that, all right.

His daughter was an hour away at the end of the peninsula, stirred, he imagined, by the dunes, her ocean.

Over breakfast he and his mother went over familiar topics.

"Golden sent him home, saying it's that or the nursing home. I didn't think he was about to die." After a pause she said, "I believe he's up there watching everything. My faith is what keeps me going, Douglas." She described the last night of her husband's life again, every word and action, what he said and what she said.

They discussed Brett's present state, the unexpectedly good summer, her extraordinary girlfriend, Beth.

"I've written to Brett," she said. "I have trouble expressing myself about all this. I can't help the way I am. I was raised in Scotland to be reserved and I am. I can't help it." She paused. "I love Brett. I wish I could do more. I can't drive to your house. I can't handle that. Brett's been to Italy; she's been everywhere. Why couldn't she come to see me?"

He cautioned her to do whatever seemed possible for her where Brett was concerned. Once it was too late, the only thing left would be regret.

They discussed other, interminable issues—her relationship with her oldest daughter, with her sister—and his mother, fragile when it came to these major themes of her life, fought her emotions. Saying good-bye in the kitchen, she said, "I love you, I really do." It was an appeal, and he reciprocated. She added, as one pleading to be understood, accepted for herself, "I'm really a good person. I am."

Of course she was a good person. And she was destined now, at the end of each day, as the darkness gathered, to suffer her heartaches and losses and regrets alone. He cared about her, he would play his allotted part in her life, and yet he didn't suffer on her behalf, he didn't particularly worry about her. Was that what Brett felt toward him? While he and his daughter were far more alike in every respect than he and his mother, while they were altogether more open, honest, *real* with each other, he was quite sure the answer was yes. As in the nature of things. With their lives before them, children looked ahead, not behind.

She met her radiation oncologist at Baystate, Alan Stark, and liked him, which was encouraging. On Saturday night she brought games to Conway: a new croquet set and a rig that produced gigantic bubbles. Brett didn't have the patience for croquet in the ensuing contest, although the rest of them became temporarily obsessed. The bubbles drifted over the darkening lawn like weird immense creatures or floating worlds—multicolored, shape-shifting, short-lived.

A small white water-filled balloon hung in the window over the kitchen table when he came downstairs in the morning. Brett, who'd stayed the night, had been up since five-thirty, alone in the quiet Conway dawn, and the balloon was from her. "A bird, small as a leaf, sings in the first sunlight," she wrote on it. On the opposite side, she wrote, "If the wind means me, I'm here. Here." The bottom said, "8/24/92 Love, B."

That morning, at Brett's insistence, they all took a long, leisurely walk down a dirt road in the shade of grand old maples—past the old cemetery, all the way to the South River, where they waded into the clear, cold water. She was winded climbing the slight uphill path from the river. The thinness of the back of her neck beneath her bright red hair hurt him.

She and her mother went out for groceries in the afternoon, and Brett returned with new white Reeboks. "Don't you *love* them?" she said excitedly, displaying the shoe. "I feel stronger and bigger. I feel like running." She marched off down the drive to try them out. She seemed better now than she had when she'd bought new running shoes on Haight Street almost a year earlier—shoes she needed for the long road to recovery. He loved her enthusiasm. She couldn't run, of course.

His next thought shocked him: she'll never run again. Never. Please get to use them, he thought, get them dirty.

She called at noon the next day, another Monday. "I feel awful. I feel like I need a blood transfusion. My energy is zilch, my heart is racing. Last night I had unbearable leg cramps that wouldn't quit." She'd been to Baystate that morning for a blood draw. At four she would return to see Stark. At one she was seeing her therapist. On Tuesday morning she was scheduled for a gallium scan and a platelet transfusion. She'd be at the hospital all day. Her life of procedures, tests, mini-traumas: to what end? That's what made it so impossible now. She hoped to elude pain.

He kept recalling one of her recent drawings: the arm and shoulder of a swimmer raised in midstroke. Except the invisible figure was swimming through earth, not water, the arm thrust up through dark grass.

It's so hard.

He was frightened. When he and Holly stopped at her apartment in the evening—Brett was making dinner, and the place smelled powerfully of garlic—she was anxious that the cramps might return that night. When he mentioned driving to Maine—he and Holly tentatively hoped to get away for a couple of days—she said, "I don't know where I'm going to be." Her hospital routine these days didn't even leave her time to work. Beth returned from jogging, so they soon left the two young women to their supper in the wonderful apartment, filled with everything that was so much them, he thought, their private, resonant world.

Brett's mood had been portentous. The silence between them as they drove home was deafening to him. How useless they were! How helpless! He could feel his wife's anguish twisting in her tighter, tighter. At last he said, "Brett is going to die." In a moment he added, "These months have been wonderful, but we know ... We have to try to prepare ourselves ..."

The truth was he couldn't conceive the thing happening, not really; he couldn't conceive that one day she would no longer be here—at her desk, on the other end of the phone, coming through the door. At the most visceral level, his daughter's fate, if that's what it was, remained stubbornly unimaginable to him.

How would she do this? How would they do this?

At the end of August the spell of oppressive humid weather gave way, following a night of rain, to unusually cool, clear days. Boyden cut the lower field to begin the last mowing of the season. Gangs of crows careered boisterously over the land like bandits. He walked down their road in the still evening, breathing in the scent of newly mown hay. Autumn, he thought. Looking at the benign sky, he said his daughter's name aloud. The heartache: all that was yet to be but that she was not to know, that they were not to share with her, sustained by her keenly appreciative take on things, comforted and strengthened by her heart and mind. Never.

They didn't know what to expect. But when he and Holly met her at the apartment the last night in August, Brett sparkled, fresh and vivacious. *It's the lipstick*. She was dressed up for dinner with her parents: a blue-green jacket over a cotton sweater, the small sterling-silver perfume decanter around her neck, Beth's linen pants. Gleaming new shoes, chestnut brown with brass ornaments, had the effect of a daring surprise.

"Do you like them?"

Yes. *Loved* them.

He hadn't managed yet to take her out for dinner alone. When the present occasion arose, for example—Beth was out with Edgar—both he and Holly wanted to be with her, and Brett wanted to be with them. They walked through the center of town, always animated with young people.

"So do you feel at home in Northampton?" he asked.

"These streets are like an extension of my living room," she said.

The restaurant was the one where almost eight months before

they'd met her out on the town with Mary. They were seated very near the table they'd had that winter night. She was doing all right, she thought, but the pain became intense at times. Her oncologist advised her to take more of the anti-inflammatory he'd prescribed. He'd been struck, reaching for a glass in her apartment, by the array of prescriptions in the kitchen cabinet: all summer long she'd been doggedly counting out numerous drugs several times a day.

That weekend Gabby Silver and her friend Miriam had visited from New York. Miriam was studying architecture in Jerusalem.

"Jerusalem sounded great," Brett said.

The night before, Lisa Bernard and a friend, both from Stanford, had spent the night.

"They're already like a couple of doctors," Brett smiled, "with their nice clothes and good watches. They plan to buy a cottage in P-town next year."

Friends checking in as summer drew to a close, he thought, before the next hectic, invigorating season swept down on them. His daughter sounded unambiguously happy for her friends' good fortune, as if it no longer hurt her to hear her contemporaries talking about plans, careers, futures. She had moved on to another place. Her life was *now,* this moment, charming her parents in a restaurant, feeling pretty glamorous.

Back at the apartment they looked through photograph albums Brett had compiled of the summer. One was devoted to Italy. Another contained snapshots of her and Beth in the light-filled apartment, at a party with friends, on Monhegan, or in Vermont. There were many pictures, as if the accumulation of images validated her experience; each moment that was printed, safe in a snapshot, provided conclusive evidence.

He wandered into her studio and looked out the window to the lighted town: her view.

Everything I love is here.

Girls were already beginning to return to Smith, she said. God, they were a riot, the parents, the station wagons full of stuff, the nervous excitement. "They look like children to me now." It hadn't been that long ago—a few years was all.

"I may audit a course," she said. Just for fun, a distraction, while Beth was still busy with her courses. All summer, Beth, someone who'd mostly been involved in the arts, had been diligently taking intensive courses in chemistry and math, prerequisites to another career. She'd done well and intended to continue down that path, wherever it might lead.

Brett was especially looking forward to an Olga Broumas workshop to be held at the poet's home on the Cape in mid-September, and she hoped Mary Burger would go with her.

Oh, she almost forgot to tell them, she'd run into S.J. today, right in downtown Northampton visiting an old friend. Of course, she had planned to see Brett. They were getting together tomorrow. "She was great, the same as ever, happy to see me."

Driving home he said, "Wasn't she incredible tonight? She looked beautiful."

Holly was looking straight ahead. "I'm in awe of her," she said.

8

AUTUMN

They walked to the cove at the south end of the island to begin their tramp around its perimeter. The ocean was calm. Cormorants and seagulls sailed over the shore or stood on the black, barnacled rock formations that extended into the water. On their trip out the day before, aboard the *Laura B.,* Holly had been trying to see the boat ride through Brett's eyes, she said—the receding land, the swells, the emerging island. Now, as they hiked toward the cliffs on the east side of the island, observing the dense dwarfed spruce here, lichen-covered granite, moss, tide pools, they were silent. He knew what his wife was thinking. This landscape, so much a part of their past as a young family, was powerfully bound up with their daughter. She would never set eyes on it again. They knew that.

Holly tied her wool sweater around her waist. "My blood feels sluggish," she said. "I don't have the energy for this today."

In fact, she was fit and particularly liked a good walk.

By the time they reached White Head, she said, "I can't continue." She moved farther back from the dizzying edge of the cliff. "I can't get my breath." Pressing her hand to her chest, she said, "I have such a pain here." In the last several months, she'd often mentioned pain in her chest, which she described as heartache.

He urged her to take deep, slow breaths, try to relax, she was all right. Once she was calmer, they walked from the promontory back to the island's lighthouse, which overlooked the village.

"We have to figure out how to live with this," he said, "just as Brett has struggled to do that. You have to go on living. You have to take care of yourself." He didn't think she had heart disease, but he was willing to believe constant stress could make you sick. Holly had been seeing a therapist again for a while, but therapy seemed less helpful as the loss of her daughter became more real, and she finally gave up on the sessions.

"I can't help how I feel."

"We don't know what we're facing. We don't know what the loss of Brett is going to do to us or how we'll actually experience it. She's still here. We're going to see her when we get home." Their ultimate grief awaited them; they weren't there yet. They had to carry on just as their daughter did, day by day. If possible, they should try to benefit from these two days away.

Returning to the village, they walked through the small graveyard at the foot of the lighthouse. Starling, Pierce, West, Stanley. Just then, reading gravestones from another century, he shrank, recoiling, from the abstract idea that intruded: his daughter's remains. He couldn't possibly see her name on such a stone.

He called her as soon as they got home. She'd been running a fever for the past two days. When he mentioned IV antibiotics to control whatever was occurring, she became annoyed. "My white count is nine hundred and it's never going to be higher. I can't go into the hospital every time I get a fever. McKee knows what's going on."

Outside, he looked up at the dense green wall of woods, the birch and maple and oak still verdant. He wanted her to have autumn— Come on!—he wanted her to see another fall. This was too soon. They weren't ready, he thought. They would never be ready.

"Last night I experienced drenching night sweats," she reported the next day. She'd spent the morning at the hospital.

When he and Holly entered her apartment that evening, she was sitting in the white-cushioned armchair. She wore a red wool peaked cap on backwards, a red plaid flannel shirt that had been his, blue jeans, and the new Reeboks. McKee had called her late in the afternoon, she informed them. She didn't have pneumonia, according to the X-ray. But her platelets were lower than ever, despite a recent transfusion, so it seemed platelet transfusions weren't going to work. She'd have to begin medication to prevent bleeding. She continued to take several prophylactic drugs and the anti-inflammatory for pain. McKee's call—the platelets—had her down.

He touched her face and brow. "You feel cool right now."

She showed them the books she'd purchased lately: a biography of Neruda, one of her heroes, and Mary Oliver's *New and Selected Poems*. "Her poetry is wonderful," she said. "You should get this." Oh, she'd had a great visit with S.J., incidentally.

Beth had been doing stretching exercises in an open area of the room behind them. The moment she went out for her jog, their emotions surfaced. Compressing her lips, grimacing, Brett fought tears. She'd been doing so well, and now, so suddenly . . .

"I didn't know it would be like this."

"What do you mean?" he asked.

"My body just not producing what I need to stay alive, dwindling down, so I'm vulnerable and completely helpless and can't do anything." She'd imagined there would be some new development, the disease invading a vital organ, for example, not this insidious decline, her body failing to make blood cells.

During the transplant, they'd been able to keep her counts up until her marrow took over. Now . . . platelets didn't take. Brett's discussion with her doctor had struck her with the force of a realization: so this is how it will be. Just days before, going out to dinner with them in her new shoes, she'd seemed so far from where she was today.

He and Holly had pulled chairs next to her, and each of them had their arms around her. At least there wasn't the pain that she'd suffered in January, he suggested, the pain that smothered her so completely she was unable to be here at all. That pain was what she'd feared.

Brett nodded. And yet that was the irony: she'd been feeling too well to believe the end was drawing near.

"I don't want to be melodramatic about it," she said, "but it's like the summer is over." The worsening symptoms, the onset of fevers accompanied by harrowing night sweats, had struck only with the change in the weather. September.

Now I'm always going to hate this time of year.

"We have to talk about what's happening," he said. "Dying. When we're together, especially if you're feeling good, no one wants to talk about it, but we must. I don't want you to be alone, to feel more alone than you have to be."

"It helps me to talk about death. To be able to talk about it." She added, "I don't want to be in the hospital. You and Beth are going to have to learn to do some things because hospice can't do it all."

Beth soon returned, flushed and youthful and strong. *Like a sapling.* Her unstinting and selfless devotion to their daughter was evident in every word and gesture between the two women. All they had endured together, their private sorrow, was like a near yet inaccessible country. Tonight, as he and Holly said good-bye, their young faces were somber.

When fever persisted for several days, accompanied now by pain in her lungs, Brett and her doctor decided she should go to Baystate Medical Center, after all.

She was relaxed, even cheerful, when they entered her room at the hospital. She hadn't changed out of her own clothes and didn't intend to. Apparently they didn't know what they were going to do with her here. She described herself as neutropenic. That word! They walked the corridor with her, and although they'd never been in this building before, the feeling was sickeningly familiar. There was one bone-marrow transplant patient on the floor, she informed them—the first at Baystate.

That night he awakened with vivid images of her in his head—greeting them at the door in San Francisco last winter leaning on a cane, striding through Northampton, where the streets were like an extension of her living room, sitting in her apartment in the red cap and new Reeboks—and fear for her washed over him.

The next afternoon, Labor Day, she had come to the end of her patience by the time he and Holly turned up at the hospital. "I've been sitting here all day," she said, infuriated, "*wasting my time!*" No one had suggested doing a damned thing for her. At least she could be receiving red blood cells, but the doctor on duty hadn't ordered the transfusion yet. "Why can't anyone do what needs to be done here?"

Moments before their arrival, a woman had been screaming in a nearby room, and that shook her up, she said. "The first thing I thought of was a bone-marrow biopsy, but then the woman began to sob hysterically." Evidently an elderly person, the matriarch of the family, had died, and what Brett had heard was the daughter's lamentation. Soon the corridor was active with people of all ages—the extended family—and the next moment, before he could get to the door to close it, a large woman was bodily carried down the hallway, shrieking, by two men.

Startled to tears, Brett said, "I've never seen that before. That pain. I feel sorry for them. The woman is gone, but the family . . . I hope it won't be like that," she said. "Screaming, all that."

"No, we cry but we don't scream."

"I don't want to be here," she said. "I've wasted the whole day." She'd called McKee, who also thought it was reprehensible that they hadn't given her the transfusion yet. They managed to reach the resident on duty this Labor Day by phone, and the young man, a Dr. Dash, a small, tightly knit, handsome guy about Brett's age, soon arrived at her room. Okay, he would order the transfusion. Then, from a telephone in the room, he called McKee at home to discuss what other course of action might be appropriate. Brett's low-grade fever had been constant. For some time Dash mostly listened. "I think I get the picture," he told McKee finally. He turned to the patient and her parents.

There was no point, he and Dr. McKee agreed, in putting Brett through a course of antibiotics, which would mean at least a week to ten days in the hospital. Given Brett's present vulnerability and her prognosis, she would only come down with yet another fever. Would she then return to the hospital for more antibiotics, which were bound to be further debilitating? Her white count was 600. It wasn't going to improve.

"You could die in the hospital," he said. His advice, like McKee's, was to go home and live what time was left. Of course, home was where Brett wanted to be. No, Dash said in answer to the question he put to him, there was never going to be a time when Brett should necessarily enter the hospital—no matter how high her fever ran.

Quite matter-of-factly, the resident took it upon himself to say, "You know, a fever isn't a bad way to die. You just go to sleep."

It wasn't the words, he thought—he had said as much himself— but the way the young man had spoken them. Dash's tone was confident, easygoing, emotionless. He could handle this tricky situation— dying young—just as competently as he'd managed every other aspect of his medical training. The woman before him was basically his own age, yet it was obvious that Dash couldn't begin to identify Brett as a member of his generation, his world. *I'm just like you.* He couldn't begin to imagine himself in her position. She had been singled out, marked. She wouldn't be troubled, would she, to hear a peer still wet behind the ears allude to her death as if it were no big deal—as if she had surely gotten used to the idea by now. Bravely facing up to death, as he probably perceived his immediate task, he didn't have the faintest idea what was going on here. He had no notion of what he didn't know.

I think I get the picture.

When Dash left the room, Brett broke down.

I didn't know it would be like this.

McKee had told her the prudent thing was to go to the hospital. They'd imagined that a life-threatening infection could be controlled. No, there was no future in being confined to the hospital, taking harsh drugs that would leave her even weaker. Given her condition, one thing or another was bound to prove fatal. There was nothing to be done. When Brett had spoken to him earlier in the day, Al McKee had not been prepared to be so brutal.

"It sounds like I could die next week," she cried. "I've never felt so hopeless."

She'd come to an acceptance of her death, she'd told them, beginning some time after the transplant. Her life since then had been a journey of acceptance, she said. Yet her pain now, the heartbreak, was raw. She didn't feel sick enough . . . to die.

"There's no cure for anything," she cried.

The three of them collapsed in an entwined heap.

Gradually recovering, as so often before, they began to talk calmly. Dash, for all his brashness, had a point. Thank God Brett hadn't come to Baystate because of pain—the smothering, killing pain.

"I'm free," she said. "Fragile and free." No more hospitals! Free to live!

"You've fought so hard," he said. "You've done everything you had to do." He added, "The four years have been grueling, but there have also been wonderful times." With each new assault on their faith and hope, they'd found themselves increasingly blessed by an awareness of connectedness and love.

She nodded.

"Apart from the normal bullshit," he said, "everything before Hodgkin's was great as far as I'm concerned."

"Smith seems a thousand years away," she said. "Good, but far away."

"You've had the summer. These months have been so important for everyone. You've done a lot."

"I'm still going to be here," she said. "I'm just going to be hotter than usual."

Eve was expected on the weekend. Thinking of her old girlfriend provoked fresh tears. "Our lives are so different now. Eve is so happy." After a silence, "I guess I won't be able to go to the Olga Broumas seminar now."

The Olga Broumas seminar had acquired symbolic importance for her: a meeting with a mentor. He suggested she call the woman and talk; perhaps that would demystify the situation.

"What are you thinking?" he asked, following another silence. He wanted to know.

"I want to get home and work. I want to do my work."

Brett's blood arrived. At eight, when Beth turned up with Chinese food, their daughter gave her an utterly open, loving smile. "Sweetie!"

He and Holly drove home in a kind of stupor. They'd thought there could be more troubleshooting, more crisis intervention. There was no more. Linker had said six to nine months, knowing Brett's marrow was bound to be very weak by then. At the end of her marrow, he thought. September was the ninth month.

Brett was exasperated when they spoke Tuesday. She hadn't gotten home from the hospital until four in the afternoon. She felt rotten.

"How about coming out to dinner soon? We'd like to see you."

"I know that, Dad."

"Tomorrow then? You could bring your work with you."

"No, I need to work here."

"All right. Shall I call you in the morning, or will I wait to hear from you?"

"I'll call." Abruptly, she hung up.

But she called back at nine in the morning. "I'd like to come out for the day, but I need to work."

"Good, I'm on my way."

At her apartment he noticed a new drawing. A naked figure in the lower half, her hands clasped behind her back, faced a horizon where countless individual fires, like distant bonfires, burned on a vast field of black. One fire was somewhat detached from the others, closer to the standing figure. She'd become quite expert at portraying her distinctive body. She'd made the drawing the night before.

"They finally saw something in my lung," she said, "and prescribed an antibiotic, but I want to hear from McKee before I start taking it."

"We'll call from the house."

On the drive to Conway she said, "I had the strangest experience last night." She was lying in bed with her eyes closed, but awake, completely awake, when suddenly, like a deck of cards being fanned, she saw numerous photographs of herself as a child and, more bizarre, there were childhood photographs of Beth and other friends—snapshots of children that she recognized but had never actually seen before. The show lasted for possibly three minutes, she estimated. "It was fascinating and disturbing at the same time. The phone rang and I got up to answer it but realized it wasn't real. Very clearly, I heard a voice say, I'm looking for Brett Hobbie."

That wasn't all. Still in bed and still fully awake, she was looking toward the window when she saw thousands of bubbles, like dust or like bubbles under water, beads of light, millions of them forming shapes in the air. "It was incredible. I woke up Beth and I was staring at all this and trying to describe it to her. She became frightened."

Subsequently Beth referred rather lightheartedly to Brett's spooky hallucinations—the photographs, the voice, the shape-shifting beads of light—but her description of the incident, and what had frightened her, was more explicit. Am I dying? Brett had asked. And of the vision of light in the window: Are they angels?

Sitting in the Conway kitchen, Brett confided, "I blew up at Beth yesterday. I wanted to be alone. With myself. I can't talk about everything all the time. I don't want to be always talking about it. I'm experiencing this. It's my life; it's happening to me, I *know* it, and I can't *share* it. I need to be by myself, you know, and try to understand what's happening. It's like the difference between walking in the woods alone or being with someone. I need simply to *be*." Other people now often sapped her strength. "Anyway, it was crazy to take it out on Snapper. We're fine now."

She spent the day at the long table in the tall, sunlit dining room, alone, working in her sketchbook.

He spoke to McKee, who advised that Brett take the antibiotic, which might clear up her lung and affect the ongoing fevers. He also believed radiation therapy, intended to reduce disease in her abdomen and her hip and perhaps alleviate pain, along with other symptoms, was clearly worthwhile. Following the day with Dash, Al McKee sounded somewhat reassuring.

After some hesitation, his publisher in New York finally decided to use Brett's drawing for the cover of *The Day*. They intended to use a blown-up detail of the drawing on the cover and reproduce the whole image as a frontispiece. A print of the jacket arrived on the Saturday of another gathering in Conway. It was a powerful cover. Brett's excitement made the whole labor of the novel worthwhile as far as he was concerned.

But—everything now double-edged—she would never see the book, he thought. She'd never walk into the bookstore on Main Street or Pleasant Street and see it sitting on the shelf. Pick it up, turn to her frontispiece, sniff the new pages. All that! Yet this detail must have seemed trivial to his daughter, if she thought about it at all, a small item carried along in the avalanche of loss.

Eve visited for four days. "She's exactly the same," Brett said, as though amazed that others could go on so unchanged. He took their picture as they walked around the yard together in Conway, holding hands, talking. Brett wore the green jumpsuit she'd worn that Saturday night in June. Her face was disturbingly pale, slightly puffy. Now she felt the disease progressing, she said, putting pressure on her lower torso, her upper legs. She felt bloated. She looked at things now, he thought—her mother's garden—with deliberate care, as though to fix the memory, preserve it. Later that evening he watched his daughter as she stood alone in the south yard watching the moon come up over the tall white pines that bordered Boyden's pasture. A full harvest moon.

When Eve was alone with him on the terrace for a moment, she said, "We were naive." The change in Brett this trip was heartbreaking and scary.

"We were always entitled to be hopeful," he said. The cure rate for Hodgkin's was high. Brett's disease had always responded to treatment. No one imagined it would recur so aggressively. In a moment he said, "You may not see her again." As recently as a year ago he couldn't have imagined the life in which he would make such a statement to Eve.

"I plan to be here," she said.

"Things could happen quickly."

Soon after supper Brett said she was exhausted—she looked it—and she wanted to return to Northampton.

"Have you called Olga Broumas?" he asked.

"Oh, I'm going," she said. The seminar was the following weekend.

The next day she and Beth and Eve attempted to drive to Vermont but turned back when Brett was afflicted with stomach cramps. She took an Ativan and slept much of the day, Beth reported later. That was new: sleeping the day away. Each day, he felt, was slightly more difficult than the one before; there was the sense, as in that Kurt Weill song, though infinitely graver, of days dwindling down to a precious few. He couldn't be with his daughter constantly—that wasn't what she wanted or needed—but he was afraid to be away from her. The need to hold tight mirrored the need to let go.

Holly said, "I'm going to die when Brett dies. I feel like my heart is cracked."

Holly met Eve in Northampton by chance, and Eve talked about Brett's wish to be alone now. "I have to let go of Brett," she said, "but *she* has to let go of everything. She has to prepare herself to lose everything."

Eve was great, Brett told him after her friend had left, Brett loved her, but four days this September had been a long visit. Her fevers seemed to have stopped for the time being, and maybe the anti-inflammatory was finally working, because her pain was somewhat improved. The bloated, full feeling was uncomfortable, however, and she was eager for radiation to begin. She intended to spend the day with Beth; they hadn't been alone together for a while.

"Enjoy the day with Beth."

"I will."

"One of us will be down Friday to take you to Springfield."

"Okay."

Looking through his journal he came on this time the year before. That very day, September 17, with Brett newly released from 11 Long, they'd walked through the park before continuing on to the clinic. Linker gave her an inspiring report—her counts were excellent—yet Brett remained subdued. That was the day she purchased the running shoes on Haight Street, a scene he remembered vividly, in part because of the poignant contrast between his daughter, diminished by her ordeal, and three other young women, who were having fun, typically vibrant and invincible-seeming. He was surprised to find that resonant detail had been left out of his account of the day. Because the observation had been too painful, he wondered, or too obvious to deserve mention?

Then, their last night in San Francisco, dinner at Zuni's, she appeared metamorphosed, beautiful. One year ago.

. . .

He arrived at Baystate Friday afternoon to keep Brett company. Holly had been there with her in the morning. Although his daughter might never be stuck in the hospital again, she wasn't altogether free of the place either. She was seated in the corner of the outpatient solarium, receiving blood and platelets again. Everyone else here, reclining in comfortable chairs in a large semicircle, bags of suspended liquids dripping into their wasted arms, was elderly. While he hated to see her in this room, among these people, Brett seemed relaxed today.

"I've decided I can't get to the Olga Broumas thing, after all," she told him, "but I still wish I could."

"It might have been awfully disappointing," he suggested. Meeting with a half dozen strangers determined to win favor and get their money's worth. He was glad she'd given up the idea.

Plaid shirt, shorts, a hooded, zippered sweatshirt, the new Reeboks. Thin legs, freckled knees. She had a new haircut. He mentioned the running shoes she'd bought this time last year on Haight Street.

Brett said, "I'm glad I'm not there anymore."

She could no longer button her jeans, she said, because her abdomen was so swollen. That morning she'd coughed blood, and her gums had bled, her platelets were that bad. They wanted to postpone radiation because her white count was so low. But when was it going to be higher?

"I want to get a CAT scan later today," she said, "to see what has grown." That was at her insistence; the doctor hadn't ordered it.

"Maybe you could skip that until they decide what action to take." The appropriate radiation therapy hadn't been determined yet.

"I want them to have a clear picture of what's happening." She had to continue doing all she could do. When the chalky barium-like substance arrived, she dutifully swallowed it in anticipation of the scan.

"When do you expect to see Eve again?" he asked.

"Not for a while. Maybe December." She added, "Ellen is planning to come in November, after she returns from France."

November, he thought. December. "With your white count so low, anything can happen suddenly."

"I know that, Dad." She added, "I wonder when I should stop eating fruits and vegetables."

They discussed the possibility of Brett's having an exhibit of her work at Smith, possibly this fall. He'd already made some preliminary phone calls but hadn't yet found anyone who seemed helpful.

By the time Brett had completed her transfusion there was only one elderly woman left in the room. They walked to the radiology department, located in a newer building, and settled down in the waiting room. It was almost five. Brett had been here all day.

"Have you made out a will yet?"

"No."

"Just leave me everything."

"Yeah, right."

She told him stories about Beth's sweet, ancient Granddaddy, age ninety-three or so. He had a Ph.D. in biology, and until recent years he'd been very sharp. These days, though, there were unhappy lapses and mishaps. Once, wishing to be helpful, he used vegetable oil to wax the kitchen floor. He filled the bird feeder with cat litter. Now, it seemed, he didn't remember what fall was all about. Entering the house the other day, he'd reported the phenomenon of falling leaves as though it were an amazing first. Brett was fond of him.

Perhaps he understood the old man, he thought, driving home toward dusk—Beth had relieved him—for this year he also felt he was seeing the fall, as it inexorably advanced all around him, as if for the first time, as if it had never happened before.

Since Beth was away, and Jocelyn, as she did every weekend, had come from Manhattan to be with her sister, Brett spent Saturday night in Conway—an ordinary evening, including a movie. How could it be ordinary? Sunday morning, he drove to Northampton to pick up her medications so she could remain with them for the day. Brett awakened with some pain and nausea, however, and she didn't improve as the day wore on. Sitting in the sun didn't feel right. She wasn't up for a country ride. In the midst of everyone's cheerfully going about their business, she decided by noon to return to her apartment.

"It's a beautiful day, and you're all so happy," she said. "You all have things you want to do. I need to be in my own place."

He called her at five-thirty, concerned that she'd been alone all day, even when that was what she claimed to want. "Would you like to come out for supper? I'd love to come and get you."

"No, I feel out of it, mainly tired." She intended to have some soup and go to bed. "I just want to be here tonight."

"Okay, I guess I can understand that."

"I hope so. Do I need to explain it?" Then she wanted to speak to Jocelyn, who she realized was probably disappointed.

Many people wanted to be with Brett now. What was becoming clear—there wasn't enough of Brett to go around.

He picked her up the next morning to return to Baystate. A new week, Monday morning; this was her work, he thought, the body that had betrayed her. She wore a pale-blue jumper over a T-shirt, with a denim shirt jacket over that. Incongruous with her young outfit, she shuffled this morning, bent stiffly from the waist. The pain in her left backside now was the pain she'd experienced for so long on the right side prior to the transplant. She'd been going to the UCSF pain clinic then, taking anti-inflammatories constantly. For months they'd been unable to find evidence of Hodgkin's.

A young man in a brown suit was leaving radiation as they arrived. The two symmetrical bald patches on the back of his head, where his neck met his skull, were the same telltale marks Brett wore following her initial six weeks of radiation therapy in 1989. She'd thought the world of her radiologist that first year of treatment, Francine Halberg, whom she hadn't seen since.

"They're very good here," the young man assured Brett, pausing on his way out. He was already halfway through his treatment. "Everyone is very good," he said. "Good luck."

His daughter smiled politely. Everyone else here this morning, like the other day at the solarium, was forty or fifty or sixty years older than she was. She had to swallow another pint of barium-like liquid. She did what she needed to do, period.

He raised the question Jocelyn had been struggling with lately— whether she should return to live in Massachusetts for the time being. Brett's response was unhesitating. "If she wants to move back here for herself, okay. But just for me, no. I don't want that responsibility." She felt very close to Joce, she said. "The present routine of visiting on weekends seems fine." But she understood her sister's uncertainty and anxiety. "I'll call her tonight."

Her simulation today, the targeted fields of radiation treatment clearly marked out on her body, went all right. Their conference with Dr. Stark, however, was ambiguous.

They looked at the results of her recent CAT scan in his office. "It was wise to have the scan done," he said, "because there has been a change. What we're looking at is like slices of white bread, right?" He pointed to swelling in the lower left of one of the ghostly images displayed on the light box. He assumed that was Hodgkin's. The other problem spots were lymph nodes in the pelvic region. *Something* was causing interference with her kidney, and he pointed out the darker area in the picture, which indicated that the organ wasn't emptying fully. Given the extent of Brett's prior radiation, there were strict limits to the therapy he could safely administer. He might alleviate some pain in the left hip. The difficulty with treating the pelvic area was further damage to her marrow. Her white count couldn't go much lower than it was. "I don't know the answer," he said. The daily routine of radiation was bound to be fatiguing and to make her more vulnerable to infection, yet she couldn't go around with her present pain either. He would talk with McKee, but Brett would have to make the decision.

With difficulty she shuffled to the car.

"Want to take me to lunch?" Brett asked brightly, as though she'd just had a great idea.

She was talkative and relaxed in the sunny restaurant in downtown Northampton, filling him in on certain friends and her hospice nurse, Carolyn, whom she adored. Small talk, really, just sitting there at their table for two. Her hands shook noticeably, not from tension or drugs but from physical weakness, she suspected. She couldn't stop the shaking. Her heart rate felt as rapid as a bird's. There were small dark spots like pinpricks visible above her T-shirt: low platelets. Her lunch was a large deluxe hamburger.

She preceded him out of the restaurant, slightly stooped, shuffling past the largely young crowd here like an infirm elderly person and not giving a damn for the looks she received. The night they'd briskly walked to the restaurant for dinner, Brett in those new shoes, looking fresh and well—that had only been three weeks earlier. Where would they be three weeks from today?

Back at the apartment she showed him her latest charcoal drawing. A female torso, in which the center of the chest was a window that framed a serene scene—a brilliantly full moon over peaceful water. On the other half of the diptych a lily reached, arching, toward the figure.

As he left her place, Brett's masseur, a thin, vigorous man in his thirties, was bundling through the door with his portable worktable.

It was easier to be *with* her. It was easier to bear one day's unfolding into the next if you could be with her. Were the days now easier for Beth, he wondered, than they were for Holly and him, left with their memories and imaginings in Conway? Being with her in the moment—riding in the car, having lunch, talking about nothing much—felt safe, possible.

. . .

McKee advised Brett to receive radiation to both areas—her back and the pelvic region. Let's get it over with, he said, and keep our fingers crossed. Rather than treating her disease according to the rules, he was treating *her,* he explained. When Holly took her to Springfield the next day, Brett's pain forced her to revert to the wheelchair, and she seemed unusually tired and frail.

Friday morning, yet another fair fall day, Brett called before nine. "Beth had to go to school," she said, "and I don't want to be alone."

He let himself into the apartment half an hour later and followed the sound of her voice—Hi—to the living room. She was lying on her side on the striped couch, a loveseat, her legs drawn up, napping. Movement meant pain. Blue sweatpants, a bright blue top.

"I'll let you rest," he said.

I don't know what I'm doing.

He fussed quietly in the kitchen, cleaning up a few dishes, wiping the counter. What did he feel? If she needed to sleep, he didn't want to disturb her, but his daughter lying there now while he aimlessly . . . In an hour Carolyn, the hospice nurse, arrived with a colleague. Brett sat up and responded lucidly to Carolyn's questions, anticipating most of them. The back pain was more incapacitating, her pelvic area so swollen that whatever she ate made her feel full. She listed the medications she was taking and how often.

Carolyn spoke gently and her smile was to be believed. "Are you feeling hopeful about the radiation?" she asked.

"I've always responded in the past, so I expect it to help. But I don't expect the pain to be completely gone."

They talked about a book on dying, written by two hospice nurses, that Brett had been looking through. They hugged good-bye warmly.

Brett ate a full plate of various take-out dishes he'd picked up at an Italian deli. He'd brought recent photographs taken in Conway for her to see. The whole family posed before the fragrant arbor of honeysuckle. Brett went through them quickly, without comment, and decided to keep one picture of herself seated at the end of the long dining table, sketching, and another of Eve and her together in the backyard, near a small umbrella-shaped tree. He'd also brought snapshots of himself; he needed something for the flap of his book and wanted her opinion.

"I don't think your face should look like a mask," she advised.

She inadvertently raised her shirt, stretching, and he was startled at how swollen her abdomen had become. As she walked, tentatively, to the bathroom, revealing her lower back as she massaged it, he observed the radiation oncologist's constellations of markings, black, blue, and red—indecipherable symbols.

Later they sat in the corridor of the radiology department for an hour, waiting for the CAT scan. She'd taken a Dilaudid pill to cope with the pain of lying on her stomach during the test, and that made her sleepier than she was already. Disturbingly, sleep was all she seemed capable of for the past few days, she said. She was able to read some—the Neruda biography—but she hadn't been able to sit at her drawing table at all.

When three medical school students hurried by in their white jackets, she said, "Lisa Bernard." It had been Lisa's ambition to become a doctor since the sixth grade, when she and Brett were best friends; lo and behold, she was doing it. "Couldn't you see Nathaniel running around here in a white coat?" she asked.

She was in the scan for half an hour, and she looked beat when she was wheeled out.

"How did it go?"

"Bad."

They found their way through the maze of corridors to radiation therapy. Another wait.

She seemed to be getting mixed signals from friends now, she told him. She was disappointed when Mary didn't call to tell her about the Olga Broumas seminar, for example. "I had to call her to find out."

"Maybe she didn't know if you'd want to hear about it, she felt uncomfortable calling when you'd been unable to go."

To Brett, Mary seemed to be withdrawing a little. She had the impression on the phone lately that Ellen, too, was distancing herself. And Richard had developed a new awkwardness around her, a solemn tone of voice that wasn't real.

"It's hard for people to know how to be with you now," he said. They didn't know what she wanted from them, what was helpful and what was bound to be interfering or disappointing. Everything had become more difficult and frightening. Suddenly a close friend wasn't sure what her role was.

She nodded.

Whatever vibes Brett was getting from her friends, it was also true that she hardly had time now—precious time—to hold up her end of relationships. Four days with Eve had seemed long. Two hours with someone less important was two hours too long. She had already begun to let go of people in her life, just as, months before, she'd relinquished significant friendships in San Francisco. Eventually—how long? he thought—her world would be reduced to a very few.

While Brett was in radiology, Stark approached him in the corridor. "This is growing," he said in an up-front New York accent. "The tumor in the back has grown since last week." His eyes were sympathetic. "I'll irradiate these areas, then I don't know what else I can do." Holding up his open palms, he said, "It's in God's hands." He used to read fiction, he went on, but he gave up on it after his partner died of a heart attack at fifty-one. "Fifty-one," he repeated, shaking his head. "Dead."

He repeated Stark's words to Brett as they drove home. *It's in God's hands.* His daughter looked at him. "Did he say that?"

Once past Northampton on the interstate, the drive to Conway was lovely, the first glimpses of color visible. Brett wanted to stay outside when they reached the house at about four-thirty. The Dilaudid had worn off completely, she said, and she was more awake and alert than she'd been all day. It was cool enough to require a jacket, and she pulled on his red wool tam-o'-shanter. He pushed her down the field in the wheelchair—the spanking new Reeboks on the footrests—to the long stone wall that he had restored over the course of their first five or six years here. With Holly and Nathaniel and Ben, the dog, they walked west along the wall, under birch trees, to the split-rail gate. From there they had a good view of the lower fields, their narrow serpentine road, bordered by maple and birch, disappearing into dark woods, two mounded hillocks rising to the north, the fall color just appearing in individual trees. The air was fragrant.

"It's beautiful," Brett said. Her thin hands rested calmly in her lap.

Nathaniel pushed her over to the road and then back up to the house. Brett and her brother remained out on the terrace by the herb bed, talking. Observing them for a moment from the kitchen window, he could see her questioning her brother, listening as Nathaniel talked, then advising him, or rather, artfully offering her considered opinion, smiling. This older sister, he thought: his son's immeasurable loss.

Brett was still in bed when he let himself into the apartment at eight-thirty Monday morning.

"I want to sleep for another hour."

"Okay, I'll be in the other room."

Less than an hour later she called him back to the bedroom. "Would you call McKee and leave him this message? My abdomen seems more swollen, and now I have pain there when I cough or urinate. Also, my urine is an unusual bright yellow, and I have a strange vaginal discharge, which is uncomfortable. And tell him I can't help sleeping all the time."

He called several times: busy.

Brett got up and dressed herself in baggy pants, a blue sweater. "My wardrobe is getting limited," she said. Her freckled face was somewhat swollen, puffy, but she didn't look bad in the face. She hobbled, bent over, to the sunny living room.

"Would you get me my cereal and my pills?"

Beth had left a bowl of cereal and a handful of pills on the kitchen counter with a note reminding her to take her medication, as if she might forget.

"I never would," Brett said. Disfigured, immobilized, in pain, she carried on with what had to be done. Her attention to detail and her determination to question everything happening, to get everything straight, was typical of the way she'd been all her life. She ate her breakfast.

How do you know what to do? a friend had asked him recently. He answered, You don't.

She soon lay down on the couch, unable to keep her eyes open. "This is how I felt with Gabby. I had nothing to say to her." Gabby Silver had visited on Sunday.

He sat in the caned rocking chair near the white bookcase Brett had filled with narrow-spined volumes of poetry. She'd singled out specific poems of a Swedish poet for him to read, as if it were her responsibility to entertain him. He couldn't follow what the man was saying. While she lay there sleeping, he browsed through other books: Wendell Berry, W. S. Merwin, Olga Broumas, Mary Oliver, James Wright. The kittens she and Beth had adopted in the spring were now more like cats and exasperated him, tearing around the room in bursts.

At noon she sat up and ate a bowl of rice in order to stomach more pills. When she lay down again, he said, "Do you hate this sleepiness?"

"Being unconscious all day? I guess so."

Nathaniel arrived to take his sister to radiation. The drive back to Conway, like these fall days, had become another element in the unfolding sorrow.

Brett returned to Conway with her brother following her therapy. She curled up on the small couch in the kitchen while Holly got their meal together. Surprisingly, her appetite was good.

"I haven't decided where I want the memorial service to be," she said as they sat at the table after eating. "Somewhere in Conway, I guess."

"It could be here on our hill," he said. They hadn't talked about this before, and her statement startled him. "We could raise a tent."

She thought that would be good. "I've decided I want to be cremated, not buried."

Yes.

"I don't know about scattering ashes," she said.

Maybe they could take her ashes to Maine, he suggested, the ocean, and release them from a boat or a cliff. They'd find the place that seemed absolutely right.

She nodded.

"It would be wonderful if you could plan the service as much as possible," he said. Choosing the poems, the music. That might be good for her, and it would be a gift to everyone present.

Yes, she wanted to do that.

Holly said she'd like to get one of those large, wonderful stones from the Maine coast, rolled smooth by the sea, and have it engraved for a marker. . . .

"That's a nice idea," Brett said.

Driving to Northampton, Holly sat in the backseat so that Brett could stretch her legs up front. He drove. They were quiet as they sped south on 91.

Brett said, "Turn on the radio."

The song was James Taylor's "Up on the Roof," which sounded sweet just now and seemed to belong to an earlier time in their lives, everything different. The sense of them all listening to the lyrics—"When this old world starts getting you down"—Brett listening to this out of all the possible songs as they drove in the dark, moved him. He was aware of her sitting next to him, looking out through the windshield. What was she thinking? There's a place to go: up on the roof. He wanted to reach out to her and found he was reluctant, afraid she wouldn't want that, wouldn't respond; and the instant he understood his hesitation, he reached across the narrow space between their seats, his eyes on the road, taking her hand, and she clasped back. They held hands until he pulled the car up before her building. He kissed the back of her hand before he let it go, and she gave him a smile.

Her phone call the next morning was unexpected because he knew Beth was going to be home for the day.

"I'm so *miserable*." It was a shattered, despondent cry. "Everything feels like it's getting worse. It's so hard to get up feeling like this every day."

Each time she'd let him hear the rawness of her despair he was initially stunned, at a loss. "Brett, you've been amazing, facing all this. I don't know how you do it day after day." To him the wonder was that he'd seen her grief so seldom.

Now she sobbed as though she'd discovered another door to her heart, which she'd just opened, that morning, awakening. "I just feel so awful. I set goals for myself each day, living in the day, but now I can't do those things. I can't write or draw."

"You can't write?"

"My hands shake so much. I can't concentrate, I can't stay awake. It's happened so fast. I don't know how it could be so fast." For all the implicit pain of recent days, she hadn't expressed her astonishment in so many words. "It's hard to go from walking everywhere and doing everything to not being able to get out of bed."

He imagined her lying in her bed just then, sunlight illuminating the room.

"I know," he said.

"I just want time to do my drawing. To do *more*." Then, as if she refused to be caught entertaining illusions, she said, "I'll be ready to make the transition, but I didn't think . . ."

He'd overheard Holly telling a friend over the phone that Brett often seemed serene, as if she'd found the way to accept her life as given. No, she hoped to do more work, to live in the day, each day, longer. What she felt this morning was anything but serene.

"Do you want me to come down? I could be there almost immediately."

"No, Beth is home today." She hadn't spoken to Beth yet this morning—she had gone out on an errand while Brett was still asleep—but she expected her soon. "I just wanted to call, to talk, because when I woke up today . . ."

Anxious to comfort her, he thought that perhaps the only possible solace was to be found, as before, in the insurmountable truth of the matter. "Your pain and frustration about not feeling better . . . you just want to feel well enough to get around again and to work, to draw . . ." He paused. "Maybe you aren't going to." Maybe there was a way to let the frustration go because . . . it wasn't going to get better.

Brett said, "I know."

"We're hoping the radiation will offer some relief so you can go on. But maybe it won't."

"I know." She was no longer crying.

After a silence, he asked, "Would you like to come out here today? We could just sit outside."

"I'd like that. Maybe Beth will bring me out after we've been to Springfield. You and Mom think of a place I can go in the wheelchair. On your walk."

When he hung up the phone, he collapsed, terrified for her.

I'll be ready to make the transition.

Awakening alone to another brilliant fall day, knowing in every part of your body that you were dying.

October 1. Geese overhead, the sound first, then the wavering line. Several flocks of geese. When Brett dropped a new pain medication from her daily regimen, the profound sleepiness that had oppressed her for the past week lifted, and she seemed better than she'd been.

Awake! The inexorable momentum of events seemed to let up. Maybe radiation would make a difference, after all; maybe there would be more good time. Thursday night she and Beth even went to the movies. Friday evening she called to report on her day. She'd resorted to liquid morphine for severe pain and was still feeling stoned. Richard had driven her to radiation. Her white count was 700. She'd been running a fever, sometimes as high as a hundred and two, so one oncologist wanted to hospitalize her for IV drugs, but she and McKee decided, as before, no. She was taking an oral antibiotic. Radiation was difficult, as usual, but she got through it. She didn't feel there'd been any change from the treatment. Stark said, Come on, tell me there's been a one percent change, and she said, Okay, there's been a one percent change, but she didn't feel it.

Her voice, under the influence, was relaxed. "You sound well," he told her.

"Well, I'm not. I'm flushed, feverish, wiped out, in pain. I just called to bring you up to date."

Saturday was warmer than it had been, balmy. Holly and Jocelyn went to the valley to run errands and returned with Brett, wearing a blousy jumper her grandmother had made her over a red cotton turtleneck. Above the Reeboks, no socks, her ankles were swollen. She sat in the wheelchair on the stone terrace and wrote in her journal. Her hands, for whatever reason, had stopped shaking. Later, when he looked out the window, she and Jocelyn had moved down under the maple tree by the picnic table. Jocelyn, on the bench of the table, facing Brett, had one hand on the wheelchair. Her full young face, even at this distance, was tragic. Because of the height of the arm rests, Brett's thin shoulders were hunched. As he watched them, they wiped tears from their faces. Later yet, on his way to the kitchen, they were in the same postures under the tree, but now animatedly talking and laughing. Unusually, it was Jocelyn who was telling the story to her older sister's amusement—narrating, he learned later, her recent adventure of the hurricane on Fire Island. Their pleasure, he thought, just being together.

262

He and Holly and Brett drove through Conway and Ashfield on dirt roads canopied over with tall trees just beginning to change color. They rode in silence. They turned onto a road the whole family had discovered together ten years earlier when they'd first bought the Conway land and before they'd built their house. The road was still the same, although it had been a golden tunnel then, more than it was today. In snapshots from that outing, Brett's long hair was the color of the trees.

It was as though every moment now was the end of something. What are you thinking? They passed a small cape nestled, no less, among its trees, and Brett let out an involuntary "Oh." He knew the place represented the sort of dream she and Beth had once envisioned for themselves.

When they returned to the house he said, "How was that?" referring to their modest foliage tour. The question amused her, as if he'd said, Was that enough? Will that do? Right after dinner, exhausted, she wanted to return to Northampton.

Monday, when Holly returned from spending the day alone with Brett, she had the distracted, at-loose-ends manner of someone who'd been away for a long time, whose journey had changed her.

Wednesday, the seventh day of October. He entered the apartment at one in the afternoon and found her in the bedroom. A hug and a kiss. She'd been sleeping all morning. It was likely now that part of the fatigue was a result of liver disorder, enlarged nodes impinging on that organ so it functioned less efficiently. Her pallor today was tinged yellow, as were the whites of her eyes. She wore blue sweatpants and a charcoal sweater.

"Would you like me to help you with your shoes?"

"No, I can manage." She pulled the Reeboks onto her swollen feet. She needed to take her medications. Something to promote blood clotting had been added because of her hazardously low platelets. Down the corridor to the elevator in the wheelchair, out to the car. The sunlight wasn't kind: her short red hair less vibrant, her face slightly discolored, her lips pale. God, he thought.

This weekend, she reminded him, she and Beth were going to Boston to attend a Stephen Levine symposium on dying. Talks, meditations, healing encounters.

"Maybe your mother and I should do that."

"It's sold out. I mentioned it to you a long time ago," she said. Tickets were $120 each. She and Beth had purchased theirs weeks ago, as soon as they'd heard about the meeting.

He was anxious about her going at all but kept it to himself. "I hope it's a wonderful weekend for you. All you could hope it to be."

"Me too."

He missed the Birnie Avenue exit, so they had to drive into the city and double back to the hospital.

Yesterday, after radiation, she and Beth had gone over to the Italian market district of Springfield, she said. "It was nothing fancy but real. The Italians shouting at each other," she said. "If I closed my eyes, it took me right back." To Italy.

They parked in the physicians' lot; they knew the code. She had to get out of the wheelchair to cross from the asphalt over grass to the sidewalk.

Waiting in the radiation department, they turned to the subject of her friends again. The new solemnity Richard seemed to have adopted was a drag. "I want to say to him, Come back. Don't be this way." And Mary. "Recently, on the phone, she didn't have anything to say to me. A blank. At last she said, I don't want to tire you by keeping you on the phone. I felt, You aren't tiring me. It's just strange."

People were afraid of what was happening to her; they weren't good at it. He was sure Mary meant what she'd said.

"About the weekend," he said, "would you like us to come to Boston anyway? We could take you and Beth to dinner one night."

"No, we see this as a special time to be together. We live together, but it's not the same. There are always people dropping by. We need this time."

"Soon this routine will be over," he said, "and there will be no reason to come back here." The course of treatment was scheduled to end next Wednesday, one week from today.

"Then I want to live. Now I feel like I'm dying, not living. Dozing off all the time. I want to be living awhile more—doing what I want to do and need to do."

While she was receiving radiation, he sat staring at the wall. *Then I want to live.* As in the past, it so happened that the other people waiting for treatment this afternoon were old. None of them looked as ill as his daughter did today.

G lancing at the time in the car, she seemed dismayed. "It's three o'clock already." The day gone—another day.

"By this time next week you'll have completed your last radiation treatment," he repeated encouragingly. No more daily trips to the hospital.

"That will be the end of my suffering," she said. "I can't stand this."

"You've suffered enough."

She looked at him. "How do I look? Is my face puffy?"

"No, you look okay. Your face looks remarkably well really." Except for her coloring, the result of a malfunctioning liver.

"I think I've gained ten pounds in two weeks. There's something extreme going on."

Entering the living room of the apartment after the dim hallway was like stepping outside again.

"Aren't these trees beautiful?" she said.

The ash outside the east window had changed overnight. With the first frost it would drop all its leaves the same way: at once. To the south a sugar maple, whose crown rose just above the window, had turned the red-gold of bittersweet.

"Take my picture with the tree behind me," she said. Beth's small automatic camera was on a nearby table. A white quilt with an orange diamond pattern, especially seasonable, had been laid across the back of the armchair Brett sat in. She assumed a relaxed posture, an ankle resting on her knee, her hands in her lap, the inflamed tree behind her.

"Are you going to smile?" he asked.

She did.

Snap.

Beth returned, wheeling her bicycle into the apartment, and they decided there was time for a walk before Brett went on to her appointment with her masseur. He pushed the wheelchair up the block to Green Street. At the end of Green, they crossed under a chestnut tree and Brett asked Beth to gather some of the gleaming smooth nuts for her. He picked up a horse chestnut and slipped it—forever—into the pocket of his plaid jacket, a horse blanket purchased in St. Louis over twenty years ago. His daughter at seven! She would be gone and he'd still have the damn jacket. Brett held her head back looking at the canopy of tall trees, taking in everything. Where the road inclined downward between the perennial gardens and the pond, he let the wheelchair roll and ran behind it.

"Dad!"

She directed their walk through the lovely garden, the hundred-year-old Camperdown elm there against a wall of evergreens. Under the large ginkgo tree, Brett took Beth's hand. He'd never seen someone walking along holding hands with a person in a wheelchair, he realized. He was grateful to guide the chair, making the hand-holding possible.

As they walked through the quad before Burton Hall, to the south of Wright Hall, Brett said, "I feel so attached to this place." She added, "I'd be so different if I went to college now. You have to wait ten years before you know enough to be yourself."

Perhaps her life there seemed like ten years ago, though she'd graduated from Smith only five years before.

On an impulse, as they crossed Green Street again, Brett wanted to stop at the admissions office. Three prospective students, dressed for the occasion, were waiting for interviews. Brett collected brochures. "I remember getting these things in the mail," she said. "I had a boxful." She read aloud from one of the booklets as they continued down the street—inspiring phrases about preparation for the future, fulfillment, what gave life meaning.

He left them at the building where Brett's masseur practiced his soothing art.

"Bye, Dad."

The fall foliage along the highway as he drove north was in full bloom, as if the world was in its glory.

Now I'm always going to hate this time of year.

Will I?

I feel so attached to this place.

He reached into his pocket for the horse chestnut. He had it.

Al McKee returned his call and gave him an assessment of his daughter's state. The jaundice as well as Brett's sleepiness persuaded the doctor that her liver, impinged upon by disease, was deteriorating. The vaginal discharge suggested a fissure between the bladder and vagina, also the result of the tumor, causing a leak. That development was another indication that the disease was growing rapidly.

He asked the doctor, "How long does she have to live?" He'd asked that question once before. Everything was different now.

"I don't think Brett will be here in two weeks."

He controlled his voice, he controlled his heart. "How will she die?"

"She'll become bedridden, she'll sleep more and more. Undoubtedly she'll develop a pneumonia. We can provide morphine to relieve the anxiety of breathlessness. Then, eventually, she'll pass away."

"She's been faithfully going to radiation each day. Is there any point in continuing that?"

McKee didn't see any point in it. "Brett should be with her family now."

Which raised the question, Why hadn't McKee already spared her the time-consuming, debilitating daily routine? But he let that go. "She and Beth are planning this trip to Boston to attend a Stephen Levine conference. Is that advisable?"

"If they need that for closure," McKee said, "that's their affair. But it could happen there. It could happen at any time. That would be very difficult for Beth."

They said good-bye.

Closure. Two weeks? Brett, he thought. Brett.

He called the apartment and spoke to Beth. Fortunately Brett was just then occupied with a family friend—showing Susan Little her work. He conveyed the essence of his talk with McKee. He hadn't realized . . . There was no medical reason to continue radiation, a hated routine that would cost them the rest of the day, another autumn day. Why not just go out and have the afternoon to themselves? On the other hand, he realized it might be easier and wiser to follow through with the anticipated plan rather than spring this on Brett so suddenly.

"She may be afraid not to follow through," he said.

"Right," Beth said.

"Do what seems best for Brett. Go to radiation if skipping it would be more upsetting."

At pains not to interfere, he had to ask: Did going to Boston this weekend simply involve unacceptable risks? Maybe it was more important for Brett to stay here and visit Jocelyn, who was returning, as usual, to see her sister. It would be devastating for everyone if something happened away from home.

Beth listened. "I'll talk about it with her. While we're on the phone," she said, "Holly's been fixing up a room for Brett. I want you to know that she wants to stay here."

That wasn't an issue.

"I didn't want Holly to be disappointed or upset about that."

Holly had, in fact, painted and done over what had been Nathaniel's room in the event that it might become useful eventually—if Brett was confined to bed, in need of constant attention, for a prolonged period, for example. No one knew what would happen or how it would happen. But no, fixing up the room had more to do with Holly's nervous energy than it did with actual expectations. She wanted what Brett wanted.

"I hope you'll come out this afternoon," he said, "instead of going to Springfield, but do what you think is right." Otherwise, they'd all meet together that evening, as Brett had planned, with the counselor from hospice.

Brett called a little later. "Well, I didn't go to radiation, because you called ten minutes before ... But we aren't going to come out," she said, "so we'll see you tonight."

"What are you going to do?"

"I'm just going to go out and sit somewhere. Over near the pond maybe. Out into the green," she said.

"What are you planning for supper?"

"A sandwich or something. Nothing special. So, six-thirty."

"Okay, see you then." He said, "Enjoy the afternoon." That sounded absurd, but he meant it.

"Bye, Dad."

Now, he thought, facing no more to do, knowing the end of her life could come at any time. Just then she sounded calm—her parting "Bye, Dad" briskly upbeat—going out into the bright afternoon.

In fact, she was pissed off at him. As soon as Beth had gotten off the phone with him, she had repeated to Brett what McKee had said, and that threw them for an emotional loop, as Susan Little described it later. They weren't prepared to not go to radiation—to face the end of that option so suddenly—and the suggestion that Brett just skip it was a frightening and confusing jolt. Beth must have felt the same dilemma he had and so she put the question to Brett directly. But why did he have to call McKee? they asked. Why couldn't he leave it alone? Why? Even now, he was interfering, he wouldn't stay out of it.

That afternoon, among other sights and sounds, she watched some moments of a women's soccer game on the Smith playing fields. Her sport! The redhead with quick feet.

Norma Dana, a likable woman in her thirties, began by asking each of them how they felt about the news they'd learned that day. Two weeks. Instinctively, he resisted group encounters conducted by self-proclaimed guides, especially when the group was his family, immersed in the greatest pain of their lives, and the guide had never met them before. Brett wanted the evening, though, and he had come here open to possibilities. In answer to Norma's question, he said that McKee's words appalled him, even though they'd been living with this inevitability intensely. He felt he was facing the unknown. Brett was here, and he didn't know what it was going to be like when she wasn't here. None of them had ever done this before.

Holly and Beth both expressed how they couldn't be prepared for what was coming.

Nathaniel's response was more positive. When he learned what the doctor said, he told them, he went around the house gathering objects that represented Brett and her relationship to him—natural objects, symbolic mementos. He was going to fashion small bags of leather, medicine bags, he called them, to hold the things he'd collected. One bag would be planted under a tree for his sister, and the other bag would be for him to keep. Nathaniel was eloquent as he described his intention, and his emotion was contagious. Brett got up from the couch and embraced him, smiling, proud of her little brother.

Changing the tenor of the meeting, his daughter said she needed all her strength now for what lay ahead; she could no longer feel responsible for other people's needs. Brett was letting go of her body, Norma elaborated, and we had to let her go, let her know that it was all right, that she could stop taking responsibility for our feelings, stop worrying whether we'd be okay, and so on.

He, her father, identified with her too much, Brett went on; she had to be a separate individual. "You too, Mom," she said. She couldn't always be telling him what the doctor said, responding to his questions, his need to know. He had to give her control of her life, to let her do what she must without asserting his needs. She hadn't gone to radiation, for example, because he called and gave them McKee's view. She became confused, and then it was too late.

But—he was stung by her reading of the situation—he'd only called because he knew how much she loathed the hospital routine, couldn't wait until it was over. He wanted to spare her another pointless, punishing afternoon. And he'd urged Beth to pursue the day as scheduled if that seemed . . .

This debate, he thought, now—how absurd . . .

To Brett the afternoon typified the way in which his suggestions were actually decisions that he'd already made, which took control away from her. She was disappointed in McKee, as well; the fact was he'd already told them—Brett and Beth—how near the end she was.

Norma, as referee here, succinctly established that they, the parents, had "given Brett permission" not to worry about them.

Next item on the agenda.

The counselor wanted each of them to tell Brett what lasting gifts they had received from her. Again, the question exasperated him, as though each of them could suddenly say what none of them quite knew. Their spontaneous responses seemed inadequate. Brett was born when he was only Nathaniel's age, and there had been twenty-seven years, which had everything to do with what they'd just been talking about. There was too much to remember, a world. When the question came to Brett, she was more prepared than the rest of them. Her mother's gift to her was her energy and the ability to be thrilled by life. Beth had taught her trust and love. With her brother she shared a spiritual bond; she knew he would always be with her, and she would be with him. When she thought of her father, she said, she thought of all the things they'd always done together, a host of images; she thought of his passion and determination and how much he loved her.

They would leave here tonight with the understanding that they could do this, Norma told them, they could *let go,* and Brett would be free to *let go of her body.*

When they stood to say good night, Brett said, "I'm not getting up, because my back hurts." She'd been thoroughly alert and articulate throughout the three-hour session. She'd smiled and even laughed tonight, despite the strain, more herself than she'd seemed for some days.

He stooped down to give her a kiss, embracing her.

"Do I look like I'm going to die this weekend?" she said to him, as if asking, Do I look like I'm going to climb Everest? She had made up her mind to attend the Stephen Levine conference despite McKee's reservations.

"No," he said, "and not in two weeks either."

She called early the next afternoon. She wanted her mother to meet her at three-thirty to look for a dress, something large and comfortable but attractive, for the Boston occasion. Richard had just arrived to take her to radiation therapy. She couldn't stop until she'd finished the prescribed course of treatment, done all there was for her to do. She couldn't fail to fulfill her obligation to herself.

Following the trip to Baystate, she was too wiped out to accompany her mother shopping, but Holly managed to find a lovely dress in one of Northampton's small shops. She was trembling with excitement, she said, as she approached Brett's apartment with her gift. As always, her daughter was effusively appreciative.

She'd told him she'd call to say good-bye before they left for Boston, and that evening she did.

"We're leaving a little later tonight than we planned so I can sleep on the way."

"It will be another adventure," he said.

"My lungs feel different," she mentioned as though in passing. "There's something there." Then, "All right, we're off!"

9

SNOW

Saturday.

Beth called before nine. They didn't go to Boston, after all, she said. Brett's breathing had become difficult during the night, and this morning there was a disturbing amount of blood when she coughed. Beth had called McKee, who said it could be pneumonia; platelets might help.

The doctor wasn't prepared, he thought, to tell them not to try.

"So we're going down to the hospital now." Beth's voice was restrained, her emotion in check. She would call as soon as there was something to tell them.

His back was rigid. I want to be with her again, he thought. Then: I don't want her to suffer.

When she called back, Beth advised that the four of them—Jocelyn had returned from Manhattan the night before—come to the emergency room. They endured the half-hour ride in silence. Behind the wheel, he felt he was driving his innocent family straight to the edge of a cliff, and there was no way out of it. They waited until the on-duty oncologist, someone who'd seen Brett before, was free to speak to them.

"I've never seen Brett so sick," he said. Surely it was pneumonia.

She'd been given morphine. "I don't believe she can live more than two days. We'd be happy to have her here at the hospital."

No, they wanted to be together in Northampton.

The doctor led them into a general examination area, and they entered a small off-white space enclosed by curtains, everything here the muted color of the pulled curtains. Brett lay on her back on a narrow bed. The sight of her—pale, jaundiced, her skin waxen, her lips bloodless—was appalling. An oxygen tube was attached to her nostrils; her breathing was labored, shallow. She was dying.

Beth, exhausted and mournful, sat on a chair toward the foot of the bed, watching her girlfriend.

"Is that Dr. Miller or who?" Brett asked, and her voice was intimate, warm, quiet.

"Richardson," Beth said. The years of their ongoing dialogue led Beth to take Brett's mental stamina and tenacity for granted.

He bent over his daughter, and she opened her eyes fleetingly, suddenly aware of others in the room, and muttered spontaneously, "I love you." As though she were on a train just then beginning to move forward while they stood on the platform—as though she were hastening to utter her final farewell while they could still hear her.

"You're going to get blood and platelets," he said softly, leaning close to her face, "then we're going home."

"To Northampton," she corrected him. Then more clearly, "I want to go to Northampton."

She hadn't explicitly discussed with her parents where she wanted to be, he realized, although Beth had made her wishes clear. He nodded. "Yes, Northampton."

The doctor soon moved them into a large room, fitted out with various apparatuses, where they could have privacy. A nurse efficiently hooked up a bag of platelets and an IV antibiotic. Intent to get Brett out of the hospital as soon as possible, they were able to accelerate the transfusion process considerably by exerting pressure on the plastic bags of blood products.

Rousing herself, Brett asked, "What's happening? Am I getting platelets?" Moments later, matter-of-factly, she said, "Have we discussed what the alternatives are when I stop breathing?"

"I don't think there are alternatives, babe," Beth said. "I think it will be time to go." She began to cry, and Nathaniel held her.

Later, speaking with difficulty, Brett explained to them, "I know it seems strange to be getting blood and platelets at this point, but if it makes me more comfortable . . ."

The nurse wanted to give her more morphine. She wasn't in pain, however, she seemed only semiconscious, and so they decided no. When Brett grasped the discussion, she said, "I don't want morphine. I'm very sensitive to it."

They drew chairs close to her, each of them intermittently touching her, her leg, foot, her face, the top of her head, as she lay with her eyes closed. Each of them wept at different times as they silently sat there, racked by some memory, by the recurrent realization of the time that had come. As if struck by a staggering pain, Holly lifted her head, her hands clenched in fists, the veins in her arms and throat prominent, and emitted a sound from between bared teeth that he'd never heard her make before. They attempted to comfort one another.

Beth said, "This is the day we met in Santa Fe three years ago." October 10.

By four in the afternoon she'd received two units of blood, a bag of platelets, and the antibiotic. With the infusion of blood, color returned to her cheeks and lips, a visible blush. By the time she was moved to an ambulance gurney, she was awake, altogether alert to her surroundings. She knew she was leaving the hospital, never to return. Leaving the hospital and everything it represented, to go home, as she wished, to die. She'd never been in an ambulance before.

Jocelyn and Nathaniel went ahead in Beth's car. Beth and Holly accompanied Brett in the ambulance, and he followed in the Volvo.

No one knew what would happen.

. . .

She sat in her bed with pillows stacked behind her. The nurse from hospice had inserted the needle for the subcutaneous morphine pump into her left thigh, although she didn't require morphine and wasn't using the device. The oxygen machine, essential now, droned on not far from the bed, which made him think of his father, although very little about what was transpiring here recalled his last days with his father. Brett seemed fairly comfortable. People were in and out of the room for a while—the nurse, the oxygen person, Beth or Holly—but eventually, by chance, he was alone there with his daughter.

He lay on the bed beside her. Her face was the same face he'd known all her life, basically—her eyes, the straight bridge of her nose, these lips. Her presence in his life was huge. "Thank you for all you've given me," he said.

Her head on the pillow, the cannula in her nostrils. She smiled faintly. "If it wasn't for your constant cheering . . ."

He asked, "What do you think will happen?"

"I think I'll be whooshed into the All," she said. "There is no self." She added, "I'm ready to *pass on,* whatever, but I don't want to be in pain." She knew how unimaginably you could suffer.

"I don't think there's going to be pain," he said.

Following a pause, she said, "I don't want to be a person again. It's too painful."

To be brought to that assessment of our lot, he thought. "It was a wonderful summer." After all the suffering, they had the unexpected respite of those months, ever since the trip to Italy. "I'm so grateful for that." He'd taken her hand. "You've been a wonderful daughter."

After a moment he asked, "Are you anxious about seeing people?" There were a number of people who would want to see her now, if possible.

"Yes, but I'll see Janice, briefly, and Richard. I'd see Mary for an hour. She'll be offended," she said. She was clearing a place for herself where she could concentrate her energy on the last thing. She didn't need to see people.

She was fully conscious and entirely composed. He asked, "Are you thinking or not thinking?"

She said, "Daydreaming."

Jocelyn and Nathaniel had gone to Conway to get various things for the night. The moment they returned to the apartment, Nathaniel sat at the dining table and began making his medicine bags. That needed to be done. Once he figured out the desired shape, he made a pattern on paper, then used that to cut the leather. Taking good care of himself, Norma said when she came by to see if anyone needed anything. By the time it was dark, Nathaniel was seated on a low stool at the head of Brett's bed, sewing his leather pouch by the light of the table lamp.

Brett only wanted water. Food was out of the question. The rest of them ate take-out Chinese, wolfing the steaming food from plates on their laps as though ashamed that appetite persisted. Edgar joined them.

Beth's parents made an appearance, which was appropriate but awkward. He had no patience for the amiable small talk that ensued in the living room: a movie, Alaska, the impending presidential election, the new season unfolding outdoors. In the tall east-facing windows, fireworks burst in the night sky above the town, the climax of the outdoor Italian Festival being staged in Northampton that night.

Brett asked to see her brother and sister. Some time later, when Jocelyn returned to the living room, she reported that Brett had heard the sociable evening prevailing in the other room and wanted to come out and sit with everyone. She joined them—Nathaniel pushed the wheelchair, while Edgar carried the bulky oxygen contraption—wrapped in a flying-geese quilt, smiling. He missed the remark she made that won a laugh from the Wilsons.

"Oh, look," she said, noticing the unnatural purple light just then opening like a flower in the sky.

A nature discussion was in progress. Bill Wilson was saying something about salamanders or the hibernation of frogs. Jocelyn told a story about a large turtle that snapped threateningly after it had been decapitated.

Brett closed her eyes. Beside her, he gently rubbed her shoulder. "Are you listening to this provocative talk?" he asked.

"Yes, about snapping heads and frozen frogs."

General laughter.

She had come home from the hospital to die.

She decided to return to the bedroom. Sitting there was too hard. And soon after that the Wilsons and Edgar departed.

As he was saying good night to his daughter, she asked, "Where are you sleeping?"

"We'll camp out in the living room."

Beth slept with Brett. Nathaniel stretched out in his sleeping bag in the corridor, and Jocelyn was on a futon in the studio, where the air seemed to vibrate with Brett's presence. Her wall of pictures, her bookcases, her mementos, her drawing table, her art, her notebooks. Brett's beautiful room.

"What was Brett saying to you when she wanted to see you?" he asked Jocelyn. It wasn't his business; he wanted to know.

Joce said, "She told us she feels peaceful. She just doesn't want pain. She asked what we thought happened after death. She thinks you disappear into a calm blue atmosphere, and your energy goes out into this vastness somehow." Jocelyn said this in a hopeful, believing way.

"She asked us if we were afraid of getting cancer," Nathaniel said. "She said, I would be if I were you." And she mentioned friends whom she feared would be diagnosed with cancer eventually, a weird intuition of some kind. "But she doesn't think Joce and I are going to get it."

No one knew what would happen, or when, or how exactly. She led; the rest of them attempted to measure up to her calm and bravery, and that made a difference. Was she relieved that the dying was almost over? There had been the almost unendurable suffering of winter, the wrenching return to New England, followed by the charmed respite of summer, then these weeks of dying, her body insisting she couldn't be, which made living, the pain of losing everything, unbearable. Did death at last seem more desirable than this dying? Relief that it was almost here? Her demeanor, every word and action, argued the truth of what she'd said: she wasn't afraid.

That doesn't mean I'm not sad.

He and Holly slept on a futon in the living room. The cats, barred from the other rooms, tore around them for a while. He didn't foresee sleeping, but he did sleep briefly at some point. A half-dozen times he heard Brett cough during the night—harsh, stressful coughing that persisted for minutes—then the muffled murmur of words between her and Beth, their two commiserating voices, followed by silence.

Early in the morning, while everyone was still asleep, he and Holly drove to Conway to look after plants and animals, make some phone calls, change their clothes. The foliage was peaking.

"I wish Brett could see this," he said. Then the sentiment seemed stupid.

"She'll never come home again. To Conway."

"I can't believe this is happening." He added, "It is happening."

These simple dumbfounded statements reflected bewildering emotions. He didn't know what he thought. Sitting next to his wife, driving up the road, observing trees, seemed bizarre. He felt he was still in Northampton, in the apartment with his daughter. His mind was there while his body was in the car, coping with the crude rush of the outside world.

They didn't linger at the house. On the way back to Northampton, Holly wanted to stop for apples. Of course, he thought, it's the season for apples.

When he entered Brett's room, she was sitting up, more thoroughly awake and alert than he'd found her on the recent mornings he'd spent here with her. He leaned toward her from the end of the bed and she looked back, dismally.

"I have so many ideas for new drawings," she said, "and I can't do them." That morning she and Beth had completed the videotape of Brett talking about her drawings, a project they'd been working on for a while. She wanted to complete as much as possible today.

"Would it be any comfort to talk about them on the video?" he said, and that struck her as a plausible suggestion.

She asked Beth to get her notebook from her desk. Then, referring to her notes and gesturing with her arms and hands, she described several additional pieces of art for the camera, work that existed in her mind but that she wouldn't be able to finish.

The phone. Beth told Mary not to come now but to find a way to say good-bye there, in Cambridge, to do something for herself. Brett didn't have the energy for visitors.

His mother, his sister Janice, and her husband, Paul, were due to arrive from the Cape that afternoon. Brett was prepared to face them, but how? he wondered.

He sat beside her on the bed.

"On the sheet of paper stating your wishes," he said, "you mentioned distributing your ashes between Maine, Conway, and Grafton . . ."

"Grafton? No."

Yesterday when he'd entered the apartment there had been a large sheet of paper covered in red ink on the living room desk, which began, "These are my last wishes . . ." Beth's handwriting, he assumed, because it wasn't Brett's. They must have been working on that Friday night under the pressure of advancing breathlessness. There was the detail concerning ashes. She would leave her art to her parents, her collection of poetry books to her brother. . . . Beth would distribute other things. Beth had since removed the document; it clearly represented hasty, incomplete notes. There was no mention of Brett's note-books, for instance.

"Do you remember dictating your last wishes?" he asked.

"No." She called Beth from the other room. "Sweetie, I don't want my ashes in Grafton."

Beth was immediately reassuring; she understood.

They attempted to discuss what she did want. She could imagine her ashes in Maine, Brett said, but where in Maine? Corea? Acadia?

They would go there and look until they discovered the perfect set-ting, he said. A cliff maybe, over deep water.

She nodded. The idea of a stone marker from Maine appealed to her, but where would they put it? "I don't want to be in that cemetery," she said, referring to one they often passed in Conway. She asked, "Am I going to be alone?"

He raised the possibility of a family plot, but when they abandoned the topic, nothing had been resolved.

They talked about the memorial service. Could she think of poems or music, or would she rather they did that themselves? Surely they knew what would be right.

At last she said, "I don't want to talk about this anymore."

Beth lay on top of the bed, and he sat on a stool nearby.

"Can we talk about the notebooks?" he asked. He was reluctant to keep coming at her with questions, and yet . . .

Brett was very clear. She and Beth had talked about it. Whatever notebooks and so forth were in Conway would remain in Conway. Beth would keep the notebooks that were now in Northampton with Brett.

To him, of course, the notebooks were her, her voice, more than anything else that would remain, except the art, which was altogether different. "All right, I'd like a copy of them," he said. "Is that pos-sible?"

Brett was ambivalent. "My journals have always been a very private place to me," she said. "How would you like that—someone reading your journals?"

He thought she was concerned that her privacy would be exploited somehow and told her that wouldn't happen. Moments after he left the room, Beth came after him.

"Brett is anxious about the notebooks," she said.

"I'm not afraid they'll be exploited," she told him, back in the room. "I don't want them read. By anyone."

"I didn't realize that's what you meant." He promised her he wouldn't read them. There would be no copies. Then, thinking out loud, he asked, "Do you want us to destroy them, burn them? The ashes could be mixed with your ashes." Later, he was astonished to recall he'd made such a statement to her; the intimacy between them at the time allowed it.

"No, I'd like them to be preserved—as objects," she said.

He regretted that he'd made her think about this at all, giving her yet another moment of anxiety, for God's sake, even now. And yet the notebooks were a detail he and Beth had to get straight, and it hadn't occurred to him that Brett would be anxious. There could be absolutely nothing in those notebooks, nothing in all her passionate scrawled pages concerning her or him or anyone else, that would disturb him—nothing. He knew her.

Sitting up in bed, Brett read to her brother and sister from the *New and Selected Poems* of Mary Oliver. At the end of another poem set in nature, she looked up and said, "After a while it feels like you're drowning in a swamp, doesn't it?"

Appreciative laughter.

She then read a Pablo Neruda poem and asked them, "Do you like it?"

An obese nurse, a part-time weekend substitute for whom hospice work represented some extra hours, lumbered into the apartment impatiently, evidently stressed out by the demands of her day.

"How do my lungs sound?" Brett asked her after the nurse had listened.

"Not bad, considering."

She didn't know how to operate the subcutaneous morphine pump and had to make several phone calls, each more taxing than the last, before she figured it out. She set the device to administer a modest automatic drip with a manual bolus as needed. Brett was insistent about understanding just what she was getting.

"I'm worried about eating," she told the nurse. She hadn't eaten for three days. "Should I be eating?" The question was prompted, he imagined, by how relatively better she'd been feeling all day. Was this . . . dying?

Norma Dana, recently arrived, stepped into the doorway. "You don't have to eat, Brett, unless you want to."

His daughter looked at her.

"Should I remove the IV, or will I be getting more blood?" The intravenous needle that had been inserted in the emergency room was still in her arm. "I probably will," she said wearily.

"Actually, you probably won't need it," Norma said. "And you can always get another one."

So that element was removed.

When the nurse finished her duties, he led his mother, Janice, and Paul—they had arrived about the time the nurse did—into the bedroom. They had never been in Brett's distinctive and comfortable apartment before, although they were surely too anxious just then to notice the place. His mother hadn't seen her granddaughter since the Christmas prior to the spring recurrence and the transplant, Brett's last Christmas in Conway, as they knew now, and the last Christmas of his father's life. She hadn't seen her granddaughter or spoken to her since everything had changed.

Brett reached her arms out to them, smiling. "I'm so glad you came," she said.

He left them alone, returning to look in from the doorway a little later. Janice knelt at the head of the bed and his mother sat on a stool, each of them holding one of Brett's hands. She told them she felt peaceful and loved. Now she reached for her black notebook, found the page, and read them a short passage that ended with a line about how the beauty of *these leaves* was their dying. She looked up, as though startled by her own words. She'd written them on Thursday as she sat under a tree on the Smith campus, the day she'd skipped radiation therapy to go out into the green.

It was a brief audience. His mother, seated in the rocking chair in the living room, was bereft, her face crumpled. When he approached to comfort her, she pushed him away, too oppressed to be touched, he thought.

"She's going to a better place than this. I have to believe there's something. There must be," she said grimly.

Eve called from San Francisco. Later he asked, "How was that?"

His daughter raised her eyebrows at him. "Saying good-bye on the phone?" She didn't intend to speak to Eve again. It was too hard. The original flame, he thought.

Lisa Bernard called, quite by chance apparently, so he brought her up to date on what had occurred so suddenly. Brett was unable to talk to her. Lisa said, "Send her my love."

What was it like for these young women imagining their friend now?

Jocelyn sat at the round dining table beneath her self-portrait, the painting Brett had had the whole time in San Francisco, writing in her journal with concentrated fury. Writing, writing!

Nathaniel wouldn't leave the apartment.

Later, when he and Holly looked into the bedroom, growing darker in the fading afternoon, Brett was still propped up against the pillows, sound asleep, and Beth lay beside her, also napping. They were holding hands. The expression on their daughter's face was peaceful.

"They're beautiful," Holly said.

They felt all right about returning to Conway for the night. It was important for Beth and Jocelyn and Nathaniel to have time with Brett without them around. They could get back at a moment's notice. Janice made the meal while Holly and his mother looked at photographs of the summer. After supper the first presidential debate was broadcast, but he found it intolerable to watch. They didn't talk about Brett and went to bed early.

He awakened at two-thirty and was unable to fall asleep again, gripped by fear, the intimation of a black void, for his daughter and for himself. Was there some way he could be with her? Was he failing to grasp some opportunity that still awaited him?

I didn't know it would be like this.

Janice had thought to stop in Northampton on the way to Connecticut, but Nathaniel called in the morning to say that Brett couldn't see her. She had said good-bye, and she couldn't do it again. Janice understood. "You get selfish," she said of her own wishes.

That morning Brett told Jocelyn, "I don't know what to do with my body."

At random he picked a Northampton funeral service out of the phone book. Pease. On the recommendation of the director there, he called Victoria Safford, the minister of the Unitarian Society in Northampton, and she came to the apartment early Monday afternoon to discuss a memorial service with them. An intense woman in her thirties with short hair, clear, thoughtful eyes, and a resolute mouth, she struck them, within the hour, as the ideal person to conduct Brett's service. Rather than present an agenda or shepherd them in any way, she listened to what they wanted to do. By sheer chance, it seemed to him, the right person had appeared at the right time. The meeting reassured them: the service they would create in Brett's memory would honor her. They would hold it in the handsome Unitarian meeting hall.

Victoria spent a brief time alone with Brett in the bedroom. As he walked the minister downstairs to the front door of the building, she said, "Brett is *far* wiser than her years." For it was a cliché, wasn't it, to make that observation about people facing death at an early age? "An aesthetic sense seems to radiate around her," she went on. "She's strong; she has definite ideas of what she wants."

Brett had been impressing them for some time now, he said.

"I'm the same way she is," Victoria Safford said. "It's in the blood."

Autumn leaves that Jocelyn and Nathaniel had gathered on their morning walk through the Smith campus decorated Brett's bedroom walls. The oxygen droned rhythmically between the bed and a bookcase.

"Hospice gave us a little blue book to help us understand dying," she told him. "It described the stages—you stop eating, drinking, breathing. I'm confused. I have a definite loss of appetite ... but it's always been easy for me not to eat. I don't know if my not eating is a sign of dying," she said, "or fasting." Like the day before, she felt too awake, too present, to be so near the end of her life.

"What would you like to eat?" he asked her.

"Is there honeydew melon? Something mushy and sweet."

There was melon in the apartment. Brett's first mouthful produced a startling smile.

"It feels strange not to call Mary. After all our communing over this very time." She added, her brow crinkled, "But I don't think I have the energy to be sincere."

"You can't be anything else," he said. But he knew she meant something more profound than honesty or good faith.

Beth had been dealing with phone calls from various friends. "Can't they understand that we've said good-bye," Brett said. "I can't keep saying good-bye."

"I'm glad you saw your grandmother."

She nodded, sitting up in the bed. "I just wanted to hold her the whole time, but she seemed too fragile." She'd told her grandmother that it had taken a lot of courage to come and see her. When her grandmother protested, Brett said, Well, it took a lot of courage for me to see you. "Dad, rub my neck. Squeeze it in the middle."

He massaged her thin neck with one hand, holding the top of her head with the other. Her soft red hair. Glad she'd asked him for something.

In a few minutes she said, "Thanks, Dad."

Bewilderingly, to Brett more than to anyone else perhaps, she felt better today, not worse. Rallying. Later that afternoon, she wanted to sit in the living room, which was so much more pleasant than the bedroom. Nathaniel carried the oxygen machine while he maneuvered the wheelchair. She now wore a salmon-pink T-shirt of heavy cotton and purple satin shorts. She pulled on her gray fleece top in the large room.

"Would you take my picture with the tree out the window?" she asked her brother.

Nathaniel snapped the photograph and then a second one of Brett and her father. That didn't seem particularly strange at the time. Snapshots.

Holly and Jocelyn had gone to the grocery store.

Beth returned from a walk, or had she been napping in Brett's studio? Earlier she had come into the apartment bearing two large bouquets of flowers—mixed chrysanthemums and white gladiolas—which made a notable impression in the room. Now she went to Brett, who sat in the wheelchair looking out the tall window at the view: the brilliant maple, the sky, the distant range of New England mountains. Beth placed a hand on her shoulder. "Today is our anniversary, sweetie," she said. It was the day they'd initiated their relationship during their whirlwind tour of the West, headed for a fresh start in San Francisco. "Our third."

Brett, summoning a voice of delight, announced, "It's our anniversary!"

He and Nathaniel decided to leave them alone. With Beth's small camera he unobtrusively snapped a picture of the two women sitting there looking into each other's eyes—the vulnerable back of his daughter's head, the shoulders hunched in the tall-armed chair, Beth's loving, stricken expression. From new love in Bryce Canyon they'd come all the way here, a journey to the interior as treacherous and enthralling and transforming as any expedition into an unknown territory.

He and Nathaniel walked through the Smith gardens to Paradise Pond, then down the well-worn path along the western edge of it, through a cathedral of towering trees, luminous in their fall colors. The people out here strolled as though blissed-out, their lives imbued all of a sudden with something beautiful. The past three days had imprinted a gravity on his son's smooth, youthful face. The boy hardly seemed to notice the people around them or the spectacle the others were enjoying. Nathaniel bore no relationship today to the students his age, twenty-one, who looked either inexplicably bored or excessively and mysteriously animated. He didn't know what his son was thinking; he didn't want to add to the confusion by trying to find out. Nathaniel was within himself somewhere, somehow managing—like the rest of them.

"Today," Nathaniel confided, "Brett asked me, How can I go through the day like this? Waiting, doing nothing, in bed."

"What did you say?"

"I asked her if she wanted to die now."

He looked at his son, who was focused elsewhere.

"In the morning she could almost think that, she said, but no, she said she wants to take in as much as she can while she's feeling like this—without pain—to take in colors, the light, the change in temperature through the day. She told me she'd like to go outside," Nathaniel said.

He put his hand on the boy's shoulder.

As they walked above the pond, returning, they passed a granite bench, given in someone's memory, at the foot of a venerable sycamore, and it was suddenly clear to him that this was one thing they could do. Holly came walking through the garden in her skirt and wool jacket, to all appearances an attractive woman in the middle of her life, he thought. She had come outside so her dying daughter could be alone with her girlfriend. Yes, she agreed, a memorial bench would be good.

The sight of young women hurrying to the library, to class, to a rendezvous, back to the dorm ... their mostly earnest faces, everything ahead of them! While Brett lay in her apartment nearby, waiting for her life to end. No one knew. That amazed him, as they approached her building, and he looked from the busy, innocent street to the windows of her apartment. No one here on the sidewalk knew what immense event was taking place there, two stories up, right in the middle of everything.

When Charles Linker, for example, said six to nine months or Al McKee said two weeks, did they have any idea what they were talking about? The answer was no. No one knew.

They were together, the six of them, in the high-ceilinged white room. It was dusk, they had not turned the lights on, and the fall sky in the schoolhouse windows was dramatic. There was music playing, a man's gentle voice, accompanied by acoustic guitar, sweet, peaceful. Brett's choice, a little-known singer she'd first heard at The Iron Horse that summer. The music had been playing when they'd first returned from their walk, and they quietly sat down, respectful of the mood they'd entered. He listened without quite hearing the words. Brett, in the wheelchair, and Nathaniel, beside her in the rocker, embraced each other for the duration of a song. Holly and Jocelyn sat on the couch with him, watching them. Beth sat in the armchair. Dusk, the sky, the music, the six of them, their silence. This moment! he thought. This moment!

When they unclasped, Nathaniel was in tears, but Brett was smiling at her brother lovingly.

"Look at the sky now," she said.

Later, lights on, he sat on the couch writing, his desperate scribbling, and Brett asked someone to get her journal, a black bound sketch pad of unlined pages. She wrote on her lap, seated in the wheelchair, the oxygen machine humming in the room. He didn't wonder at her wanting to write. It was like her desire to have photographs taken that she would never see. Part of living was getting it down on paper.

Eve called and Holly spoke with her for a long time. When she rejoined the rest of them, she said, "Eve sounds helpless, wanting to be here and not knowing what to do. She said she spent the day reading all the poetry you used to read together," she told her daughter.

Brett said, "She can't let go until I'm gone."

Earlier in the day Beth told Gabby Silver and Jocelyn Emerson that they couldn't come now. Do things in your own way, Beth told them.

He asked Brett if she'd like them to use passages from her journal for the memorial service, such as the reflection she'd read aloud to her aunt and her grandmother the day before. She flipped through the pages, and when she found the passage, she read it aloud again, then pouted, dissatisfied. "I don't know. I know so many beautiful, great poems that are complete," she said.

She dozed, eyes closed, in midsentence, her hand and the pen stalled on the page of the notebook. Then, alert again, she read what she'd written. "I can't write," she said. "I go back and it doesn't say what I mean. How strange." She seemed almost amused.

The kittens, more like cats all the time, darted around the room in spurts.

Noticing the bouquet of white flowers again, she said, "Our anniversary! Oh, Snapper, I love them."

It was almost seven o'clock. "What are you having for supper?" she asked.

They were planning to call out for a pizza. "Do you think the smell will bother you?" Brett hadn't eaten, except for the slice of melon, since Friday.

She didn't. Looking at her swollen bare feet on the footrest of the wheelchair, she said, "My feet look like scones."

They watched the moon rise in the window.

"I want to make going outside tomorrow a goal," she said. "It's so easy to lie in bed all day. I'm so tired."

Lisa Bernard called from California, and Richard, who'd been away for the weekend, assuming Brett was in Boston, called from down the street. Each time, Beth left the room to talk to them.

"It's too tiring for Beth," Brett said. "She does too much. Don't they realize?"

They wolfed their pizza and salad with beer, and the smell didn't bother her. They rented a movie and sat there watching, pretending to watch, although it soon proved unwatchable, as far as he was concerned, and everyone kept dozing off, especially Brett. She and Beth reclined on the hospital bed that had been delivered earlier in the day and now stood in the middle of the living room. The movie wasn't something they needed in order to sit there together, but they'd all agreed to it. Perhaps they wanted the end of this day to feel, as much as possible, like an ordinary evening. Soon after eleven, with everyone practically asleep as it was, he and Holly decided to return to Conway.

I want to make going outside a goal for tomorrow, he thought, awake hours later. *I want to take in as much as I can....* She'd been amazing all day. *Aren't I having a good day?* He wanted her to be spared more suffering—spared before more suffering began.

In the morning, she was in the grip of a more profound fatigue, compounded to some extent by the morphine Beth had given her during the night to help her rest. She attempted to go over the details of the memorial service, Jocelyn told him, but found it difficult to focus. Her therapist, a woman named Andy, came by but only remained for ten minutes or so because Brett couldn't stay awake.

He and Holly entered the living room. Reclining in the hospital bed, their daughter appeared to be sleeping.

She opened her eyes. "Hi."

"I've brought you some roses," Holly said. She had picked a lavish and impeccable bouquet of seafoam roses that morning as the sun was rising. She placed them on top of the white bookcase, which contained Brett's books of poetry, beneath the large reproduction of Leighton's *Flaming June,* a sumptuously romantic nineteenth-century picture of a young woman in a golden transparent garment who appeared sensuously asleep. The woman in the painting had Brett's coloring, her former hair, and Brett's classic straight-bridged nose.

Today the color had drained from her face, and the whites of her eyes were more yellowed. Her thoughtful eyes.

"My chest hurts," she said. "In front and under my wings." Temper flared in her face. "I'm angry. I don't want pain." She didn't want what she had to do now ruined by pain.

"I hear you've selected the poems you'd like," he said. Jocelyn had told him they'd made a list of possible poems—Oliver, Neruda, Rexroth, Berry, Gary Snyder, Roberto Juarroz.

"I didn't really make final choices. You'll have to choose the ones I want." She meant everyone would. There was a song she definitely wanted played, though, Jane Siberry's "Calling All Angels." She looked at him, frowning. "The only trouble is they used it in a movie."

He didn't know the song.

Beth had recently encountered Albey Reiner, who said he'd like to see Brett if that was something she wanted. When he arrived, Brett said, "I want to be alone with him." They had only met that one time the previous winter, before Brett had made up her mind to return to New England.

The four of them—he and Holly, Jocelyn and Nathaniel—walked through the Smith grounds again. He'd called the college that morning and been informed that there was only one available site for a memorial bench on the campus. After some uncertainty, they located the spot: a small, grassy terrace on the south side of Wright Hall, beneath a honey locust, above a bank of azaleas, and overlooking the wide lawn before Burton Hall. It was a relatively private, roomlike enclosure at the center of the campus just above the gardens. A young California redwood towered above the spot to the southeast. Yes, they agreed, this was the place.

"I'm going to walk into town," Nathaniel said. "I need to look at people."

He and Holly and Jocelyn continued under the grand trees along the pond, walking through leaves, the air fragrant. They made a loop up through a residential street and back toward Elm Street. He seemed to be all right, briskly walking along, then without warning found himself going to pieces as Tenney House, where Brett had lived at Smith, came into view.

Reiner was with Beth in the studio, and Brett appeared to be sleeping in the living room, when they returned.

She opened her eyes. "We didn't talk," she said. "He just held me. I couldn't talk."

The pain in her chest was severe. He suggested a shot of morphine and she agreed. As he pressed the button, the automatic injection device emitted a discernible sound. Two milligrams. Reiner stepped back into the room. Brett raised her arm in a wave and managed a smile for him.

"See you soon," he said, kissing her forehead, and left.

She looked at Beth, who stood at the foot of the bed. "I haven't seen *you* for a while," Brett said lovingly.

Later, Beth, Jocelyn, and Nathaniel went out, and Holly sat with Brett while he wrote in his notebook, determined to get whatever he could think of on paper. When Brett coughed now, unable to get anything up, it was agonizing, her chest tortured. Holly helped her onto the commode. He took her wrist and felt her pulse racing under his fingers. She looked at him. Her eyes seemed larger and her pale skin, faintly freckled, appeared gold-tinged, taut across her face. To him she looked beautiful; she was beautiful.

She turned her head to the south window. "I want to feel the sun," she said, adjusting her position.

He opened one window wide so she could experience the air. A brilliant shaft of afternoon sunlight reached her lap, and Brett sat wondering at the warm beam with her fingers, holding it like a precious object. Turning her head, she followed the light up toward the south window, as though looking for a way out, a way out of her suffering, looking beyond the room and them, detaching herself.

She was mostly sleepy.

Jocelyn and Nathaniel returned with more autumn leaves, glossy horse chestnuts.

"Totally," Brett smiled. An expression of highest praise.

He and Jocelyn, seated in chairs by the bed, continued to scratch in their notebooks.

"What's everybody writing?" Brett asked.

"I don't know what else to do," he said.

"It's a way to differentiate one hour from the next," she said. When a siren sounded outdoors, she added, "Something you're writing caused that to go off."

She was concerned about Beth, whose days were so jam-packed with friends calling and everything else. "She does too much." But then she said, "Beth can do it. She can do anything." She looked at her sister and asked, "Do you love Michael as much as I love Snapper?"

He closed his notebook and set it aside. From her bed, his daughter said, "I'm glad you got out what you needed to. I like to write things that come to me—like messages, images, insights—not just what happened."

It was six o'clock, another day gone.

That evening Richard visited her only briefly, Brett fading in and out of sleep, her strength clearly waning. Richard read her a Rexroth poem, the first poem he'd ever read her, he said, when they met just after she'd graduated from college.

Michael arrived from New York and had his time with Brett. Then Jocelyn, Nathaniel, and he returned to Conway for a square meal and a night's sleep. Jocelyn, especially, looked exhausted, her pink freshness temporarily washed out. He recalled the struggle and confusion of his father's death. The man went on living for days after the day his death had seemed imminent. It was as though you had to struggle for your own death. Brett was alive, she was here, and death remained unknown, remote, like a rumored destination that became all the more impossible to imagine the longer one journeyed toward it.

He sat at his daughter's drawing table in the room that had become, after a brief interval as the master bedroom, her studio. "10/13/92," he wrote, "Tuesday." Beth was with Brett in the darkened living room; they wished to be alone now. Holly was in the bedroom, talking with two of her friends, her pillars of support, telling them everything she needed to say, telling them about Brett that day, and her other children, and her feelings, confident that she could say whatever came to the surface, that they wanted to know, they wanted to listen, and that everything she said was important.

The white Formica desktop was blackened with Brett's charcoal. There was a full moon in the schoolhouse window to his left, behind the trees and buildings of the town. He'd been in the room many times, of course, stood in her window, but he'd never sat at her desk before. How she surely loved working here, he thought—tall in the saddle— her music playing, the town at her elbow. Her wall before her.

He looked at each image she'd taped up here: photographs of friends and family and places, reproductions of paintings and sculptures, postcards of all kinds, many from Italy. A snapshot of herself as a little girl on a swing or sitting at her mother's drawing table. Her parents on a mountain in the Adirondacks. Her brother and sister. Eve. Beth. The wall was another work of art as far as he was concerned.

The last time he'd gone into the living room, Brett said, "You're still writing?" It was all he could do, he replied. And now, as he sat there, he considered how futile his effort was. He wanted to get it all down, everything that happened, but of course there was no such thing. He couldn't get what occurred between Brett and others—her mother, her sister, her brother, Beth, and the rest. He couldn't get down what she felt and thought or what this was like for her, what dying was like. He would only know that when he was dying. He couldn't get down what he was failing to see at that moment by not being with her. No matter how many pages he filled, exhaustively recounting everything that came to mind, his crude summary of what happened was hopelessly inadequate. Yet he was afraid not to do it. It was imperative to get the substance of these days down in whatever form, down in his notebook, where it was safe, where it could not be lost.

The sound of her coughing was the only sound in the silent apartment. He clicked out her desk lamp and sat in the dark, more like twilight, looking out the window. Her room, her moon there.

The two women were on the hospital bed, settled down for the night. He gave her a kiss. Her forehead felt cool. He placed his head against her chest: her heart beating too fast.

"Good night."

"Good night," she said.

Holly was lying in the small bedroom, staring at the ceiling. Leaves taped to the wall. The Georgia O'Keeffe poster of the great oak, if that's what it was, reaching to a starry sky: Santa Fe Chamber Music. That went back to when Brett and Eve were together.

"What are they doing now?"

"Trying to sleep."

Throughout the day Brett's breathing had become more shallow, difficult, so that now she hardly had the strength to cough. Coughing had become more like a groan. They lay in her bedroom, listening.

He must have dozed off, because sounds of agitation awakened him—groaning, stressful breathing. He went into the living room and Holly followed. Brett was sitting on the edge of the bed with Beth. She seemed out of it.

"She's all right," Beth said. "It's the morphine." Beth had hoped an extra dose would help her sleep through the night.

A slight moan accompanied each breath she took. "I love you, Beth," she muttered repeatedly.

They laid her back in the bed, and he and Holly returned to the bedroom. Brett's agitation continued, and the sound of Beth's voice either questioning or reassuring her. By daybreak their daughter's struggle seemed constant—dozing, then waking to fight for breath, which sounded like agony to them.

Holly said, "It's barbaric." Why did a person have to fight to die? How long?

At six-thirty the two women appeared to be sleeping, and he and Holly quietly let themselves out the door.

In the parking lot, the sight of a man and a woman dressed for work, scraping frost off the windshields of their cars, was bizarre to him. They didn't know! Another sunny blue fall day also seemed outrageous. They got coffee and something to eat on Pleasant Street, returning to the apartment within the hour. Her building, he thought, looking up at her corner, the blank reflecting windows of her studio, the living room.

Brett was sleeping, reclined in the raised bed.

Beth went into the bedroom for a nap. She'd been up all night.

He called Smith and told the woman he'd spoken to several times already that they'd seen the proposed site for a memorial bench on the south side of Wright Hall, and yes, they wished to claim it. He'd be in touch.

Brett opened her eyes and saw him watching her and held her arms out to him. He embraced her. With slurred speech, as though she hadn't attempted to form words for a while, she muttered, "I love you." Just as she had on Saturday in the emergency room, uttering the essential good-bye while there was still time.

A health-care aide from hospice arrived, a woman younger than his daughter, and busily looked after her, thoroughly swabbing out her mouth, clotted with dried blood from the night's struggle, applying ointment to her lips, checking on her needs. Brett had come to the end of needs. She hardly seemed aware of this attention. Promptly the aide was off to her next patient.

Brett struggled to sit on the side of the bed, with her feet on the floor. Resting her elbows on the food tray, she held her head with both hands like a person in despair, although this anguish was largely physical. It was the same posture his father had repeatedly assumed that long day in the hospital on the Cape, battling for his next breath. Did sitting up represent a flight instinct, or was it simply more comfortable? He sat on her left-hand side and held her. Soon, she lay back in the bed, her head against pillows. Several times she attempted to speak, but the words were unclear. She still wore the salmon-colored T-shirt and the purple satin shorts.

He happened to answer the phone when Eve called from San Francisco. "I was dreaming of walking with Brett to all the places she liked to go in the city," she said, "walking fast like when she was strong and healthy." Eve felt she was definitely there with Brett, there in Northampton. She would be there for the memorial service—positively. "Would you tell Brett, if possible," she said. After he hung up he realized it was only seven o'clock in California, which accounted for the sleepiness in Eve's voice. She must have just awakened, he thought, from the dream she described.

Holly sat by the bed studying her daughter's face. *I want to take in as much as I can.* Brett appeared to be sleeping, not suffering. Her breath came slowly. The room was as bright as the out-of-doors, blue sky in the windows, the trees there. The sort of day when the physical world seemed *in focus,* a heightened clarity, all the way to the Holyoke range on the horizon. Beth's white gladiolas, Holly's pink and white roses beneath the vivid *Flaming June*. He looked at his watch: 10:45 A.M. Then the jolt, like a current pulsing through his brain: Brett was dying!

Never, he'd never thought she would die.

Beth went to her scheduled therapy session, wheeling her bicycle out of the apartment. When Jocelyn and Nathaniel arrived and saw their sister, they immediately took up their places near her. No one said anything. How did all that was happening appear to them? he wondered. Their big sister, the one who had always gone before them and brought back news from the world out there.

The four of them sat with her. They watched her breathe.

Carolyn had been Brett's regular hospice nurse for most of the summer, and that was a lucky matchup. Brett was crazy about her. She arrived around midday. Ironically, as it struck him, she'd been away for the weekend attending the Stephen Levine symposium in Boston. Carolyn's demeanor was impressively calm. She seemed to smile with genuine affection for her patient as she went about her business, gently checking Brett's vital signs.

He wondered about the automatic morphine drip—was Brett getting too much? Carolyn told him Brett's state had nothing to do with morphine; she was nearing death. Surely within the next forty-eight hours, she said.

He and Jocelyn and Nathaniel were on the left side of the bed, while Holly sat on the right. Carolyn said she'd like to sing, if that was all right with everyone. She knelt by the bed then, next to Holly. Startlingly, in a brave, full voice, beautiful and wrenching to him, she sang directly to Brett "A Song of Passing," a composition she'd written, they learned later. "You are leaving ... set your spirit free ... take your wings and fly ... soar beyond the skies ... sorrow cuts me through ... let go ... I'll remember you. . . ." He caught only fragments of the several verses. The power was in her voice. The song cut through their fragile composure, and their grief poured out.

Brett reclined in the bed in a sitting position, her mouth slightly open, the oxygen cannula affixed to her nostrils.

"She can hear," Carolyn told them. "She hears you, although she doesn't seem to."

He hoped she'd heard Carolyn's song. He imagined her listening somewhere in her consciousness, wonderingly and keenly appreciative.

Beth entered the room, having pedaled her bike across town, and clung to Brett's nurse, sobbing hard on the woman's shoulder.

It was Carolyn who suggested they each take a moment to be with Brett and say good-bye. Given their present state, he didn't know if they would have thought of that themselves.

They withdrew to the hallway near the front door so that each person could be alone with her. Jocelyn went to be with her sister first. Beth and Holly embraced. He was near the front door, hoarding his pain maybe, holding on to something, when Carolyn came up to him, and he collapsed over her small body. He felt her taking deep breaths, attempting to calm him.

"How can someone have their heart torn apart like this?" she said.

Brett lay in the bed with eyes closed, and Jocelyn was beside her, leaning over her, bravely telling her sister . . . what exactly?

He and Nathaniel came together in the hallway, and his son's hard, strong body was racked by sobs as the boy clung to him with powerful force.

"Dad."

They clung to one another, stumbling from one embrace to the next, and he felt the heat of their suffering, the heat of their pressing bodies and wet, reddened faces, and the animal smell of their bodies and breaths.

Nathaniel spoke to Brett next. Jocelyn went to the kitchen, and he followed his daughter and held her. Her grief was ravaging her, consuming her.

It's too much for one person. I can't hold it.

"You've been wonderful," he told her. "You're going to be all right. Brett isn't suffering."

He and Holly took care of their children before they took care of each other. That was the pattern, as though what comfort they had to offer should be put to the best use. As though inhabiting the same house of misery for so long had numbed their ability to comfort each other. Or maybe they took their mutual concern for granted; they didn't need to express it here.

Carolyn had left the apartment.

Beth had her final moment alone with her beloved companion. And then he went in to her.

The room was still bright. Brett lay back as before, sitting up, her head on pillows, her eyes closed, her breath coming slowly. Her fair arms lay on the sheet beside her body, her hands relaxed. He knew her face so well, every detail of her face, and yet there was so much to absorb.

"Thank you for your life," he said, "thank you for being such a wonderful daughter. You've meant everything to me." He held her. "You've done all you can do. There's nothing more to do. It's time, it's all right to let go. Open your wings," he said, recalling Carolyn's song. Later, he was unable to remember all he'd said to her in those minutes. He said, "You'll always be in our hearts, we'll always love you." He said, "The time has come." He said, "I love you." He wanted to say good-bye and it was all right to leave and they'd be all right somehow. He told her what decisions had been made: that her ashes would be cast into the sea off the Maine coast—they would find the spot—that there would be a bench placed in her memory on the Smith campus in a quiet, beautiful area. Did he see the faintest nod when he said that? He told her there would be a wonderful memorial service and everyone would be there. He said good-bye.

There was a difficult small sound in her throat as she lay there with her eyes closed, and he was suddenly anxious that her mother have time with her.

He said, "Your mother is going to say good-bye now. And then we'll all come back and be with you."

Distinctly and unmistakably, Brett said, "Okay."

Her mind!

He and Beth came together in the hallway while Holly was with her daughter. He thanked her for being who she was, this remarkable person, all she'd done. "You've been extraordinary these years. I know Brett loved you."

"I love her so much," Beth said.

Their faces were damp, and the smell of hair and breath and flesh was like the odor of their grieving. They were animals who knew what suffering was.

"I believe she made her peace with this," he said. "She understood and accepted that this was her life."

"I know she did," she said. "The only thing that really made her angry was pain."

The five of them gathered around her. He sat behind his son on the left side of the bed. Holly and Jocelyn were on the right, and Beth was at the foot of the bed, holding Brett's strong-looking feet in her hands. They placed their hands on her; they pressed their faces against her body. They'd come to the unknown place that no imagining could anticipate or reveal. They'd entered—and it felt like a space, a sacred room—the final hour of Brett's life.

"You've done all you can do," he said. "There's no more to do. Let go. Be at peace, Brett. Now you can be at peace. It's all right."

Her struggle to die was a struggle to give up breath. Her rapid pulse was visible in her throat, beating like a tiny creature struggling to be set free. Could her young body persist against her will? Carolyn had told them how important the will was. They could help Brett pass over by letting her go. He remembered his father's stubborn will.

At some point Nathaniel and Beth changed places, so that Beth was at the head of the bed. "It's okay, sweetie. You can go. Let go. Be with the angels."

"We're all here with you," he said.

They were there with her, yes, and she was alone.

The time had come, and he wanted her to be released. He wanted her consciousness, her knowledge that she was dying, to come to an end. He wanted the dying to end.

"You can let go. You're not this body."

He asked them if he could take a last picture of Brett while she was still alive, and no one objected. Nothing they did seemed strange then. The instant he snapped the picture of Brett surrounded by her family, the camera made a faint whirring sound, automatically winding up the exposed film.

He and Beth repeated their litany of loving encouragement and re-assurance. Then, just when he believed her pain and anxiety were over, Brett became agitated. She forced herself to sit up, moving her legs so that she sat on the edge of the bed, directly in front of him. She muttered unclearly. They were alarmed. She reached her arms up and let them drop on his shoulders, leaning forward, resting her head heavily on his shoulder. She raised herself in seeming discomfort, and Beth hastened to hit the morphine pump. Brett collapsed over him again, and he supported her with his shoulders, listening to her stressful breathing against his chest. They didn't know what she wanted or what it meant.

"Do you want to lie back now?"

At last she assented, and they laid her back on the bed.

He moved to the other side of the bed with Holly. Jocelyn was at the foot of the bed, directly behind him, and Beth and Nathaniel were on the left.

"Be at peace. The pain is over. Be free, Brett."

When he attempted to shift her upper body to make her more comfortable, she sat up again, startlingly, reaching up with her long arms. Now she placed her weight on both Beth and Nathaniel. She struggled to speak.

"It's okay, hon, it's okay," Beth pleaded.

They were there with her and she was dying. She knew. Sitting up straight, she reached and pulled the oxygen cannula from her nostrils. Suddenly, with her head erect, Brett opened her eyes, but wide, extraordinarily wide. She appeared to be looking out the east window of the apartment at the autumn sky. This lasted long seconds. They knew she had come to the last moment of her life. They gently settled her back on the pillows.

"You can go now," Beth said. "It's okay."

"We love you."

Her eyes were half open, her lips were parted, and her countenance was peaceful. Brett's breathing had altered, so that now, instead of slow, congested breaths, her breath was a whisper, faint, very shallow, hardly a breath at all.

Raising her hand to her mouth as one aghast, Jocelyn cried, "Oh, my God." She began to sob hard.

He reached an arm behind him to hold her.

Nathaniel stared at his sister in wonder, crying.

In the lowering afternoon light, Brett's skin appeared not jaundiced but golden really, and her eyebrows were tinged lavender. Her eyes, looking straight before her, appeared peaceful, even serene. A single tear ran from the outside corner of her right eye down her smooth cheek.

"You can go now," Beth whispered once more. She leaned forward and pressed a kiss to Brett's parted lips.

They watched each breath grow smaller, breath after final breath. They watched. At last no breath came.

He reached forward and closed his daughter's eyes. It was three-forty in the afternoon.

They covered her body with their hands and faces, stricken. Sobbing, Jocelyn asked, "Is she *dead*?"

Nothing had prepared them for where they were now. In an instant they had moved from the sacred intimate room where each of them had been determined to do his or her part to an infinitely lonelier, more frightening place. Life without Brett. No Brett, ever again. Never. She had died, she was gone.

They decided to bathe her and dress her, make those final preparations themselves; they all wanted to do that. It wasn't something they'd thought about earlier. Beth got a bar of Brett's favorite soap, a white basin of water, and white washcloths for each of them. He and Nathaniel lifted her while Beth put a clean sheet under her. The limpness and weight of her warm limbs, this lifelessness, was so strange. He gently bathed Brett's face, Holly her long, smooth legs, and Jocelyn her feet. Nathaniel was especially diligent about removing every trace of the morphine needle from her thigh—the residue of tape. They were calm. They removed the salmon-colored T-shirt and Brett's purple satin shorts and looked at her naked body—her full breasts, her long, slender limbs and slender waist, the fair triangle of her pubic hair, her peaceful face, her beautiful hands and feet. A telltale callus on the middle finger of her writing hand reflected her intelligence and passion. Her closely trimmed fingernails. Her earlobes. Her lips. The scar from her laparotomy, the first major surgery, was a straight vertical line from sternum to navel.

"She's so beautiful," Jocelyn said.

Beth carefully washed her armpits and beneath her breasts. She removed a diamond earring and the ring, a simple silver band, she had given Brett. That would go into one of Nathaniel's medicine bags.

They dressed her in the earthy-green leaf-patterned dress with the large carved pearl buttons. Brett's favorite dress—the dress she'd worn that night in San Francisco when she and Beth had come to dinner at 111 Buena Vista East just before she entered the hospital to undergo the bone-marrow transplant. *I desire to live.* They'd all gone up on the roof, and he'd taken a picture of her in that dress, with her new leather jacket over it. *What pleasure life is.*

They lifted her astonishingly limp body in stages, all helping to get the dress on; then they sat with her, touching her, holding her.

The manner of Brett's death, the sense of peace on her face as she died, seemed a final gift from her. Each of them said they felt that.

Beth called hospice, and Carolyn and Norma soon arrived.

Holly was concerned about the evening chill, and so they pulled the dark tights Brett had usually worn with the green dress over her lower body. They placed a pillow under her head and wrapped her in the Irish-chain quilt that Brett's grandmother had made. They folded her hands over her most prized shell. They decided to let the rhythm of the day dictate when Brett's body would leave them: at dark. Then there was no more for them to do. They sat with her for the last time.

Jocelyn lay beside her sister's body and smoothed her hair and held her. "She feels the same as ever," she said.

Dusk invaded the room.

The man from the funeral home arrived at six-thirty. They spread the quilt inside the wine-red funeral bag, then he and the man lifted his daughter's body from the bed and placed her on the quilt, the shell in her hands, the pillow under her head, and the quilt wrapped around her again. They wished her body to be transferred to a coffin for cremation just as it was. The man zipped the bag up to her shoulders, but he didn't close it over her head; she appeared to be wrapped in a bunting. They each kissed her again as he maneuvered the gurney to the door. Then she was gone.

Jocelyn said, "I thought after Brett's death I would be destroyed and lost, but I feel enlightened."

Maybe they all felt that—for the moment.

Once they'd exchanged the day's last embraces here, once Edgar had arrived to be with Beth, they had to leave that room which seemed like a place of safety; they had to walk outside. The world as they'd known it, the world with Brett living in it, had ended.

. . .

Snow silently fell all day; it fell through the night and continued into the next day, dry, drifting snow, the second substantial snowfall of this first week of the new year. Late in the afternoon he skied the trail he regularly walked during all seasons. Up through the woods to Fisher Meadow, which was bordered by silvery stands of sugar maples and beech and gave a view of New England hills to the north; then through more woods, climbing to Parker's pasture. From there the uphill trek flattened out and led to several downhill runs. The thrust of his skis through fresh, untouched snow, kick and glide, was some kind of excitement, the physical exertion, breathing deep, a release. The beauty of the quiet woods, so transformed in snow, which outlined the branches of every tree today, and made the smaller smothered hemlocks look like winter gnomes, was almost unbearable to him.

I don't want to be a person again. It's too painful.

It had been a year and almost three months since his daughter died. Her constant presence in his life had remained all the more vivid, increasingly vivid and intense, for he was engaged in writing a memoir of her long struggle with illness. In the manuscript, he was now approaching his daughter's last birthday, her courage on that occasion, approaching again, nine months from that birthday, her death at twenty-seven.

In just a few days her birthday would be upon them. January 11. Twenty-nine, he thought. To have seen her at twenty-nine!

Beyond the hunters' lean-to, at the crest of a gradual incline and before the trail ran downhill, he came to a narrow passage enclosed by snow-laden hemlocks, almost cavelike, where the stillness seemed deeper. He stopped.

Are you here? He listened to the silence of the woods. Help me, he thought.

Soon he shoved on. From the large pasture he had to retrace his path back through the woods, but it was all downhill now, which made it seem a different trail altogether. He came out into Allis's field, and crossed a stone wall, buried in snow, into the lower mowing of his property. From there, across the white, undulating fields, beyond bare trees that stood out starkly against the sky, he could see their house at the top of the rise, its distinctive snow-covered rooftops, the three chimneys. Their house of grief, he thought.

The morning after her death, he remembered walking outdoors, looking up at the sky, the maples there in all their colors, and thinking her name. Panic came over him. He would not be able to see her or speak to her *today.* The thought that she no longer existed wasn't believable. Months later, and more than a year later, the fact of her death continued to strike him at times with the force of an unanticipated and astonishing realization. Never to see her or speak to her again? A cold paralyzing dread, the sickening lostness a child might feel as he became aware of unrecognizable surroundings, would engulf him. Her presence, synonymous with her absence now, was everywhere!

There's nothing left that I was.

Months later, and more than a year later, looking back, he didn't know how she sat there in those final days waiting to die, or how they sat with her. How did any of them do any of it? His subsequent suffering and grief made his relative composure at the time seem absurd, a temporary insanity. Her dying had seemed more a conscious act than a passive succumbing—and they had endeavored to be as heroic as she was.

He was haunted by her aloneness and his failure, after all the years of being there in whatever way he could for her, to alleviate that. He awoke and looked out at the morning, as he lay in bed, and imagined her awakening to another day, immediately aware of her body—*I'm going to die*—and he became terrified for her, his pulse racing. The promise, implicit in every aspect of her growing up, was that she'd have her life. She had always confided in him, despite her frustration with him. She had looked to him most of her life. He couldn't save her. In the end, was he even much comfort? He wanted to be with her again, he wanted more time, he wanted to understand more, to do more, to hold her.

Awakening he thought with revulsion, I'm alive and Brett is dead.

The phone ringing in the house was always, fleetingly, her. An alarm.

What was it like for her, those last days and moments? The sight of them coming and going in the apartment? Their insistent voices telling her it was all right, let go? He'd know what it had been like for her to die when he was dying, he thought, but then he considered, no, he would never know what it was like to be dying at twenty-seven.

Their house of grief with its solitude, its woods, its sky with moon and constellations, its memories—everything they needed to suffer their loss. He indulged in quasi-rituals of grief in which he would play the music that he associated with his daughter—the music she'd chosen to play that Monday before her death, for example, the last music she'd listened to—while he looked at photographs of her, all the photographs, going back to her youth, but especially snapshots of her recent history in San Francisco, especially photographs of the last summer, including all the photographs of Italy—her radiant happiness in Italy!—of Conway and Northampton, and the last roll in Beth's camera, the shots of his daughter's final days. Her clear, sorrowful, intelligent eyes as she looked directly at the camera, seated in the wheelchair before the flame-colored maple tree in the window, waiting to die. The awful knowledge in her eyes. The last picture on the roll of film—Brett surrounded by her mother, Beth, her sister and brother—had come out blurred, as though taken through a rain-streaked window, which was all right with him. He wanted that picture, but it seemed right that the moment it depicted wasn't plainly visible.

Another night, as he listened to her music, he would look at the charcoal drawings, seeing them more clearly each time. An exhibit of her work, he thought, was what she would most want.

Neither he nor Holly were prepared to watch the four-and-a-half-hour video Beth had made of Brett over the last months and weeks of her life. He was holding that in reserve, he told himself, for some future time when he would long to have his memory of her—the sight of her on film, the sound of her voice—more vividly awakened. No, not now.

The house was replete with all the treasured accoutrements of heartbreak. Her books, which often contained the inscription of her name. Numerous scraps of paper stuck out of her many volumes of poetry; each marked poem was like hearing from her again—a message. All Brett's marvelous, usually funny, and informative cards and letters to them. Her young, strong, positive voice! And all the cards and letters *from* them, which Beth had returned to him in a large file folder. Their daughter had saved everything they'd ever sent her. The correspondence on both sides throughout those hard years was always hopeful.

Brett's ashes, gray and white and blackened fragments of bone, were kept in a pine candle box, which had the proportions of a miniature coffin, by chance, and had been a gift to Brett from the man who had built their timber-frame house. They decided to wait for the right time to take her remains to the Maine coast. They would know it when it came. To Holly, the box of her daughter's ashes when she held them, as she sometimes did, had the dense, compact weight of an infant.

One day Beth brought them another wooden box, which contained all the exotic and mundane shells Brett had found on both coasts and in Europe and the Caribbean. Searching through the box early one morning as it lay in a slant of sunlight on the kitchen table, Holly discovered a strand of glinting red-gold hair long enough to persuade her that it was a strand of Brett's hair from before cancer, from the days of Brett's robust, gorgeous health.

From the opulent bouquet of flowers at the memorial service, Holly took a length of ivy and rooted it in water. Within the year her inspiration resulted in a flourishing plant, from which she continued to cultivate new ivy plants.

And the notebooks, too. Beth had given them the notebooks. They were more than she wanted, possibly, or she believed they were more rightfully his, or she gave them up out of compassion for him; Holly had told Beth how much Brett's journals meant to him. She delivered them bound together by a blue satin ribbon, eight notebooks of various sizes and shapes and bindings. They sat on a table in the room that had been Brett's bedroom. He hadn't untied the ribbon. At first he believed he would read them eventually, provided he had the nerve to break his promise, hungry for contact with her, eager to know whatever he could know. Now he believed he would never read them. He'd become protective of her privacy, and it had nothing to do with the promise he'd made her.

Beth retained the things from Brett that spoke to her most resonantly. And Jocelyn and Nathaniel each had what they needed, he hoped, to hold their lost sister close. Brett's life had been ascetic, her possessions few, yet when nothing could be enough, less was more.

Each family occasion that arose, each birthday, and of course the absurdly charged holidays, with their built-in burden of sentiment and memories, became at some point a ceremony of remembrance. They were four now, even while Michael usually made five and Beth often made six.

From the south side of Wright Hall you looked west to the perennial gardens or south across the wide lawn before Burton Hall. They'd chosen a Gloucester bench, a classic design with a high raked back and contoured seat, intended, according to the brochure, to withstand "the tests of time, weather, and heavy use." The gray stone embedded in grass at his feet possessed a granite finality.

Snow

Snow

IN MEMORY OF

BRETT HOBBIE

January 11, 1965–October 14, 1992

To Bloom Is To Be Taken Completely

Brett had used the line from Jorie Graham as an epigraph in a journal from her junior year in college.

The first spring without her was another passage. She was here, he kept thinking, right here with them, in her linen slacks, her vivid shirt. Tulip, lilac, robin, bluebird—each living thing pierced them with renewed loss, freshening their sorrow. And summer, the first summer, unusual months of drought seemed to mirror their grief, remembering.

A morning in September he found Holly at the kitchen table in a state of anxiety, almost panic.

"We left Brett's body too soon," she said. "We should have stayed with her. We left her alone; we let her be taken away."

He didn't know what to say to her. Fall was coming down on them.

They'd imagined this first anniversary of her death would be the time to drive to the Maine coast and commit her ashes to a deep place in the Atlantic. Now that the time had come they found they weren't ready to let the ashes go.

The morning of October 14, he and Holly walked through the Smith gardens and up the stairs to the small lawn on the south side of Wright Hall. It was the same sort of beautiful fall day, crisp and blue, it had been the year before. Beth was sitting on the teakwood bench, wearing Brett's brown leather jacket. They were happy to find her there. Both his and Holly's relationships with Beth had evolved over the past year as the three of them realized how much they needed one another.

. . .

As winter approached, the project he had embarked on, the memoir, began to repel him. It was as though his daughter's life before cancer had been erased by the past four years. Her life wasn't to be reduced to nothing but pain and suffering. He stopped working on it.

The day after Christmas Beth came out to Conway to join the family for dinner and stayed the night. They talked about the past year and they talked about their plans, the possible future. Nathaniel intended to pursue a life of adventure. "I want to *live,*" he said. Jocelyn and Michael were working hard toward an exhibit of their work in their rented loft in New York, a first show for both of them since they'd left the shelter of school. Beth had recently taken her MCATs and was now applying, at twenty-eight, for admission to medical school. Her experience with Brett had changed her life for good.*

After everyone had gone to bed, he went through the house turning down thermostats and turning out the lights. In the mud room, he picked up Brett's leather jacket from the chair where Beth had left it. He hadn't noticed what Beth was wearing when she arrived and he hadn't expected to find the jacket here. For an instant it was as though the presence of the jacket meant Brett was in the house. Oh God! Not to know of her brother's adventures or Jocelyn's art or Beth's ambition to follow the path of Andy Leavitt and Al McKee. He picked up the sweater Beth had taken off with the jacket, and it took a moment for him to realize that it was his daughter's zippered cranberry-red sweater—the sweater she'd been wearing, with new black corduroy pants, when she greeted them at her apartment door the agonizing Christmas they had flown to San Francisco to be with her. The last Christmas. It was the very sweater he'd recently described in the chap-

---

*As of June 1995, as the proofs of this book were being corrected for the printer, Beth had just completed her first year of medical school at Tufts, Jocelyn's first show at the Tilton Gallery in New York was soon to be notably reviewed in *Art News,* and Nathaniel had just set off on a solo rock-climbing tour of the country, traveling by motorcycle from Massachusetts to California.

ter he'd last been working on. He'd forgotten the sweater still existed. He held it, kneading the strong, enduring wool with his fingers, then he brought it to his face.

The sweater he'd been trying to recall in his manuscript: here it was in the house two years later! He took it for a sign.

Then the snow began—two tremendous snowfalls the first week of the new year—and he began to ski late in the afternoon after working on his resumed manuscript, which now had a name. His thoughts remained with his daughter, so going out into the silent woods felt like communing with her. The snow seemed to have rescued him, an unexpected ally. And the snow continued, the winter of '94 continued, with constant bitterly cold temperatures and repeated snowfalls. Snow piled up in swirling drifts around the house, blew past the windows of his room, a white maelstrom, so their solitary place felt all the more isolated and cut off, which was what he wanted. He kept going out, striving through the frozen white woods and across the windswept fields as he approached again his daughter's death—striking out each afternoon, the sun already low in the sky, so that it began to feel like he was searching for her. Each time he went out he stopped at the same place in the close shelter of dark hemlocks—Are you here?—and appealed to her, asking for help, forgiveness, listening to the wind that moaned over the trees.

The snow and the cold went on into February, and he wanted it to last. In Fisher Meadow, gusting wind raised small tornadoes of snow that danced over the large pasture like manic wraiths. The undulating slope of Parker's mowing loomed golden in the western light and looked like a body, he thought, massive contoured flesh, a being. He often returned just at dusk, coming down through the woods in the partial dark, back to the snowbound house, a prison this winter, in which they did nothing but work, Holly said, although it was also their place in the world, a haven, where a fire burning at night in the large hearth could make a difference, where their heartbreak could be lived. Late nights he walked outside, stomping down the road, the cold burning his face, the snow glinting in moonlight; and Orion always brandished his sword in the unbelievable sky.

The month of March, as if conspiring with his wishes, began with a blizzard, a nor'easter, just as he was embarking again on the last weeks of his daughter's life, the last fall. He'd begun writing in June; he'd get to the end within the month, he saw, if he could bear to do it. The labor of the book, he realized, had been a way to hold on, and he was reluctant for it to end. Entering his workroom now was like going into a room where his daughter was dying, another room where she was dying again.

The anticipation of spring made him apprehensive.

The idea of flying to Italy as soon as this is over. She'd written that in a letter to them at the start of her treatment at UCSF. She got to Italy, he thought.

He was warm as he plowed down the trail on skis for perhaps the last time this year. Past the hunters' lean-to, he stopped in the place he always stopped, where the trail narrowed and was canopied with hemlock boughs. Are you here? He closed his eyes, and the picture was of her face at the moment of her death. He thought of the candle box containing all that was left of his daughter's body, all that was left of this entire person—the box sat on his wife's dresser in their bedroom—and he thought, She was here and now she is utterly gone; she was alive and now she's dead. Her life, everything that was Brett, is over and done with, and there is no more. . . . And the dread, the black, cold lostness that came over him, was something that could be fatal, that could make living impossible.

He moved out from under the dark green branches and continued, pushing hard down the trail of thawing snow. The skiing was over.

The light behind the trees was spring light. And he'd come to the end of his manuscript, at least for the time being.

The idea of flying to Italy . . . He and Holly had the idea they should do that this spring if they could swing it. The last card they'd had from Brett had been from Tuscany, and the last words on the card, the last written message to them, so perfectly her, were the perfect words.

I feel light and full, surrounded by beauty, and please come here sometime. Love, Santa Bretta.